W9-BMC-653

Bloom's Modern Critical Interpretations

The Adventures of Huckleberry Finn
The Age of Innocence
Alice's Adventures in Wonderland
All Quiet on the Western Front
Animal Farm
The Ballad of the Sad Café
Beloved
Beowulf
Black Boy
The Bluest Eye
The Canterbury Tales
Cat on a Hot Tin Roof
Catch-22
The Catcher in the Rye
The Chronicles of Narnia
The Color Purple
Crime and Punishment
The Crucible
Cry, the Beloved Country
Darkness at Noon
Death of a Salesman
The Death of Artemio Cruz
The Diary of Anne Frank
Don Quixote
Emerson's Essays
Emma
Fahrenheit 451
A Farewell to Arms
Frankenstein
The Glass Menagerie
The Grapes of Wrath
Great Expectations
The Great Gatsby
Gulliver's Travels
Hamlet
Heart of Darkness
The House on Mango Street
I Know Why the Caged Bird Sings
The Iliad
Invisible Man
Jane Eyre
The Joy Luck Club
Julius Caesar
The Jungle
King Lear
Long Day's Journey into Night
Lord of the Flies
The Lord of the Rings
Love in the Time of Cholera
Macbeth
The Man Without Qualities
The Merchant of Venice
The Metamorphosis
A Midsummer Night's Dream
Miss Lonelyhearts
Moby-Dick
My Ántonia
Native Son
Night
1984
The Odyssey
Oedipus Rex
The Old Man and the Sea
On the Road
One Flew over the Cuckoo's Nest
One Hundred Years of Solitude
Othello
Persuasion
Portnoy's Complaint
Pride and Prejudice
Ragtime
The Red Badge of Courage
Romeo and Juliet
The Rubáiyát of Omar Khayyám
The Scarlet Letter
A Separate Peace
Silas Marner
Slaughterhouse-Five
Song of Solomon
The Sound and the Fury
The Stranger
A Streetcar Named Desire
Sula
The Sun Also Rises
The Tale of Genji
A Tale of Two Cities
"The Tell-Tale Heart" and Other Stories
Their Eyes Were Watching God
Things Fall Apart
The Things They Carried
To Kill a Mockingbird
Ulysses
Waiting for Godot
The Waste Land
Wuthering Heights
Young Goodman Brown

Bloom's Modern Critical Interpretations

Upton Sinclair's *The Jungle* *New Edition*

Edited and with an introduction by
Harold Bloom
Sterling Professor of the Humanities
Yale University

Bloom's Modern Critical Interpretations: The Jungle—New Edition

Bloom's Literary Criticism
An imprint of Infobase Publishing
132 West 31st Street
New York NY 10001

Library of Congress Cataloging-in-Publication Data
Upton Sinclair's The jungle / edited and with an introduction by Harold Bloom.—New ed.
p. cm.—(Bloom's modern critical interpretations)
Includes bibliographical references and index.
ISBN 978-1-60413-887-0 (hardcover)
1. Sinclair, Upton, 1878–1968. Jungle. 2. Sinclair, Upton, 1878–1968—Political and social views. 3. Chicago (Ill.)—In literature. 4. Working class in literature. 5. Immigrants in literature. 6. Social problems in literature. 7. Political fiction, American—History and criticism. I. Bloom, Harold.
PS3537.I85J973 2010
813'.52—dc22
2010009945

Contributing editor: Pamela Loos
Cover design by Takeshi Takahashi
Composition by IBT Global, Troy NY
Cover printed by IBT Global, Troy NY
Book printed and bound by IBT Global, Troy NY
Date printed: July 2010
Printed in the United States of America

10 9 8 7 6 5 4 3 2 1

This book is printed on acid-free paper.

Contents

Editor's Note

My introduction reluctantly admits that *The Jungle* (1906) is a period piece: To read it, one puts one's uphill shoulder to the wheel and feels proper gratitude to Upton Sinclair's book, which helped give us the Pure Food and Drug Act of 1906.

G. S. Balarama Gupta calls for a reevaluation of Sinclair as a humanist and a propagandist, after which William Bloodworth explores the influence the novelist had on that great American pastime, eating.

Matthew J. Morris notes the ways the book both embraces and rejects a Howellsian realism, followed by Steven Rosendale, who applies an environmentalist sensibility to the novel's strivings.

J. Michael Duvall inevitably traces the alimentary and scatological processes at work in the novel, while Orm Øverland marks the evolution of Sinclair's protagonist from Lithuanian immigrant to American socialist.

Giedrius Subačius then explores Sinclair's sources and the implications of centering the novel on a Lithuanian family, after which Michael Moghtader takes on discursive determinism in *The Jungle*. Elizabeth Kraft concludes the volume by tracing Sinclair's reforming impulses to the great Samuel Richardson and his *Pamela*.

HAROLD BLOOM

Introduction

In his 90 years, Upton Sinclair wrote 90 books, almost got elected governor of California (1934), and died knowing that he had helped pass the Pure Food and Drug Act of 1906 and had lived to be Lyndon Johnson's guest observer on the signing of the Wholesome Meat Act (1967). That is hardly a wasted life, though *The Jungle* is now only a rather drab period piece, and the other books are totally unreadable.

Morris Dickstein and Emory Elliott between them have done as much as can be done for *The Jungle,* which I have just reread with curiosity and revulsion more than six decades after my first encounter with the book. I dimly recall having found it both somber and harrowing, but I was very young, and both experiential and literary sorrows have made me more impatient with it now. American naturalistic writing can survive a certain crudity in style and procedure; Dreiser, in particular, transcends such limitations in *Sister Carrie* and *An American Tragedy.* But Sinclair has nothing of Dreiser's preternatural powers of empathy. What Sinclair tries to do is simply beyond his gifts: His people are names on the page, and his inability to represent social reality makes me long for Balzac and Zola or even Tom Wolfe.

Time is cruel to inadequate literature, though it can be slow in its remorselessness. The young have a remarkable taste for period pieces; I note that my paperback copy of *The Jungle,* published in 1981, is in its thirty-third printing, and I suspect that most of it has been sold to younger people in or out of class. I meditate incessantly on the phenomenon of period pieces, surrounded as I am by so many bad books proclaimed as instant classics, while John Crowley's *Little, Big* (1981), a fantasy novel I have read through scores of times, is usually out of print, as it is at the moment. Patience, patience. The Harry Potter books will be on the rubbish piles, though after I myself am gone, and *Little, Big* wll join the Alice books of Lewis Carroll and Kenneth Grahame's *The Wind in the Willows.*

As a literary critic who has covered the waterfront for a while now, I find the mountain of mail that comes to me instructive, even though I cannot answer it, or even acknowledge it, if I myself am to go on reading, writing, teaching, and living. The two constant piles of vituperative missives come from Oxfordians, poor souls desperate to prove that Edward De Vere wrote all of Shakespeare, and Harry Potterites, of all ages and nationalities. The rage of the partisans of the Earl of Oxford, though crazy and unpleasant, baffles me less than the outrage of the legions of Potterites. Why are they so vulnerable to having their taste and judgment questioned?

No matter how fiercely we dumb down, led in this by the *New York Times Book Review* and the once-elite universities, period pieces seem to induce uneasy sensations in their contemporary enthusiasts. On tour in Turin, several years ago, I found myself talking about my *How to Read and Why* (the Italian version) at an academy for writers called the Holden School, in honor of Salinger's hero. When the school's head, my host, a novelist, asked me why my book said nothing about *The Catcher in the Rye,* I gently intimate that I considered it a period piece, that would go on, perhaps for quite a while, but then would perish. Honest judgment has its costs, and I was shown out rather coldly when I departed. All critics, I know, are subject to error: My hero, Dr. Samuel Johnson, nodded in the terrible sentence: "*Tristram Shandy* did not last." And yet I wonder, as I age onward, what it is in us that makes us so bitter when period pieces expire, if we are one of the survivors of a dead vogue?

G. S. BALARAMA GUPTA

A Note on Upton Sinclair's The Jungle

Upton Sinclair appears to have suffered considerable critical neglect though, paradoxically enough, he remains one of the most widely read American novelists abroad. This is obvious from the fact that, except Floyd Dell's critical biography (to which, incidentally, an Indian student of American literature finds it almost impossible to have access), there seems to be not a single full-length study of this stunningly prolific writer, and further, not many literary historians have found it necessary to devote more than a couple of lines to him, and that mainly to denounce him as merely a hack writer. While most of Sinclair's critics admire his indefatigable vitality and colossal productivity, they tend to dismiss him as a mere muckraker and a superior journalist who has produced didactic political potboilers which are no more than fiction-coated tracts.

The proper approach to Upton Sinclair would be to view him as a humanist who was a sincere soul with a firm belief in the perfectibility of man, and so lashed out mercilessly at all the evils of modern life, hoping that some day happiness and justice would be restored to mankind. A trenchant critic of capitalism, which he believed was the arch enemy of social equality and human progress, Sinclair made it his life's mission to expose, to excoriate all forms of sham and organised greed. *Oil*, *King Coal*, *Boston*, *The Brass Check*, *The Moneychangers*, *Wet Parade*, *The Goose-step* and *The Goslings* are just a few

---

From *Indian Studies in American Fiction*, edited by M. K. Naik, S. K. Desai, and S. Mokashi-Punekar, p. 125–33.

of those scores of novelistic attacks which he carried on till his last breath. Whatever else Sinclair's detractors may say against him, even his bitterest critics would not question his sincerity: his entire life was a series of sacrifices for the noble cause of helping his suffering fellow men realise their essential human dignity and rightful happiness.

For the satisfaction of critics who insist on all art being its own end, it may be granted at the outset that Sinclair cannot elicit sympathy from them for he never believed in the doctrine of 'art for art's sake'. Art, according to him, is for life's sake. It is for man's sake, for the sake of freedom and justice, and ultimately for man's betterment. Sinclair is positive in his outlook to art. Not only does he believe that all art *is* propaganda—deliberately or unconsciously—but he also insists that it *should be* propaganda. He is a staunch believer in the efficacy of art in transforming the world by properly shaping man's ideals.

Thus we can safely assume that Sinclair *is* a propagandist. Putting it in other words, he is a committed writer—committed, by and large, to man's welfare. But, it must also be admitted that a great creative writer desires to make his works of art aesthetically sound and satisfying, while they also serve his purpose. It would, of course, be wrong to claim that Sinclair has always achieved this harmonious balance. But, at the same time, it would not be a generous gesture, to expect uniform artistic excellence in the writings of a man like Sinclair who wrote with amazing fluency (It is nothing short of a phenomenal feat that for some months he turned out eight thousand words a day, Sunday included!) and laboured under continual threats of want and penury. Justice requires that one must take note of a writer's successes as much as his failures.

The purpose of the present article is to analyse and study *The Jungle*, which is one of Sinclair's most significant performances, for more than one reason. It is with this book that Sinclair drew the attention of the reading public to himself as an important writer; with this he burst into fame and made a fortune which, of course, he invested (and consequently lost) in that famous Helicon Hall, a single-tax Colony at Englewood in New Jersey. It is further significant for our purpose, since it reveals both the excellences and limitations of Sinclair as a committed artist.

Apart from the topical appeal of *The Jungle* which created a national sensation when it was first published and led to the hastening of the enactment of the Pure Food and Drugs Act, its pointer and authenticity aroused immediate acclamation of Sinclair's admirers like Jack London who called it the *Uncle Tom's Cabin* of wage slavery, and said: 'It is alive and warm. It is brutal with life. It is written of sweat and blood, and groans with tears.'[1] The novel was based on minute personal observation, and all the agony of Sinclair's own privations had gone into the making of the book as he admits in his autobiography: 'For three months I worked incessantly, I wrote with tears and anguish, pouring into the pages all the pain that life had meant to me.'[2]

Like most of Sinclair's works, *The Jungle* is a crusade: it is a fiery indictment of the ruthless powers of capitalistic industrialism in general and, in particular, a grim revelation of the insanitary conditions in the Chicago meat-packing industry, which is termed with indignant contempt as 'the beef trust'.

Sinclair paints here a grim and graphic picture of the various hardships that a Lithuanian immigrant family faces in the Chicago stockyards where the entire family is gradually ground down and broken under the crushing impact of the gigantic industry.

The longest, and perhaps the bitterest, struggle is that launched by the Hero himself. Jurgis is, no doubt, lucky enough to get a job without difficulty at the 'killing beds', but it is, indeed, a horrible job: he has to sweep for long hours the entrails of slaughtered steer, with his ankles immersed in blood. He has just stepped into this ghastly universe, and the process of disillusionment has already set in. He and his family are swindled of their savings by a real estate agent, who lures them into a house which has nothing new except its coat of paint. Meanwhile, Jurgis is acquainted with the various cruel realities of the packing town. The factory turns out to be a veritable hell where decency and honesty are unheard of, and graft and competition are the chief presiding deities. The life of the workers is a continual misery, fraught with physical hardships and constant mental strain. Worry and fear are the sole fare they sup on. And, meanwhile, the inevitable happens. Jurgis meets with an accident at work, and is thrown out of his job. He is now a damaged article and no one will use it. At last he takes up a job at the fertiliser factory, full of nauseating odour. Work is a passion with him, but he is nowhere allowed to work for long. He has trouble with his boss, Connor, whom he beats up for using his wife, Ona, to satisfy his lust, and thus lands himself in jail, where he loses the last shred of hope. Released from prison, he finds his family broken up. They have lost their house for default of payment of monthly installments of rent and interest; Marija is out of work, with her hand injured in an accident; Elzbieta and Stanislovas are out of work too; and Ona, now dismissed from work, is suffering the throes of a premature child birth. Jurgis somehow manages to bring in a midwife; but not before his beloved wife has died along with her child. It is as though the light of his life is rudely extinguished: 'Dead! *dead*? And she was only a girl, she was barely eighteen. Her life had hardly begun—and here she lay murdered—mangled, tortured to death!'[3]

It now seems impossible for Jurgis to get any job in Chicago as he has been blacklisted for his assault on Connor. His hope revives when he gets a good enough job at the Harvest Trust, but just after nine days he is again jobless for there is a seasonal slump. Then, thanks to the benevolence of a settlement worker, Jurgis finds a job in a steel mill. This again revives his hope, but it is again short-lived. Little Antanas, his son and sole solace, is drowned and leaves Jurgis horror-stricken.

Now Jurgis detests Chicago for all the havoc it has wrought upon him and flees the place. He becomes a migratory farm worker; enjoying the health and freedom of the countryside. But with the end of the harvesting season, his work ends too. Perforce he returns to Chicago, and after a month's frantic search, he gets a job of laying telephone cables underground. But, ill-luck dogs his steps, and he has another accident. When he is discharged from the hospital, he is not yet fit for work, and is forced to roam the streets begging for handouts. One day, by a curious chance, he encounters a drunken youth of the Beef Trust who gives him a hundred dollar bill. In his attempt to change the bill, he is deceived by a bartender, beaten up by a policeman, and sentenced to ten days and costs. While in jail he is attracted to Jack Duane, an erstwhile jail-acquaintance with whose help he enters politics on release, and through politics he is able to find a place in the stockyards once again. He learns that Stanislovas has died from rat bites and Marija has become a whore in order to support Elzbieta and her children. Now he happens to listen to a socialist speaker's eloquent denunciation of the various injustices inflicted on wage slaves. He becomes a convert to socialism, and finds a job as a porter in a hotel owned by a socialist. For the first time in his life, Jurgis starts perceiving some meaning in life and hopes for a bright future.

Jurgis's father is luckier, for his agonising struggle, though no less bitter, is much shorter than anybody, else's. Unwilling to be a burden on the family, this honest old man secures a job in the pickle-rooms at Durham's—of course only after bribing the foreman with a third of his pay. But the work does him no good. The damp air stirs up his old cough, and he collapses after a few days.

The short life of Ona Lukoszaite, 'one of God's gentlest creatures', is filled with physical hardships and excruciating mental tortures. One is struck by the cruel incompatibility between the sweet temperament of this fragile little woman and the brutish atmosphere she is placed in. Horrified at the prospect of all her people going jobless, she succumbs to the threats of Connor, and suffers indescribable psychological torment, having had to be unfaithful to her loving husband. The worm of shame and misery eats gradually into her soul and she finds release only in death.

The life of Teta Elzbieta, Ona's stepmother, is no less painful. Her career as a servant of a sausage machine is miserable enough, but she has the additional misfortune of witnessing her children also suffer endlessly.

Marija Berzynskas, Ona's cousin, has a crueller fate. In addition to suffering all the miseries that the packing town women are generally victims of, she has the misfortune of ending up as a prostitute, since that is the only way left her to eke out a livelihood for her dependents and herself.

The tragedy is not limited to these adults alone. The children of the packing town have their share too: they are fed on adulterated milk, and are woefully undernourished. Elzbieta's youngest child, a three-year-old cripple, dies of eating infected pork. Little Antanas, Jurgis's sole consolation, becomes a victim of several diseases, and gets release only when he is drowned in the muddy waters of a sunken street. Stanislovas, when he should be going to schools, is forced to go out in the streets to earn a few cents, and he too meets with a ghastly end, when shut up helpless in a deserted building, he is eaten up by ravenous rats.

It should be clear from the foregoing description of what happens in the novel that Sinclair had brought forth a work of fiction which was as vital and explosive as a pack of dynamite designed to shatter the smug complacency of the capitalist devotees of mammonism. And it is small wonder that it administered a terrific shock to the entire nation. Here was a merciless exposure of the outrageous practices of the rapacious capitalist wolves in a gigantic and outwardly respectable industry as well as the untold saga of the endless tribulations of the dumb millions suffering barbarous persecution and ignominious privation. The novel was based on indubitable facts, and the author's fearless earnestness in dramatising them in what was destined to become one of the world's most powerful and unforgettable novels could just not be ignored. As one would expect, this powerful tragedy filled all thinking men with terror and pity, and Sinclair must have himself felt sufficiently rewarded since so much of his own indignation and pity had gone into its making. If one were to agree that 'the chief object of a novel is to facilitate the flow of tenderness in the human heart and thus refine and ennoble it,'[4] Sinclair had created an undoubtedly great novel.

It is astonishing that even a critic of, Carl Van Doren's standing should have not only complained that Sinclair's novels lack 'the merit as works of art which might have made them permanently stand out', but also said that 'Sinclair created few characters which live on in the memory and few memorable incidents.'[5] At any rate, one would hesitate to accept his statement in the case of *The Jungle*. Not only the major characters like Jurgis and Ona, but even the minor ones such as Marija and Elzbieta come out well, as full-blooded men and women, entirely life-like, because they are unmistakably taken from life. And as for the incidents, they too are unforgettable for, again, Sinclair was imaginatively transcribing the wretched drama of life being played out by the unfortunate wage slaves in the Chicago stockyards at the start of the century. And what gives unity and strength to *The Jungle*, as much as to his fiction in general, is the strong note of Sinclair's compassion for the lowly and the disinherited, the exploited and the victimised. Sinclair's primary inspiration comes from his pity for his fellow men and his ultimate purpose is the accomplishment of human welfare.

Actuated as *The Jungle* is by fervent proletarian motives, as most of Sinclair's critics have pointed out, it is not surprising that it sometimes degenerates into downright propaganda. For instance, the entire ninth chapter consists of heavy documentation concerning politics and graft that have combined to perpetuate inhuman crimes, and also minute details of the nightmarish existence of the industrial workers. It is as if Sinclair forgets for a moment that he is writing a novel and not a tract, and even quotes some of the sections of the rules and regulations governing the inspection of livestock and their products (p. 112). This only helps to thicken the colour of propaganda.

In the last few chapters, Sinclair places Jurgis in the midst of some socialists and he is made to listen to discussions and lectures on party politics and on the various atrocities of capitalists: the Beef Trust, the Coal Trust, the Oil Trust, the Railroad Trust, and such other organisations of capitalist economy are brought under fire. There is also an adulatory description of the excellent work that is being done by *Appeal to Reason*, a socialist paper. And Sinclair reports that, in a short span of a year or so, the protagonist is educated here to become an active socialist for whom there is a bright future. Obviously, this is all hurriedly done, and it is not difficult to see that Sinclair's propaganda spills over the artistic framework.

The last chapter, is perhaps, the weakest and most explicitly propagandistic part of the novel. It is, by and large, a peg to hang some of Sinclair's ideas on. It contains perorations and discussions on various subjects, such as government, marriage, prostitution, Jesus, war, competition, industrial warfare, advertising, and several other allied topics. It also includes comments on some of Sinclair's pet subjects like abstinence, vegetarianism, and the cooperative commonwealth. What makes this last chapter awkward and puts it out of focus is the fact that Jurgis is a silent auditor of all these orations, and we have reason to doubt if he understands anything of it at all. The chapter is evidently intended to convert Jurgis hastily into a socialist, but it is doubtful if he can make out anything of names like Nietzsche, Fletcher, Gilman, and Kropotkin. Sinclair himself would not come out with a defence of the ending of the novel. On the contrary, he confesses that he was so acutely hard pressed financially when he was engaged in writing this novel that he had to hurry through it, finish it somehow. In a letter (published later by Quint) to Mr and Mrs Gaylord Wilshire (Mr Wilshire was the publisher of a widely circulated socialist magazine), he says: 'I have no words to tell what a hateful and soul-destroying influence the money-question has been in my life. Suffice it to say that never have I been able to write a single thing as I would have liked to write it, because of money. Either I was dead broke, and had to rush it; or I knew that if I had my way, the public would not read it, and that the publisher would not accept it. Think of my having had to ruin *The Jungle* with an ending, so pitifully inadequate; because we were actually without money for food.'[6] Therefore, we find that the defect of *The Jungle* seems to lie, by and large, not in the realistic delineation of characters or incidents, but rather in Sinclair's failure to restrain himself from advocating his preconceived cures for the evils he condemns. The artist's job is only to *suggest* a possible solution or possible solutions to the problems posed by him, and not to impose any of them on the reader with vehemence, as Sinclair does in the novel being discussed.

While describing *The Jungle* as 'a story written out in letters of fire', Alfred Kazin rightly points out that it is idle to complain of the reformative motive lying behind all of Sinclair's literary efforts, and, says: 'Van Wyck Brooks might complain that "the only writers who can possibly aid in the liberation of humanity are those whose sole responsibility is to themselves as artists," but in a sense it was pointless to damn Sinclair as a 'mere' propagandist. What would he have been without the motor power of his propaganda, his driving passion to convert the world to an understanding of the problems of labour . . . the promise of socialism . . . and so much else?'[7] An unbiased analysis of *The Jungle* reveals that it is futile to indulge either in an unqualified acclamation or outright denunciation of Upton Sinclair. It is again Kazin who seems to give us a clue to a proper understanding of this much-neglected writer. One is inclined to agree with Kazin when he describes Sinclair as 'something more than a "mere" writer and something less than a serious novelist'.[8]

It would be a pity if what Hatcher says—in a tone obviously tinged with irony—should be true: 'He [Sinclair] has been rewarded next to Theodore Dreiser by the condemnation of more people who have not read his books than any other American novelist.'[9] To ignore a writer or merely heap condemnation on him, because he attacks vested interests is not fair. The critical acrimony generated in the case of Sinclair seems to have been mainly for the reason that he was trying to hit at the very roots of the festering American civilisation.

Manifestly, *The Jungle*, like his other works, is an act of social criticism designed to show up the evils of American society. In all such works there is always an element of passion, philosophical urgency, and exhortation which borrow their strength and wisdom from a system of thought, whether idealism, or humanitarianism, capitalism or socialism. The product of such an industry may be accepted primarily in terms of its human relevance outside its affiliation to a political philosophy. *The Jungle* reveals the horrors of a social order, which, for all its glorious basic assumptions, has, like most such social orders, developed an internal rottenness in its development. In analysing this internal disease, the author may be offering remedies which may not be acceptable. But while we discover the remedies to be unpalatable to us, it would be an act of critical honesty to recognise the wisdom of the diagnosis. That is to say, regardless of Sinclair's political leanings or ideological affiliations, a more balanced and courteous revaluation of what he has done as a social critic is, in all fairness, due to him.

Notes

1. Jack London, 'Appeal', No. 520, 18 November, 1905 (Girard, Kansas).
2. Upton Sinclair, *The Autobiography of Upton Sinclair* (London, 1963).
3. Upton Sinclair, *The Jungle* (London, 1906), p. 226.
4. Mulk Raj Anand, in a private conversation with the present writer.
5. Carl Van Doren, *The American Novel* (New York, 1970), p. 242.
6. Howard H. Quint, 'Upton Sinclair's Quest for Artistic Independence—1909' in *American Literature*, Vol. 29 (March 1957 Jan. 1958), p. 196.
7. Alfred Kazin, *On Native Grounds* (New York, 1942), p. 121.
8. Op. cit., p. 116.
9. Harlant Hatcher, *Creating the Modern American Novel* (London, 1936), p. 132.

WILLIAM BLOODWORTH

From The Jungle *to* The Fasting Cure: *Upton Sinclair on American Food*

During the Progressive Era Americans hoped for improvement in many aspects of national life besides politics and economics. One object of reform which has often been overlooked by social and cultural historians was the American diet. A quick survey of popular magazines between 1900 and 1917 will reveal dozens of articles with such titles as "Perfect Feeding of the Human Body," "Eating for Efficiency," "Modern Ideas on Food," "Sawdust as Food" and "Electricity and Diet." The progressive temper gave rise both to serious nutritional research and to food faddism. Such figures as James Harvey Kellogg of the Battle Creek Sanitarium and Horace Fletcher, a man who taught thousands of people how to chew their food differently, were widely known during these years. In particular, it was an age of experimentation with food and eating. Americans seemed more willing than ever before to raise serious questions about what they consumed and how they ate, and to heed answers provided in popular books and magazines. Vegetarianism, hydrotherapy, auto-intoxication, fasting, natural foods, raw meat diets and other dietary subjects took on public significance. Many people, it would seem, hoped to perfect the human race by applying democracy and science not only to political life but also to matters of the stomach.

One progressive figure who was more than ordinarily interested in such matters was Upton Sinclair, author of *The Jungle* (1906). In that muckraking

---

From *Journal of American Culture* 2, no. 3 (Fall 1979): 444–53.

novel and in a variety of other writings between 1906 and the beginning of World War I, Sinclair may be seen as a bellwether of American interest in the reform of food and eating habits. He also represents an unusually vigorous attempt to combine questions of food with political propaganda that ranged from merely progressive to conspicuously socialistic in its intent. Few other American writers have been as willing to make food the subject and sometimes the substance of their rhetoric.

I

> These people could not be shown to the visitor.... Their peculiar trouble was that they fell into the vats; and when they were fished out, there was never enough of them to be worth exhibiting—sometimes they would be overlooked for days, till all but the bones of them had gone out to the world as Durham's Pure Leaf Lard.[1]

The Jungle was really only the beginning of Sinclair's involvement with American food, but it was an auspicious start. Simply in terms of what it did to national eating patterns, the novel was a remarkable literary achievement. According to Waverley Root and Richard de Rochemont in *Eating in America*, Sinclair's expose of filthy processes in the meat industry reduced the American appetite for meat—at least for meat processed by packing houses—for several decades. In 1928, at the height of the pre-depression boom, the packers still found it necessary to carry out a national "eat more meat" campaign. The passage of the Pure Food and Drug Act of 1906, which in spite of loopholes and defects in enforcement was "one of the major events in the history of American food," is of course another measure of the novel's impact.[2] One wonders whether American consumers who have read *The Jungle* are yet able to buy meat products with a completely clear conscience. Perhaps it was not so much the workers in the lard that made readers dubious about packing house products as it was the chemicals, the rat droppings and the assortment of other putrid items that Sinclair pictured as eventually finding their way into hams, sausages and cans of meat.

Shortly after the novel appeared, Sinclair claimed that actually he had not been much concerned with the state of meat processing when he wrote the story. His frequently-quoted statement to this effect—"I aimed at the public's heart and by accident I hit it in the stomach"—has considerable validity.[3] His initial motivation had been the failure of a 1904 strike in the Chicago stockyards, and his concern from the beginning had doubtless been the conditions under which the wage slaves of industry were forced to work and live. Furthermore, the amount of space in the novel that is actually devoted to documenting the lack of sanitation in the packing plants is small;

in fact, Sinclair's proletarian hero, Jurgis Rudkus, leaves the plant well before *The Jungle* is half finished.

Also in several places in the novel the appearance of food serves literary purposes only, and serves them well, having little to do with muckraking. The Lithuanian wedding feast or *veselija* with which the story begins is one example; here Sinclair uses not only food but also music and ceremony to express the initial hopefulness of the immigrant workers and their faith in controlling the destiny of their own lives. They soon fall into poverty and chaos, of course, but at the wedding they are successful in creating at least an illusion of affluence and control:

> Suddenly some of the steam begins to advance, and, peering through it, you discern Aunt Elizabeth . . . bearing aloft a great platter of stewed duck. Behind her is Kotrina, making her way cautiously, staggering beneath a similar burden; and half a minute later there appears old Grandmother Majauskiene, with a big yellow bowl of smoking potatoes, nearly as big as herself. So, bit by bit, the feast takes form—there is a ham and a dish of sauerkraut, boiled rice, macaroni, bologna sausages, great piles of penny buns, bowls of milk, and foaming pitchers of beer. (10)

And much later in the story, when Jurgis rebels against the city by fleeing into the countryside—after the death of his father, his wife and his son—his momentary freedom is also celebrated in terms of food. This time it is the healthy, natural and vegetarian fare that he finds at a farmer's table: "there were baked beans and mashed potatoes and asparagus chopped and stewed, and a dish of strawberries, and great, thick slices of bread, and a pitcher of milk. Jurgis had not had such a feast since his wedding day" (213).

Yet in spite of Sinclair's statement about aiming at the public heart—and in spite of his use of food to shed light on his characters and their circumstances—his claim of hitting the American stomach only by accident is not true.

The deliberate attention to matters of the stomach in the novel may be illustrated in several ways. The use of footnotes to present direct quotations from government regulations concerning the inspection of intrastate meat shows Sinclair's willingness to interrupt the flow of his story, mixing nonfiction with fiction, for the sake of authoritative documentation for the cause of pure meat. Such facts of meat inspection did not directly affect the lives of the oppressed workers who constituted Sinclair's expressed main interest. Middle-class readers would of course have recognized a direct effect on the meat they consumed. Sinclair's careful attention to issues like meat inspection provides a rather interesting contradiction of a second statement that he made at the time of his famous heart and stomach comment: "I do not eat meat myself, and my general attitude toward the matter was one of general indifference."[4]

Other aspects of *The Jungle* hardly suggest indifference toward meat. Even the passages about workers who fall into the cooking vats directs attention mainly to ingredients in a consumer product. The real danger to the workers seems slighted; the agony of those who actually fall into the vats is not even mentioned. Chapter 14 of the novel is another good example of a concern with food which seems in fact to precede Sinclair's concern with his working-class characters. The main point of the chapter is the accelerating deterioration of Jurgis' Lithuanian family after three years in Packingtown. By this time, according to Sinclair, after several deaths in the family and no relaxation of the vicious poverty in which they had been living:

> They were beaten; they had lost the game, they were swept aside. It was not less tragic because it was so sordid, because it had to do with wages and grocery bills and rents. They had dreamed of freedom; of a chance to look about them and learn something; to be decent and clean, to see their child grow up to be strong. And now it was all gone—it would never be! They had played the game and they had lost. (137–8)

Much of the story remained to be told—seventeen more chapters, in fact—but Sinclair wished this early to show the extent of their despair. Yet this chapter, with its naturalistic emphasis on the impossibility of the workers improving their situation through their own efforts, begins not with an account of the troubles of the immigrants, or even with the oppressiveness of the conditions under which they must work. Rather, Sinclair starts the chapter with several pages of exposition devoted to the subject of rotten hams and sausages which contain ground-up rats. For instance, he points out how no one ever pays the least attention to sausage ingredients: "there would come all the way back from Europe old sausage that had been rejected, and that was mouldy and white—it would be dosed with borax and glycerine, and dumped into the hoppers, and made over again for home consumption." Or that "there were things that went into the sausage in comparison with which a poisoned rat was a tidbit" (136).

In other words, Sinclair apparently felt that the way to a reader's heart was through his stomach. Once the sickening facts of meat processing were served up, he could move on to the struggle for survival that his characters were inexorably losing.

The novel abounds with other examples of Sinclair's eagerness to use his story of wage slavery and the soul-destroying jungle of capitalist exploitation as a vehicle for raking in the muck of adulterated food. The processing of "steerly" cattle which were covered with boils, of tubercular animals, or of cows about to calve; the use of tripe, pork fat, beef suet and other non-poultry items to make "potted chicken"; the rechurning of rancid butter; the doctoring of milk with formaldehyde; and the cutting of ice from pools of stagnant and polluted water are among the examples. One can easily guess why a young and fervid socialist writer at this time in America would take pains so often to attack food processing: his socialism had an obvious middle-class bias. Although he spoke *for* the lowest working classes, he spoke *to* a much wider audience. He wanted to show that not only did the Beef Trust exploit the lives of the workers, it also exploited the ignorance of the middle-class public. Food and its processing could therefore be used politically and rhetorically as a means of bridging class differences.

But Sinclair was also interested in questions of food for reasons that went beyond his immediate socialist commitments. This seems evident near the end of the novel when he digresses from his narrative to expostulate on the aims and eventual results of socialism. For this purpose he makes extensive use of a Herr Doctor Schliemann, a socialist lecturer whose ideas are presented with such sympathy and at such length as to convince the reader that they represent Sinclair's own. Schliemann speaks of many advantages that socialism will provide. Prime among these is an increase in freedom of speech. Under socialism, with its motto of "Communism in material production, anarchism in intellectual" (331), Schliemann might be able to publish a magazine for the purpose of popularizing, among other things, "the gospel of . . . Horace Fletcher, the inventer of the noble science of clean eating."

The Herr Doctor is also interested in promoting "the scientific breeding of men and women" (336), thereby aligning himself incidentally but precisely with the main interests of J.H. Kellogg of the Battle Creek Sanitarium: diet and eugenics.

Sinclair was obviously interested in food for a variety of reasons. Both the lack of food, or at least the lack of nutritious food, among the industrial proletariat and the adulteration of food consumed by all classes of Americans were obvious examples of social injustice in his eyes. They pointed clearly to the evil effects of profit, monopoly and capitalism itself. Beyond this, though, poor nutrition and unscientific eating habits were acts of race suicide.

II

> The whole modern art of cooking is largely a perversion; a product of idleness, vanity, and sensuality. It is one of the monstrous growths

> consequent upon our system of class exploitation. . . . Needless to say, this elaborate gastronomic art has been developed without any relation to health, or any thought of the true needs of the body.[5]

Between the appearance of *The Jungle* and the beginning of World War I, Sinclair's interest in American food took several different directions. One—his interest in adequate meat-inspection laws—was predictable and respectable. Given Sinclair's socialist bent and utopian hopes, the other directions were equally predictable. But when they took forms like raw-food vegetarianism and therapeutic fasting, they tended to move toward the extremes of dietary ideas in progressive America.

Immediately after *The Jungle* was published in February 1906, Sinclair devoted most of his attention to insuring the passage of the Pure Food and Drug Act. Although Jack London had endorsed Sinclair's novel as an "*Uncle Tom's Cabin* of Wage Slavery,"[6] Sinclair himself was willing for his publisher—Doubleday—to advertise *The Jungle* as "a searching expose of . . . the fragrant violations of all hygienic laws in the slaughter of diseased cattle . . . and the whole machinery of feeding a world with tainted meat."[7] Capitalizing on the public impact of his book, Sinclair proceeded to plead with President Roosevelt to investigate sanitary conditions in the Chicago packing plants. He also published articles to refute charges (largely by the packers themselves) against his novel, and he set up a publicity office in a New York hotel where he released almost daily information to the press about the progress of the battle between the American public and the Beef Trust. Eventually he besieged Roosevelt with demands for action to the point where the President sent a message to Frank Doubleday saying, "Tell Sinclair to go home and let me run the country for a while."[8] This Sinclair did only after passage of the food and drug act in June.

Although he eagerly participated in and abetted the kind of middle-class reform liberalism exemplified by the Pure Food and Drug Act, he did not entirely lose sight of his more radical socialist views. Here, too, food played an important role, particularly as a Veblenesque way of attacking the upper class as gluttonous, decadent and parasitic. No better example can be found than a 1908 novel, *The Metropolis*, a generally unsuccessful attempt to expose the lifestyle of New York's upper crust. The first description of an upper-class meal as experienced by Sinclair's then-innocent protagonist (Allan Montague) will suffice to illustrate the novelist's effort to use food as socialist rhetoric:

> It began with ice-cream, moulded in fancy shapes and then buried in white of egg and baked brown. Then there was a turtle soup, thick and green and greasy; and then—horror of horrors—a great

> steaming plum-pudding. It was served in a strange phenomenon of a platter, with six long, silver legs; and the waiter set it in front of Robbie Walling and lifted the cover with a sweeping gesture—and then removed it and served it himself. Montague had about made up his mind that this was the end, and begun to fill up on bread and butter, when there appeared cold asparagus, served in individual silver holders resembling andirons. Then—appetite now being sufficiently whetted—there came quail in piping hot little casseroles; and then half a grape-fruit set in a block of ice and filled with wine; then little squab ducklings, bursting fat, and an artichoke; and then a *cafe parfait*; and then—as if to crown the audacity—huge thick slices of roast beef! Montague had given up long ago—he could keep no track of the deluge of food which poured forth. And between all the courses there were wines of precious brands, tumbled helter-skelter,—sherry and port, champagne and claret and liqueur. Montague watched poor "Baby" de Mille out of the corner of his eye, and pitied her; for it was evident that she could not resist the impulse to eat whatever was put before her, and she was visibly suffering.[9]

Sinclair often accompanied such descriptions with information about the flaunting of sex, as well as food, among the rich: "he hesitated every time he turned to speak to the young lady beside him, because he could look so deep down into her bosom, and it was difficult for him to realize that she did not mind it" (49). Sinclair had good intentions, of course, and had actually been present at such meals, but the American reading public much preferred Sinclair to turn their stomachs by descriptions of tubercular cows. *The Metropolis* sold no more than eighteen thousand copies, and Sinclair soon began writing about American eating habits in a different and more direct way.

In 1909 Sinclair started discussing food and eating as a matter of personal experience as well as public information and political fact. A personalistic style was nothing new to him because he had long before developed the habit of publishing magazine articles with such titles as "The Confessions of a Young Author" (*Independent*, 1902), "My Cause" (*Independent*, 1903) and "What Life Means to Me" (*Cosmopolitan*, 1906). However, the burst of publications dealing with his personal diet between 1909 and 1911—two books (one co-authored), articles in *Colliers* and *Cosmopolitan*, and a series of monthly essays in Bernarr Macfadden's *Physical Culture* magazine—as well as his occasional later descriptions of what and how he ate, were probably due mainly to the example of the popular Horace Fletcher.

When Sinclair referred to Fletcher in the last chapter of *The Jungle* as "the inventor of the noble science of clean eating," he knew the enormous acclaim that Fletcher was then enjoying. Horace Fletcher pursued a peculiar American dream of health, and his success story was widely circulated in popular print between 1902 and 1914. A successful importer, Fletcher stumbled upon a unique way of eating in the 1890s when he was in his middle forties and suffering terribly from stomach trouble and other ailments. Upon being refused life insurance because of his health, Fletcher retired from active participation in business (a la Franklin) and set out to find a cure for himself. Eventually he discovered that proper eating, not medicine or doctors, was the remedy. By eating only when he was truly hungry and chewing his food with extreme thoroughness Fletcher began to lose weight and to gain strength. He also discovered that he needed only one-fourth to one-half the amount of food he had been used to eating. Around 1898 Fletcher began actively promoting his eating practices, which he called "Fletcherism," in books and lectures. Scoffed at for a while, his ideas soon became popular and people throughout America and Western Europe began to "Fletcherize" their food. Perhaps the turning point in Fletcher's quest for recognition was a series of experiments he underwent at the Yale University Gymnasium around 1902. Well into his fifties then, Fletcher proved himself capable of astonishing feats of strength and endurance. By 1909 he was a world-famous personality whose "scientific" principles were discussed at leading universities and endorsed by academic figures as respectable as William James. The American Association for the Advancement of Science made him a Fellow, Dartmouth granted him an honorary M.A., and Chautauqua selected him as its lecturer on "Vital Economics."[10]

Fletcher's principles were dangerously simple. He claimed that the human appetite could be trusted entirely to choose the right food and the proper amount of it. As far as he was concerned, carbohydrates were as nutritious as anything else; only calories counted. The basis of Fletcherism was complete mastication, with Fletcher himself chewing food so thoroughly that only the juices would enter his stomach. Except in the matter of chewing, Fletcher advised, "Trust to Nature absolutely and accept her guidance."[11] For Fletcher and his disciples (including John D. Rockefeller) this simple trust was the way to happiness and morality as well as a healthy body. Officials in London considered ways to entice the poor and the criminal to eat Fletcher-style. Managers in industry asked Fletcher for assistance in increasing the motivation of workers. Fletcher himself felt that his eating method could solve "the whole social problem" in "a single generation."

In 1909 Sinclair and Michael Williams, who had been with Sinclair in his Helicon Hall living experiment two years before and who, like Sinclair, had spent time at the Battle Creek Sanitarium, authored a book entitled *Good Health and How We Won It.* Sinclair wrote the introduction and helped edit the rest of it. Essentially, the book tried to offer recent findings in the field of nutrition, mainly those of Fletcher and Dr. J.H. Kellogg. But it also presented personal experience and, as proof positive, photographs of the authors and their families. Sinclair wrote, "We have done this frankly and simply, and we trust that the reader will not misinterpret the spirit in which we have done it. Mr. Fletcher has set the noble example in this matter, and has been the means of helping tens of thousands of his fellow men and women."[12]

The facts of nutrition in *Good Health* stressed Dr. Kellogg's notions of auto-intoxication due to undigested bacteria in the lower intestinal tract, a theory which (because of high bacteria counts in meat) led to vegetarianism. Somewhat in advance of their day, and much in the spirit of the later Adele Davis, Sinclair and Williams also dealt extensively with matters of calories, proteins and minerals. Yet some of the advice offered—for instance, the use of a cold water bottle on the stomach before meals to stimulate blood flow and appetite—was highly idiosyncratic, even silly. The general intention, though, was as noble and progressive as Horace Fletcher's. In his introduction Sinclair argued first that Western civilization was on the verge of decline: although politics and economics had shown recent improvement, there remained "those manifold and race-destroying evils known as nervous troubles, and those other evils resulting from malnutrition, which are lumped together vaguely under the name of dyspepsia, or indigestion" (10). However, if the beneficial forces of democracy and science could be applied to questions of health, the decline of civilization might be avoided. Referring to poverty and exploitation, Sinclair said:

> we see a world-wide and universal movement for the abolition of these evils. And hand in hand with this goes a movement of moral regeneration. . . . We see this movement in literature and art; we see it in the new religions which are springing up—in Christian Science, and the so-called "New Thought" movement; we see it in the great health movement which is the theme of this book, and which claims for its leaders some of the finest spirits of our times. (11–12)

Had anyone before made such an ebulliently progressive statement, linking together muckraking, socialism, Christian Science and nutrition research in one paragraph?

But Sinclair's optimism was to require a few adjustments. In fact he began to lose some of the good health that his book described as having been "won." Jack London wrote him in August of 1909 to say "'Good Health' to hand. Oh, you fakir! I hear that after publishing said book you have been sojourning and fasting at Battle Creek."[13] London was right, but Sinclair was doing his fasting under the direction of Bernarr Macfadden, who had set up an institution at Battle Creek as a rival to the one operated by Kellogg. With Macfadden's advice Sinclair was quickly modifying the ideas of Fletcher and Kellogg. He took up the eating of meat again, for one thing, but he stopped cooking his vegetables. He also fasted, as London noted, for periods up to ten and twelve days, to combat ailments like headaches, indigestion and constipation. These new diet practices became the subject of a series of articles in *Collier's*, *Cosmopolitan* and *Physical Culture* throughout 1910. His statements about fasting drew the most attention, of course, and encouraged him to consolidate his findings in *The Fasting Cure*, published in May of 1911.

In addition to changing his mind about what constitutes the best things to eat and the best way to eat, Sinclair also began to push his arguments with greater fervor. For one thing, he went into much more detail about his personal experiences, apparently willing to offer up his own body and its functioning for public inspection. For another, he became much more insistent upon the need for good health:

> I look about me in the world and nearly everybody I know is sick. I could name one after another a hundred men and women, who are doing vital work for progress and carrying a cruel handicap of physical suffering. For instance, I am working for social justice, and I have comrades whose help is needed every hour, and they are ill!

Finally, he sought publicity and joined others who believed in the efficacy of fasting. *The Fasting Cure* cites scores of successful fasts which, according to Sinclair, eliminated conditions of ill health ranging from neurasthenia to cancer. For instance, he included the case of a young man injured in a railroad wreck whose lungs were punctured: "Suffered in succession attacks of bronchitis, typhoid, pneumonia and pleurisy. Was reduced from 186 to 119 pounds, and had planned to take his life. Fasted six days, gained twenty-seven pounds, and plays tennis vigorously, in spite of having an opening in his chest. Recently walked 442 miles in eleven days" (31).

Sinclair was dead serious about fasting. "The fast is to me the key to eternal health, the secret of perfect and permanent health. I would not take anything in all the world for my knowledge of it," he wrote in his book (25). He was not alone in his praise of starving for health's sake; references to books by Macfadden, Lucy B. Hazzard, C.C. Haskell and Hereward Carrington occur periodically in Sinclair's explanations. Undoubtedly he thought that he was part of a significant progressive movement. He was cautious, however, to advise that the fast should be practiced only when a person has something wrong with him. It was not "a thing to be played with . . . for the fun of it, or out of curiosity" (40). Ten years later in his *Book of Life* (1921), an attempt to tell his working-class readers how to do everything from "how to find health" to "how to eat and how to sleep" to "what books to read," he was still enthusiastically advocating fasting. Even five decades later, in his autobiography (1962), he made public his debt to Bernarr Macfadden and—without actually advocating fasting—once again described the benefits it had brought him in his earlier life.

III

Sinclair's concern with food and diet has several explanations. The most obvious one is that he suffered personally from stomach problems, especially when he was hard at work on his books, and that he sought—and sometimes thought he had found—cures that he was willing to share with the public just as he had shared his knowledge of Packingtown in *The Jungle.* Also Sinclair's idea of what literature could deal with included anything "which is likely to be of use to other men in understanding how to live"—as he stated it in a 1928 "Credo" published in the *Bookman.*

Food also had its political dimensions for Sinclair. On one hand he was a complete progressive who felt that the public should work to correct abuses of all kinds (he was later an enthusiastic supporter of Prohibition) and that science and democracy could illuminate every dark corner of civilization. On the other hand he was a socialist, and he saw dietary excesses through the same ideological framework that he saw the economic products of labor: as a denial of equality.

But reasons of personal health and political ideas do not provide a complete explanation. Sinclair's attention to food—particularly to matters of eating—must also be recognized as a cultural phenomenon. In particular, it is necessary to take note of Sinclair's insistence on the virtue of self-discipline. His attitude toward food and eating was obviously Puritan.

Sinclair himself preferred the term "morality." As he once put it in a *Physical Culture* article, "the problem . . . of establishing a permanent civilization is one of morality. We must learn to resist temptation, and to withhold ourselves from over indulgence *even in the presence of unlimited opportunity.*" This statement provides a key to understanding his attitudes.

Sinclair did not write about food as he did because he was worried about food shortages; his use of the phrase "unlimited opportunity" reflects his infinite faith in the ability of technology to meet the needs of everybody. Nor was he at heart concerned about public wealth *per se.* In the same article where the statement about "unlimited opportunity" appears, Sinclair offered his "Golden Rule of Health"—a rule which, upon examination, has less to do with health than it does with the morality of self-restraint.

In trying to make clear how this kind of morality should work, Sinclair quoted first from William James' "The Moral Equivalent of War." Sinclair agreed with James' assertion that the nation must continue to develop "the manliness to which the military mind so faithfully clings"—but must do so without actually participating in warfare. For Sinclair, physical culture, with its emphasis on carefully controlled diet and rational use of fasting, could "impose upon ourselves those virtues of hardihood and self-control which war has bred into the race" (615). *Eating* could thus be a moral equivalent of war.

Sinclair also referred to a description of feeding habits among sled dogs in the Klondike as provided in a story by Jack London. In London's words Sinclair felt that he had support for his ideas on *human* diet. In spite of being "ravenously hungry," London's dogs eat only a small amount of dried fish once a day:

> Theirs was the simple, elemental economy. A little food equipped them with prodigious energy. Nothing was lost. A man of soft civilization, sitting at a desk, would have grown lean and woe-begone on the fare that kept Kama and Daylight at the top-notch of physical efficiency. They knew, as the man at the desk never knows, what it is to be normally hungry all the time, so that they could eat any time. Their appetites were always with them and on edge, so that they bit voraciously into whatever [was] offered and with an entire innocence of digestion.

"I should be willing to take the last sentence of that paragraph as my 'Golden Rule of Health'," Sinclair wrote, for it is "a return to the best in nature" (616). To establish civilization permanently, American eating habits needed to take several steps backward on the evolutionary ladder. Or perhaps Sinclair meant to say that you are what you do not eat.

Notes

1. Upton Sinclair, *The Jungle* (New York: New American Library, 1960), p. 102. I have quoted from the readily available Signet paperback rather than the 1906 Doubleday edition. I have made other references to the novel in parentheses, as I have done with other sources.

2. Waverley Root and Richard de Rochemont, *Eating in America: A History* (New York: William Morrow, 1976), pp. 210–11.

3. Upton Sinclair, "What Life Means to Me," *Cosmopolitan*, 41 (Oct., 1906), p. 594.

4. "What Life Means to Me," p. 594.

5. Upton Sinclair, *The Book of Life: Mind and Body* (New York: Macmillan, 1921), p. 129.

6. *Appeal to Reason*, 18 Nov., 1905, p. 1.

7. John Braeman, "The Square Deal in Action: A Case Study in the Growth of the 'National Police Power'," in Braeman, et al., *Change and Continuity in Twentieth-Century America* (Columbus: Ohio State Univ. Press, 1964), p. 45.

8. Upton Sinclair, *The Autobiography of Upton Sinclair* (New York: Harcourt, Brace & World, 1962), p. 124.

9. Upton Sinclair, *The Metropolis* (New York: Moffat, Yard, 1908), pp. 45–6.

10. See Isaac F. Marcossin, "Perfect Feeding of the Human Body," *World's* Work, 7 (Feb., 1904), 4457–60, and Horace Fletcher, "How I Made Myself Young at Sixty," in *Ladies Home Journal*, Sept., 1909, pp. 9–10, as well as the article on Fletcher in the *National Cyclopedia of American Biography*, Vol. 14.

11. Fletcher, p. 10.

12. Upton Sinclair and Michael Williams, *Good Health and How We Won It* (New York: Frederick A. Stokes, 1909), pp. 16–17.

13. London to Sinclair, 24 August 1909, Sinclair Manuscripts, Lilly Library, Indiana University.

MATTHEW J. MORRIS

The Two Lives of Jurgis Rudkus

William Dean Howells once warned that realism, like romance, would ultimately die as a truthful art form: "When realism becomes false to itself, when it heaps up facts merely, and maps life instead of picturing it, realism will perish too."[1] He meant that realism must show some of the pattern of life, instead of merely accumulating description. That is a reasonable program, although Howells chose puzzling terms: one might just as easily have aligned "picturing" with formless description, and "mapping" with a realism that discloses the underlying structure of events. What does a map do if not subordinate surface appearances to a schema of spatial relations? But Howells was stressing precisely the schematic quality of a fiction congested with details. Such a fiction, having failed to identify the true source of formal coherence in art as in life, would still aspire to meaning, but this meaning could only be arbitrary, like that which is conventionally assigned to the configuration on a map. Curiously, Howells' division of the possible methods of realism here anticipates the analogous distinction signalled by the title of Georg Lukács's "Narrate or Describe?" For Lukács, classic realism surpasses naturalism in that realist novels take on a narrative form dictated by or expressive of historical necessity, while naturalist novels, choked with description, remain formless. The true realist must "go beyond crass accident and elevate chance to the inevitable," which means dramatizing

From *American Literary Realism 1870–1910* 29, no. 2 (Winter 1997): 50–67.

that epochal conflict in light of which every facet of the man-made world assumes significance.[2] If he cannot see that conflict, though he may have the best intentions to promote reform by describing, for example, slum life, the novelist inevitably assembles discrete data whose significance he can only will as symbolic.

Lukács could thus have adopted Howells' vocabulary and said that naturalists like Zola, for all their virtuosity in description, lack the pictorial sense, and thus can only map social relations. Of course, Howells actually liked Zola, and Lukács based his aesthetic judgments on a theory of reification alien to the American novelist. Their dismissals of formless fiction coincide only in part. But this coincidence brings into focus some of the assumptions about realism that have informed responses to Upton Sinclair's *The Jungle*, a novel noted for its vivid descriptions and the ultimate formlessness of its plot, one which often seemingly "heaps up facts" in just the way that Howells (and, for different reasons and in different terms, Lukács) deplores. Sinclair must have been aware of the doctrines promulgated by Howells, and would later assent to censures of his novel which are at least consonant with these doctrines, if not derived from them. Yet *The Jungle* does not merely violate the canons of Howellsian realism, for it never quite embraces them. Rather, it remains, on the one hand, trapped within an ideal of factual accuracy which seemingly ignores Howells' call for formal harmony, while showing signs, on the other hand, of a more significant divergence from the realist program, a reclamation of romance as the indispensable dialectical counterpart of realism. In view of these signs, we must assume that the eccentricities of *The Jungle* have a constructive purpose, until they are proved to reflect poor judgment alone. The charge of "mapping" is unlikely to furnish such proof, for Sinclair arguably sets out to restore "mapping" to its literal sense: he uses spatial layouts as figures for complex social relations. When he describes how factories process meat, his description also functions as a diagram of how the ruling class corrupts democratic institutions.

This treatment of space is closely related to Sinclair's strategy of embodying capital, labor, and other abstractions in individual characters—another hallmark of what Howells calls "romance." But these authorial choices need not render a work shapeless or schematic. Sinclair's use of maps and types opens, rather than closes, the question of whether he fashions a compelling plot, one which supports the argumentative burden he places upon it. As a socialist, Sinclair believed that the environment shapes human behavior, but also that human beings may reshape their destinies. Men may not make their history just as they please, yet they do make it. Sinclair's treatment of characters, their settings, and their actions follows from this concern with the making of human beings and, or more properly within, their surroundings.

To formulate the problem of realism and romance in Sinclair most clearly, then, we begin with a closely related matter: the proper role of personal development in a leftist literature which, as such, is in some measure bound to emphasize the impersonal or suprapersonal conditions of collective action.

The most common plot in American radical fiction in the first half of the twentieth century, and particularly during the Progressive Era, depicted the conversion of a middle-class ingenue into an activist. Writers hoped, by showing such conversions, to induce similar changes in their audiences; they were also, understandably, writing about what they knew best, the processes of political discovery that had shaped their own vocations. They generally motivated these conversions by having characters observe, and if possible experience, the contrasts between rich and poor.[3] The reader, following a fictive proxy through a series of telling juxtapositions, thus confronts the evidence that American society, rotten with class differences, can be saved only by socialism.

Although this strategy—portrayal of conversion, motivated by pointed comparisons—seems natural, indeed inevitable, the contradictions of novels like *The Jungle* call it into question. Everybody agrees that the first half of the novel, which shows the suffering of the Rudkus family under a system they can neither resist nor understand, is more compelling than the second half, in which Jurgis Rudkus comes to see and comprehend the class system that has destroyed everyone he cared about, and to join the fight to change that system.[4] The concrete political effect of the novel followed from public furor over the quality of canned meat, so nauseatingly rendered in the novel's early going, and not from the later, programmatic introduction to socialist thought. Apparently Sinclair would have written a better novel in every way if he had forgotten about conversions and their motives.

Critics of Sinclair have often suggested the greatest danger of the conversion plot: if radical action is to come from the proletariat, fictions about the conversions of bourgeois protagonists, aimed at the conversion of bourgeois readers, are at best irrelevant, if not elitist. To be sure, *The Jungle* is one of the few Sinclair novels about the conversion of a worker, but critics have shown that even this story bears many traces of the detachment of its author and readers from the working class it purports to help. Michael Folsom argues that the tediously discursive ending of the novel reflects the lingering influence of its author's genteel background, which, at the crucial moment, got the better of his realist and socialist pretensions, and induced him to render Jurgis' conversion as "a psychic event, not a social or economic one."[5] This psychologization makes the newly-politicized Jurgis less threatening to the middle class reader, in that the socialism he will help bring, far from being worker-culture, will feel like an extension of "polite society"; Jurgis' silence during the novel's final theoretical exposition attests to Sinclair's continuing concern more for the "intelligentsia" than for "laboring people."[6] Thus the "tacked on," preachy quality of the final chapters reflects not merely the author's impatience to point his moral, but also his deeper political ambivalence about this moral.

Folsom's article defines a widely-shared view of the formal effects of ideology on "America's first proletarian novel." Christopher Wilson, discussing Sinclair's achievement and limitations as functions of the economics of publishing in the Progressive Era, argues that Sinclair in *The Jungle* assumes the position of a "visitor," a middle-class spectator whose detachment from the working-class tragedy he observes impairs his creative sympathy.[7] Likewise, June Howard points out that Sinclair "plays the role of the reader's guide and interpreter in an alien land" so that "the worlds of the observer and the participant remain polarized, joined only by the narrator's pity and good intentions."[8] Finally, L. S. Dembo, while joining Walter Rideout in defending the plausibility of Jurgis' conversion, finds in the best of Sinclair's later novels the same faults of intrusive spectatorship and class-condescension that Folsom and others have found in *The Jungle*.[9]

The genteel protagonists of Sinclair's later novels, and the detached observer implicit even in *The Jungle*, all embody a wish: the wish that one could see the operations of class society from top to bottom, and choose the moral and rational response dictated by the plain facts.[10] Above all, Sinclair wishes that the often invisible workings of class could become visible, indeed incarnate, and thus remediable; to show class struggle in the direct encounter of a rich man with a poor man, or in their close juxtaposition, is to show its solution, even if the encounter depicted remains one of violent injustice. The literary conventions which bring millionaires and proletarians face-to-face in this way are commonly described as "romantic" or "allegorical."[11] As we have remarked, these terms generally carry a note of derogation, at least since Howells, who expressly links them.[12] Now, when critics disparage Sinclair's willful and hasty allegories, they at least implicitly endorse an opposite method, a patient technique proper to realism. The genuinely realistic narrative follows its protagonists through the great struggles of their lives and beyond, to the last consequences of these struggles, the ultimate social causes of which permeate every lived detail of the text, instead of being compressed into one or two symbols. By this measure, the most meticulously realistic part of Sinclair's oeuvre is the first twenty-one chapters of *The Jungle*, up until the death of little Antanas. To that point, every misfortune of the Rudkus family follows organically from the conditions of immigrant life in Packingtown. Their suffering, if exceptional, is not incredible; it unfolds gradually, amid other, comparable, cases, in small matters as well as great, and despite their stubborn struggle for happiness and dignity. June Howard has remarked that an "inexorable fatality seems to pursue Jurgis and his family, so that *The Jungle* at times seems to be following the logic of the plot of decline."[13] Sinclair might well have followed this trajectory to the bitter end by letting Jurgis die, Hurstwood-style, after descending each remaining rung of the social ladder. Instead, he gives Jurgis a second life, with adventures as a tramp, a prisoner, a strike-breaker, a robber, a machine politician, again a prisoner, and finally a convert to socialism. I would argue that this second life is really no more allegorical than the first; it merely shifts its scene and themes, in order to relate the first life to a broader political context and to Sinclair's own professional experience.[14]

Jurgis' first life, closely tied to the lives of his family, centers alternately on his workplace and his home, the house the family struggles to pay off and finally loses. As long as this poising of the Rudkus household against the stockyards predominates, the Rudkuses' ethnicity counts for something in the narrative; they struggle not only to survive, but also to preserve a certain community. By the time his father, wife, and son have died, however, Jurgis has lost this community, and the significance of ethnicity and of the first spatial system succumbs along with it. In Jurgis' second life, the narrator tries to show the causes of the earlier suffering in the workings of a political machine subservient to the great industrial machine he has already described. In this investigation a new spatial system prevails, now divided among various places where organized crime and political corruption block, deflect, or poison the flow of goods and information necessary to the well-being of society. This spatial coding of social forces, like the allegorical presentation of social types, makes explicit tendencies to romance which are implicit even in the first part of the novel. The two halves of Sinclair's plot thus reflect two aspects of a single problem. In turning to the first half of the plot, then, we also take up the mix of political, rhetorical, and aesthetic theories which Sinclair brings to his problem.

I. The First Life: Description and the Melting Pot

Sinclair's criticism affirms the veracity of his fiction, at the expense of its fictiveness. Thus in response to reviewers' often vehement disagreements about the accuracy of *The Jungle*, he announced his commitment to an ideal of unmediated description: "I intend 'The Jungle' to be an exact and faithful picture of conditions as they exist in Packingtown, Chicago. I mean it to be true, not merely in substance, but in detail, and in the smallest detail. It is as true as it should be if it were not a work of fiction at all, but a study by a sociologist."[15] He reserves the right to "dramatize" and "interpret," but makes no further concession here to the impact of authorial perspective on observation, for he believes the science of socialism preserves him from distorting the world he would describe. Marx and his expositors famously vacillate between using "ideology" as a pejorative epithet applicable to bourgeois philosophy and political economy, and using it to denote a universal and constructive component of the reproduction of society; for Sinclair only the former sense exists. He expresses this rudimentary notion of ideology most clearly in an essay that antedates *The Jungle*, "Our Bourgeois Literature—The Reason and the Remedy."[16]

Sinclair opens his article by defining "bourgeois." He believes civilization is approaching the close of a "long evolutionary process."[17] For two hundred years, Europeans have been wresting "political sovereignty" away from the aristocracy; now "industrial sovereignty" must likewise be won for the entire populace, and it must be won worldwide. The class that won the first stage of this struggle and must lose the second is the bourgeoisie, and the currently ascendant literature is "simply the index and mirror" of this ruling class, with all its familiar vices. In later years, Sinclair's most disciplined muckraking would come in his "Dead Hand" series (1918–1927), tracts exposing the venality and hypocrisy of organized religion, journalism, education, and art; here he anticipates this project in a couple of sentences: "The bourgeois civilization is, in one word, an organized system of repression. In the physical world it has the police and the militia, the bludgeon, the bullet, and the jail; in the world of ideas it has the political platform, the school, the college, the press, the church—and literature."[18] While this is hardly a nuanced view of the relationship between class interests and ostensibly disinterested public discourses, it sustained Sinclair for decades of work as a socialist writer. His task was to expose "repression" in its subtle forms as well as its overt ones, and so to contribute to the world's progress toward the utopia of reason.

At first glance, this program has little to say about the shaping function of the writerly imagination, just as it begs the question of how anyone can be sure of his or her own scientific impartiality. As Earl Norton Lockard points out in his dissertation on Sinclair, "technique" is "subordinate" here, serving "primarily to make the writing clear," and this subordination is consistent with a theory which assumes propaganda on behalf of the working class to be the true end of art.[19] This theory could logically compel the writer to abandon fiction altogether, if another medium offered better results. Yet both *The Jungle* and Sinclair's early aesthetic statements do imply that fiction achieves its rhetorical ends in ways different from other kinds of writing, that novelists present their truths with uniquely literary conventions. "Our Bourgeois Literature" is a good example of the ambivalence with which Sinclair makes this implication. He initially denigrates the role of literary conventions when he accuses writers constrained to please a middle-class public of turning "all history into a sugar-coated romance," while socialist writers hew to the bitter unliterary truth.[20] But later in the essay he speaks of "the mighty revolution that is gathering its forces, far down in the underworld of the poor," showing his attachment to a figurative system in which unveiling and eruption would remedy the burial and damnation of the poor under the existing regime.[21] Such a system is more consistent with romance than with realism, to say nothing of the unmediated exposure of reality. Here, then, Sinclair makes his first dialectical leap from a program of description which merely ignores Howells, to a renewal of romance which potentially answers him.

Of course the "underworld" had long since become a dead metaphor, the isolated use of which means nothing, but we will see that this metaphor is hardly isolated in *The Jungle*. There the gustatory analogue for the writer's procedure will hardly be sugar-coating—one thinks rather of an emetic medicine—but the emphasis on a demonic world veiled by innocent surface appearances is fully consistent with a kind of romance. A further nonfictional clue to this (highly literary) imaginative system of disguises, burials, exposures, and eruptions comes in "Is 'The Jungle' True?," where Sinclair declares that "The Beef Trust is a thing which presents itself to my imagination as a huge castle, a fortress of knavery and fraud," adding that he had to "descend into the social pit" to write about it.[22] The figure of proletarian life as subterranean, and capital as a fortress, is an admission that literary conventions, and indeed conventions which antedate and survive any discussion of realism, animate Sinclair's "exact and faithful picture."

Sinclair approaches a similar admission in *The Jungle* itself, and even at a moment when he intends to emphasize the opposite, simply factual, aspect of his work. In a passage from the original serialized version of the novel, which was cut in the Doubleday, Page edition, the narrator maintains that his task as the spokesman for wage slaves is harder than the task of his model, Harriet Beecher Stowe. Her novel on the life of chattel slaves was dramatic and picturesque because the cruelty of masters and the flight of the runaway slave have great inherent literary interest, but "the lash which drives" the proletarian—economic need—"cannot either be seen or heard."[23] This complaint, consistent with Sinclair's belief in unmediated reporting, hardly does justice to Stowe's inventiveness, and its excision improves the novel. But in elaborating this point, Sinclair reveals a curious ambivalence, notably when he asks "Who can make a romance out of the story of a man whose one life adventure is the scratching of a finger by an infected butcher knife, with a pine box and a pauper's grave as the denouement?"[24] On the one hand, this question implies that Sinclair's subject matter is unromantic—he might have said "naturalistic." But the sentence also implies that Sinclair would be willing, like his precursor, to use "romance" for his propaganda—if it were available and effective.

Indeed, he admits elsewhere that he tried in *The Jungle* "to put the content of Shelley into the form of Zola"—surely the ambition of a writer who had at least considered appropriating the form of Shelley as well.[25] Further, Sinclair's rhetorical question indicates that the raw materials of his novel come from life already incipiently formed as "stories" with "denouements," and hence that the writer cannot present them without considering how they function as plots. Sinclair disavows such considerations when he pretends to practice direct description, but his fiction everywhere belies this pretense. When he describes people and places, he invariably shows how both are caught up in processes of change.

The most rich and sustained descriptions of *The Jungle* are those of the *veselija,* or wedding feast, of Jurgis and Ona, in Chapter One. Having attended such festivities during his seven weeks of research in Packingtown, Sinclair was able to show the customs of the Lithuanian immigrants in some detail.[26] In doing so, he introduces the family and establishes its utter difference from the American mainstream. But this chapter already hints that the immigrants' customs have begun to erode in America. For instance, Jurgis and Ona trust their wedding guests to contribute cash to offset the expense of the entertainment, but these contributions fall short of the expected amount. The sense of communal obligation which would have motivated the guests in Lithuania has already begun to wither under "some subtle poison in the air" of the new country.[27] The poison is the narrow understanding of self-interest, made ever narrower by the pressures of the free market. Thus the young couple starts its life together burdened with debts and baffled by social change; it is already engaged in the action which will transform it irrevocably. The same action continues through the second great descriptive set-piece of the novel, the factory tours of Chapter Three. For the family members, not privy to the commentary in which Sinclair debunks the packers' propaganda, leave the tours too awe-struck to suspect the deceit and violence they will soon find in this workplace. As a result, before they begin consciously to struggle, they slide even further from knowing and resisting their antagonists. After these tours and the family's purchase of a house in the next chapter, all of the decisive environmental factors are established, and the human experiment begins to unfold more rapidly and inexorably. The contradictions of the ensuing narrative follow from Sinclair's effort to balance the ethnic difference of the Rudkuses against the political imperative to make their metamorphosis typical for all American workers, and so to allegorize.

By the end of the novel, Sinclair ceases to pay attention to the specifically Lithuanian qualities of the Rudkus family. Their fate becomes nothing more or less than representatively proletarian. But it would not be fair to say that Sinclair's interest in their ethnic peculiarities was factitious, an opportunistic injection of color into the beginning of the story. Rather, Sinclair meant to show how industrial capitalism, among its other effects, could strip away the uniqueness of folkways as it transformed immigrant farmers into industrial workers. The house the Rudkuses buy, to their ultimate grief, is where this process of stripping-away emerges as representative. As their neighbor, Grandma Majauszkiene, relates in Chapter Six, four earlier families—German, Irish, Bohemian, and Polish—have successively bought and lost the same house.[28] Her urban archeology is highly conscious of differences among these ethnic groups; she notes, for instance, that the Irish family used political clout to stave off its doom for a while. And yet these differences cannot measure up to the regularity with which the house, and by extension the economic world it represents, works the same fateful transformations on the families. Sinclair exaggerates when he implies, by the example of this house, that every new family was destroyed by Packingtown. In reality, each wave of immigrants found a place, however slowly and painfully, in American society. Thus James R. Barrett points out that the German and Irish workers who first came to the stockyards had become "the most 'American'" and the best adjusted by 1909, while the Bohemians were on their way toward Americanization.[29] In this perspective, the outright annihilation of the Rudkus family is a figure for the cultural bleaching it would undergo if, like most families, it survived.[30]

By using this house to concentrate the social forces that corrode ethnic identity, Sinclair reminds us that naturalism is often defined as a kind of fiction which uses heavy description to promote a genetically or environmentally deterministic theory. But even the crudest materialism understands the environment to encompass more than the local physical surroundings, and certainly Sinclair's socialism is refined enough to recognize that the Rudkus house is more suggestive as a symbol than as a direct source of unexpected bills, unsafe sidewalks, and unclean water. Bad as these conditions are, they are secondary to the house's status as the intended reward for the family's labors, and its haven from a hostile world. When the family loses the house, a series of non-homes (brothels, prisons, thieves' dens, streets) takes its place, until Jurgis finds a new, indestructible family in socialism, and a correspondingly collectivized home in the hotel of Comrade Tommy Hinds. The novel's scenes of degradation thus appear as stages in Jurgis' progress from traditional to revolutionary community, which means that the setting has an allegorical function, in the novel's vision of human renewal, from the first. It also means that this allegory, far from being the negation of purposeful plotting, always emerges through an action, a process of change.

Although the Rudkus house and neighborhood are important scenes of transformation in their own right, the greatest changes unfold when the narrative moves out into the workplace. What happens there, in turn, both influences public life and is affected by it. This interplay of economy and polity emerges as the explicit topic of the novel's later chapters, but it is already implicit in the first life of Jurgis Rudkus. As early as the ninth chapter, for example, Sinclair suggests that political disfranchisement is systematically united with the family's other woes. The chapter opens with a report on how venal Democratic Party operatives induce the immigrant workers to sell their votes, and then describes how the officials thus elected allow the packers to pollute the environment and adulterate meat. But this outline of systemic corruption must remain imperfect until reader and protagonist have both felt the full subjective horror of the results. Jurgis, in particular, must experience effects before he can understand causes. And so Sinclair goes on to catalogue the special debilities incidental to each job in the packinghouses: workers in the pickle rooms contract infections, and have their fingers eaten away by acids; butchers and can-makers cut their hands up, while stampers' hands simply get chopped off. Finally, in a painful literalization of the metaphor of the American city as cultural melting-pot, workers in the cooking rooms fall into huge cooking vats, perhaps only to be fished out after "all but the bones of them had gone out to the world as Durham's Pure Leaf Lard!" (120).[31] This most extreme variant of the immigrants' forcible assimilation exemplifies how all the descriptive passages in the first life of Jurgis Rudkus are indeed allegorical, even fabulous, but hardly formless. The injuries and adulterations they detail contribute to a larger narrative: of the destruction of a family, and the poisoning of a commonwealth. We cannot understand the completion of this narrative, the tale of redemption, merely by labelling it as a failure in Sinclair's skill and patience as a writer, his rigor as a socialist, or his purity as a realist. We may, though, be able to show how his vocational trials affected the kind of allegory he wrote as he moved his protagonist out of the stockyards.

II. The Second Life: Mapping the Jungle

In the second life of Jurgis Rudkus, Sinclair offers a more complete systemic view and causal analysis of the evils of the modern industrial city. This change of focus, from the experience of injury to the elucidation of causes and remedies, brings with it an increasingly deliberate reflection on the nature of political knowledge. Although Sinclair believes in the ultimate rationality of history, and hence in the worldly efficacy of writing exposés, he is wary of piecemeal political interventions, like the arrest of individual crooked aldermen and corporate malefactors. Such interventions constitute a reformist counter-narrative which steals and blunts the truths of the socialist movement, leaving the profound structural evils of capitalism intact.[32] This co-optation may be the least brutal weapon of a ruling class which, as we have seen Sinclair saying in "Our Bourgeois Literature," still has its police, bullets, and bludgeons as well. But for Sinclair as a writer, the subtler intellectual weapons of the bourgeoisie pose a profoundly personal threat. I suggest that he became increasingly conscious of this threat as he turned to the second life of Jurgis Rudkus. This tale of proletarian education is thus also a report on historical and journalistic revisionism, and the predicament of the writer who would combat these evils. Sinclair's later chapters make most sense when seen in the light of this predicament. He is now writing about transformations of literary meaning, as well as economic and political life. Critics have had trouble seeing this widening of the novel's vision of change, because Sinclair himself, discussing the composition of the later parts of *The Jungle*, emphasized the loss of meaning, rather than its displacement. Reading the later chapters of the novel thus entails reconsidering Sinclair's discussion of what went wrong while he wrote it.

Sinclair believed that his "last chapters were not up to standard" because he had lost "both my health and my money" over the course of 1905.[33] His account of how he wrote the novel does not specify when this decline set in, or which chapters first bear witness to it, but other sources lend some substance to his claim. Sinclair reports that he began writing on Christmas Day, 1904, and worked steadily for three months. By the end of this time (25 March 1905), four chapters of the serial had run in as many weekly issues of the socialist journal *The Appeal to Reason*, whose managing editor, Fred Warren, had the first nine chapters two weeks before running the first installment on February 25.[34] Thus Sinclair composed at least half of the first life in six weeks, and several more chapters before taking his family on a spring vacation in Florida. Beginning in May with the tenth chapter, the weekly installments consist of half-chapters, until the death of Ona in Chapter Nineteen, which ran on August 26. This change may reflect a slackening of Sinclair's pace of production, a decline which would be consistent with more concrete evidence that he was becoming distracted or discouraged by late summer. Sinclair reports that he went to work founding the Intercollegiate Socialist Society "shortly before the completion of the book."[35] Since the I.S.S. had its inaugural meeting on 12 September 1905, it seems likely that Sinclair finished the novel in late September or early October. By then he had ascertained that Macmillan would not grant the request he had made in a letter on September 13 for a second five hundred dollar advance with which to rework the later chapters as the sequel to a first novel consisting essentially of the first life.[36] The last serial installment appeared in the *Appeal* on 4 November 1905, while the quarterly *One Hoss Philosophy* had carried a somewhat different conclusion to its concurrent run of the novel in October. The following January, Sinclair, having had further differences with Macmillan and four other publishers, signed a new contract with Doubleday, Page, which published the revised novel in February.[37]

Thus by the end of the serial run, Sinclair, experiencing friction with both socialist and commercial editors, was looking for ways to reconceive his task. The conditions under which the very last chapters appeared imply that they were especially damaged by this stress, as their plodding quality would seem to suggest. Warren ran the last eight chapters (including the ones that consist almost exclusively of doctrinal exposition, and are equivalent to the last four chapters in the Doubleday, Page edition) in a separate package which readers had to request by postcard, a sign that popular interest in the serial had waned.[38] It is even possible that Sinclair had seen some of the negative reader reports which were circulating at Macmillan, a factor which could have demoralized him as he wrote his didactic peroration.[39] Yet the author's merely privative view of how the novel's second half differs from its first is insufficient. Even if such a view held for the very last, homiletic, chapters, it would remain inadequate for Chapters Twenty through Twenty-Seven, the bulk of the second life. Though we may never know enough about the quotidian details of the composition of *The Jungle*, I suggest that as Sinclair experienced personal reverses in the summer of 1905, he became increasingly conscious of parallels between himself and his protagonist. But even if these reverses came too late to affect the content of the second life, Sinclair's earlier travails as a writer had predisposed him to identify with industrial workers, and this predisposition is the key to his emerging emphasis on textual as well as industrial and cultural retooling.

Sinclair was the first to discuss this identification, presenting it as a source of strength which had benefitted *The Jungle*: "I wrote with tears and anguish, pouring into the pages all the pain which life had meant to me. Externally, the story had to do with a family of stockyards workers, but internally it was the story of my own family."[40] He adds that Ona and her infant parallel his first wife Meta and their son David, both of whom were sickly, and he relates how the entire family, like the fictional immigrants, faced the budgetary constraints which come with an ambitious mortgage. So while it is always dangerous to equate writer and protagonist, the author here offers a warrant for seeing some such identification imparting vividness to the novel's early narrative of economic struggle. Leon Harris has pursued this connection into the second life, comparing Jurgis' stint as a migrant agricultural worker and tramp to Sinclair's attempt to write while living in the country.[41] Of course, observing such parallels does not, in itself, address the problem of how Sinclair's narrative generates meaning after it abandons its first spatial system. The same writer who draws inspiration from a little bit of adversity could, after all, be ruined by a lot of it; such a view of Sinclair's case would be compatible with his autobiographical assertions, but it would bring us no closer to understanding what the later chapters actually do. To gain that understanding, and finally read the maps rather than simply dismiss them, we need to consider a topos in Sinclair's confessional writings which has a sustained and thematic relationship with the topography of his novel: the use of prison to symbolize ideological error.

Sinclair describes his conversion to socialism as "the falling down of prison walls about my mind."[42] This sentence comes from an autobiography he wrote in 1932, but coincides with images which appear in his nonfiction at least as early as "Is 'The Jungle' True?," with its capitalist "fortress of knavery and fraud." Prison is a conventional, even trite, figure for illusion or ignorance, but for that very reason we may assume a certain constancy of meaning among Sinclair's uses of it. Such constancy, within a given text, is one of the distinguishing features of allegory; I am suggesting that references to prison in *The Jungle* have this allegorical consistency, but also that later works by Sinclair enable us to see these references as something more than the feverish effusions of a hurried and impoverished writer.

In *The Brass Check* (1920), his exposé of the kept press, Sinclair relates an episode which preceded, and may well have influenced, his work on *The Jungle*. In 1904 Sinclair, newly converted to socialism, wrote "An Open Letter to Lincoln Steffens," asking the author of *The Shame of the Cities* what practical remedies he proposed for the abuses he had documented. Steffens liked the letter and tried to get *McClure's* to publish it; refused, it found its way to *Collier's*, where the young editor Robbie Collier accepted it until his father, the publisher, compelled him to reverse the decision and keep the magazine free of subversive messages.[43] Sinclair renders this reversal dramatically, as a personal affront he endured while dining with the Colliers. He then describes their refusal to publish his letter as a cause of the 1919 Red Scare: if *Collier's* had "taken up the truth which I put before them, they would have conducted a campaign to make the American people see it—and to-day we should not be trying to solve the social problem by putting the leaders of the people's protest into jail."[44] Sinclair could hardly have sustained the grandiose historical claim which, taken literally, he makes here, but what matters is that he ties censorship to incarceration, and does so in connection with his vocational development. This development is a vital context for his great novel. In *The Jungle* as in *The Brass Check*, Sinclair uses the physical and ideological apparatuses of law to represent the forces that restrict radical literary expression, forces correlated in turn to the more subtle and constructive agencies that shape and distort public opinion. The series of confinements and escapes experienced by Jurgis Rudkus, however plausible in their own right, thus refer also to their author's struggle to convey through them the knowledge he had acquired about life in the stockyards, a struggle at once with a hostile publishing climate and a broader ideological environment resistant to the truths of socialism.

The episode with the Colliers in *The Brass Check* supports the view that this struggle was still on Sinclair's mind in 1920. It was presumably a fresher wound when he wrote *The Jungle*, where it enters into a scene from Chapter Twenty-Four, familiar to viewers of Charlie Chaplin's *City Lights*. The drunken son of one of the great meat-packing tycoons picks up Jurgis, takes him home, feeds him sumptuously, and gives him a hundred-dollar bill. After the young man passes out, the butler throws Jurgis back on the street; Jurgis is robbed of his hundred dollars by a bartender, whom he assaults, only to be arrested. The episode stresses human connectedness by the irony that the young man whose fortune depends on the daily exploitation of people like, and at times including, Jurgis, can casually and meaninglessly give him such a sum; it is in part a parody of private charity. It is also unapologetically allegorical, both because its characters are all types, and more narrowly because it presents Jurgis' arrest as the mere external realization of a spiritual shackling which antedates the encounter with the bartender: "all outdoors, all life, was to him one colossal prison, which he paced like a pent-up tiger, trying one bar after another" (278). This sentence, so redolent of Sinclair's apprenticeship as a hack writer, anticipates Sinclair's introduction to the chapter of *The Brass Check* about his famous interview with President Theodore Roosevelt. In the middle of a series of chapters on the publication and reception of *The Jungle*, and its deflection from its real goals, Sinclair pauses to recall his resolution and the adversity that tested it: "I was determined to get something done about the Condemned Meat Industry. I was determined to get something done about the atrocious conditions under which men, women, and children were working in the Chicago stockyards. In my efforts to get something done I was like an animal in a cage. The bars of this cage were newspapers, which stood between me and the public; and inside the cage I roamed up and down, testing one bar after another, and finding them impossible to break."[45] Sinclair's representation of the writer as a caged animal fits neatly with his admission that he identified with his protagonist. The same metaphor applies to Jurgis' unfreedom wherever he goes, and Sinclair's incapacity to help, however he writes. Jurgis' adventures reflect his creator's career: as surely as Jurgis is thrown out of the packer's mansion by the butler, Sinclair finds himself turned out of the house of Collier.

Just as Sinclair figures himself as a struggling worker, Jurgis emerges as a prototype of the proletarian writer. This emergence lends plausibility to his conversion, as it shows him assembling a narrative picture of the world he has experienced. He does so, appropriately, by moving between the extreme immurement of the convict, and the total exposure of the homeless beggar. First he becomes "free to roam the shopping district," observing its contrasts; this freedom comes after his first imprisonment, but before the encounter with the millionaire, and the confinement that follows it.[46] His compensation for this enforced, and in many ways degrading, sojourn in the wide world of contrasts is not merely an increase in street-wisdom ultimately redeemable as socialist doctrine, but also, more proximately and specifically, the acquisition of the ability to narrate. When, after further adventures, he becomes a successful beggar, he does so by constructing a "hard-luck story," of which "not a word . . . was true," but which he can deliver "scientifically."[47] He has become a romancer, in short—and one who, like a good naturalist, brings science to his narration. In the penultimate chapter of the serial, Jurgis, now a socialist, even finds his voice as an orator, joining his comrades in debate with a reactionary politician.[48] By making himself conspicuous in this way, he exposes himself to a final arrest for an assault committed in his old life, but this time the walls and bars around him will be purely physical. Meanwhile, by making his surrogate a skilled purveyor of rogue stories, Sinclair virtually admits that his own development as a writer and a socialist, and his decision to turn Jurgis' life into a picaresque tale, were positively shaped by his engagement with the great resources of romance writing.

With this engagement in mind, we are better equipped to understand the rhetorical strategy of the second life of Jurgis Rudkus. The novel certainly shifts mode and mood between the first twenty-one painful chapters, in which the Rudkus family is ground into sausage, and the next six chapters, in which Jurgis wanders about, mixing with rich and poor, and learning the ways of tramping, corrupt city politics, and organized crime. The man who can move among these different worlds is a definitive mediator among types, and in playing this role Jurgis loses all personal specificity (i.e., as a stockyards worker, as a Lithuanian). But the claim that this change of narrative method represents a loss of realism is hard to sustain, or even define; we have seen that the first half already contains a strong tendency to romance. With the close of this half, the novel shifts its focus from the family's struggle to preserve a certain community to the causes and consequences of its failure in this struggle. In the second half Jurgis has no home, but the factory remains, now part of a series of equivalent infernos, jungles, and jails, each of which symbolizes the repression of writing and memory. In this world Jurgis the adventurer is as free of social bonds as Sinclair the observer, for whom he becomes a surrogate. Before, Sinclair contrasted industrial efficiency with personal and ecological chaos; now the scenes of blockage and pollution also refer, however obliquely, to a damming-up of information, a poisoning of public opinion.

This subtext of censorship and revision enters into almost all of the novel's later maps, however schematic they appear, and however far they depart from the setting of the early chapters. For example, one of the temporary jobs Jurgis finds after his family breaks up involves helping to build a freight subway, "a perfect spider-web beneath the city" (268). Although the city council has only authorized "the construction of telephone conduits under the streets," a group of capitalists is using the contract to set up a freight monopoly; they intend "to have the teamsters' union by the throat."[49] The episode thus contributes both to the novel's titular conceit (metropolis as wilderness, complete with throat-ripping predators) and to its allied project of using the city's geography and architecture to give physical substance to the intangible evils of capitalism. For this project, the unauthorized digging is more suggestive than the Yerkes traction scandals which Dreiser was to fictionalize in *The Titan*, though these latter were more notorious, and Sinclair does mention them, too. The street railways Yerkes sought to corner were mainly elevated, and thus less infernally resonant than the tunnels into which Jurgis descends. But Sinclair has a second reason for displacing affect from the traction scandals to the buried "spider-web." For this scheme does not merely menace labor, but also perverts the city council's well-meaning effort to facilitate communication. The contractors promise to enhance the flow of information by deploying telephone lines, and deliver instead a system for transporting freight, one which will ultimately, upon the death of the union and the consolidation of the monopoly, impede the free circulation of goods and ideas alike. Sinclair regularly links these two forms of circulation and the blockages which threaten them, and this linking complements his identification of the writer and the worker. Characteristically, he dismisses the official investigation of the telephone scheme by highlighting its literary character: the malefactors may get into "gaol," but only "figuratively speaking" (268).

Prison and its equivalents are thus scenes of literary contention, scenes that the enemies of reform deny, rewrite, or at least misname. Where Sinclair the socialist sees a jungle, bourgeois political economists see Nature; where he sees an inferno, they see an efficient machine; where he sees jail and silence, they see law and necessity, the triumph of fact. Each of these re-visions leads directly to the next. For example, when Jurgis is first incarcerated, Sinclair speaks of his jail as a "Noah's ark" of crime and a "wild beast tangle" (198–9), equating prison with a jungle.[50] Later, when Jurgis is a beggar, Sinclair calls the Detention Hospital into which beggars are herded "a miniature inferno," but also, in effect, a jungle, whose residents can be seen "barking like dogs [and] gibbering like apes" (277). Hell, jail, and jungle are thus interchangeable terms, and all three are scenes of blockage, the squandering of human capital. But Sinclair's deepest insight is that mere waste is impossible: the capitalists have, rather, created vast laboratories, places of mutation, ideological as well as physical. They preside over something far more terrible, and far more wonderful, than any ordinary abattoir, just as Sinclair writes something far more complex than a botched naturalist novel.

A muckraker must show industrial conditions in their full hideousness, as the reality underlying the utopias of the political economists, and yet he must also show the efficiency of the system that exploits these conditions and extends them even to the writer's cell. In other words, his task of making the terrible transformative powers of capitalism visible is inseparable from his discovery that anything he says must take its place among existing representations—that his observation of reality is intertextually mediated. Sinclair never formed an adequate theory of the relationship between inherited literary form and realistic depiction, but the growing explicitness within his novel of the romantic animation of the landscape, and the change in Jurgis' representative function, attest to his struggle with this relationship. This struggle has been seen only in negative terms, as the reason the novel unravels. Now we can understand it as a positive adaptation of the novel's code.

Notes

1. William Dean Howells, "Editor's Study," *Harper's Monthly* (May, 1886), 973; rpt. in Edwin H. Cady, ed., *W. D. Howells as Critic* (London and Boston: Routledge and Kegan Paul, 1973), p. 83. Cited in Amy Kaplan, *The Social Construction of American Realism* (Chicago: Univ. of Chicago Press, 1988), p. 46.

2. Georg Lukács, "Narrate or Describe?," *Writer and Critic*, trans. A. D. Kahn (New York: Grosset & Dunlap, 1970), p. 112.

3. Walter B. Rideout's *The Radical Novel in the United States, 1900–1954* (Cambridge: Harvard Univ. Press, 1956), summarizes several works which share this plan.

4. See Abraham Blinderman, ed., *Critics on Upton Sinclair* (Coral Gables: Univ. of Miami Press, 1975), for a selection of critiques forming this consensus.

5. Michael Folsom, "Upton Sinclair's Escape from *The Jungle*: The Narrative Strategy and Suppressed Conclusion of America's First Proletarian Novel," *Prospects* 4 (1979), 251.

6. Folsom, pp. 259, 261.

7. Christopher Wilson, *The Labor of Words: Literary Professionalism in the Progressive Era* (Athens: Univ. of Georgia Press, 1985), pp. 133–6.

8. June Howard, *Form and History in American Literary Naturalism* (Chapel Hill and London: Univ. of North Carolina Press, 1985), p. 159.

9. L. S. Dembo, *Detotalized Totalities: Synthesis and Disintegration in Naturalist, Existential, and Socialist Fiction* (Madison: Univ. of Wisconsin Press, 1989), p. 169.

10. Dembo remarks that Sinclair's characters lack psychological depth because of his "view of the world, which to its core is rationalistic and moralistic" (*Detotalized*, 186). In such a world characters should look around them and decide to be good. The same insight prompted Lincoln Steffens to compare Sinclair to George Bernard Shaw, concluding that both represented "the economic reformers, the Socialists, who really believe in morality" (*The Autobiography of Lincoln Steffens* [New York: Harcourt, Brace, 1958], II, 605).

11. For example, Wilson argues (p. 131) that "Sinclair's sublimation of personal and poetic desire" in his realist fiction represents the lingering effects of his training as a hack writer and then as a producer of narcissistic *Künstlerromane*: "Even as he laid claim to realistic subject matter, his prose retained the heightened tones of his earlier allegories."

12. For example, he declares that "the romance . . . deals with life allegorically and not representatively; it employs types rather than characters" (Howells, "Novel-Writing and Novel-Reading," *The Norton Anthology of American Literature*, 3rd ed., ed. Nina Baym et al. [New York: Norton, 1989], p. 269). Compare a very similar formulation in the "Editor's Study" cited above (Cady, p. 81). Though "romance" and "allegory" are not identical, we may treat them as such while considering the critical discussions which shaped Sinclair's reception and, in some measure, his praxis.

13. Howard, p. 158.

14. Among commentators on *The Jungle*, Eric Homberger has taken the most understanding attitude toward what he calls the novel's shift from "naturalism" to the "picaresque." This shift, he argues, is motivated by Sinclair's "belief in the capacity for change" (Homberger, *American Writers and Radical Politics, 1900–39* [New York: St. Martin's Press, 1986], p. 43). Sinclair can hold such a belief because he belongs to a generation of leftist writers not yet alienated from society at large, as well as being temperamentally resistant to the "dehumanizing" aspects of "Darwinian naturalism" (p. 4). Although I, too, find the term "naturalism" occasionally unavoidable, my point is partly to show how it and the allied term "realism" prove insufficient as norms for Sinclair's work, insofar as they are defined in opposition to "romance," "allegory," or "the picaresque." We cannot ignore these binarisms, for Sinclair does not, but we can analyze how he creates his realism by casting out and recovering its opposites.

15. Sinclair, "Is 'The Jungle' True?," *Independent*, 17 May 1906, p. 1129.

16. See Utz Riese, "Upton Sinclair's Contribution to a Proletarian Aesthetic," in Dieter Herms, ed., *Upton Sinclair: Literature and Social Reform* (Frankfurt, Bern, New York, and Paris: Peter Lang, 1990), pp. 11–23, for a discussion of how this essay fits into Sinclair's evolving "self-authorization" as a radical writer.

17. Sinclair, "Our Bourgeois Literature—The Reason and the Remedy," *Collier's*, 8 October 1904, p. 22.

18. Sinclair, "Bourgeois," p. 23.

19. Lockard, "Technique in the Novels of Upton Sinclair," diss. University of Chicago, 1947, p. 17.

20. Sinclair, "Bourgeois," p. 22.

21. Sinclair, "Bourgeois," p. 23.

22. Sinclair, "Is 'The Jungle' True?," pp. 1132, 1133.

23. Sinclair, *The Lost First Edition of Upton Sinclair's "The Jungle,"* ed. Gene DeGruson (Atlanta: St. Luke's Press, 1988), p. 65. Hereafter cited as *LFE*.

24. Sinclair, *LFE*, p. 65.

25. Sinclair, "What Life Means to Me," *Cosmopolitan*, 41 (October 1906), 594, cited in Ronald Gottesman, "Introduction," Sinclair, *The Jungle* (New York: Viking Penguin, 1985), p. xx.

26. Sinclair, *American Outpost: A Book of Reminiscences* (Port Washington and London: Kennikat Press, 1969), p. 156.

27. Upton Sinclair, *The Jungle* (New York: Viking Penguin, 1985), p. 20; hereafter cited parenthetically.

28. See James R. Barrett, *Work and Community in the Jungle: Chicago's Packinghouse Workers, 1894–1922* (Urbana and Chicago: Univ. of Illinois Press, 1987), pp. 36–51, for a helpful discussion of this passage and the demographic realities it represents.

29. Barrett, pp. 38–9.

30. "The Life Story of a Lithuanian," narrated to Sinclair's friend Ernest Poole for Hamilton Holt's *The Life Stories of Undistinguished Americans as Told by Themselves* (New York and London: Routledge, 1990), pp. 6–20, is thus far less gruesome than *The Jungle,* although it confirms many of the novel's details, and gives a sense of the cultural sacrifice involved in successful immigration.

31. Elaine Scarry discusses Marx's similar linking of jobs and products to the injuries they cause in *The Body in Pain: The Making and Unmaking of the World* (New York: Oxford Univ. Press, 1985), p. 267; Sinclair had probably read *Capital,* and certainly claimed to know Marx thoroughly (Leon Harris, *Upton Sinclair: American Rebel* [New York: Crowell, 1975], p. 330). Compare the discussion of "dangerous trades" in Jack London's *People of the Abyss* (Westport: Lawrence Hill & Co., 1977), pp. 103–5.

32. Hence Sinclair's famous remark on the pure food laws which followed his call for more militant action: "I aimed at the public's heart, and by accident I hit it in the stomach" (Sinclair, *American Outpost,* p. 175).

33. Sinclair, *American Outpost,* p. 161.

34. DeGruson, "Introduction," *LFE,* p. xv; the bibliography to this edition gives the publication dates of the chapters (319–333).

35. Sinclair, *American Outpost,* p. 159.

36. DeGruson, "Introduction," *LFE,* xix–xx.

37. Gottesman, "Introduction," *The Jungle,* pp. xxi–xxii.

38. DeGruson, "Introduction," *LFE,* p. xix.

39. See Suk Bong Suh, *Literature, Society, and Culture: Upton Sinclair and* The Jungle, diss. Univ. of Iowa, 1986, p. 122, for more on the dates and contents of these reports.

40. Sinclair, *American Outpost,* p. 156. Compare (to name only one example) his earlier description of the "harrowing, fourteen-hour-a-day labor" which went into *The Journal of Arthur Stirling,* causing his stomach to go on "strike" (p. 123).

41. Harris, p. 75.

42. Sinclair, *American Outpost,* p. 143.

43. Sinclair, *The Brass Check: A Study in American Journalism* (Pasadena: privately printed, 1920), p. 24. This book also confirms, incidentally, that Sinclair counted Howells as an important leftist literary forerunner (pp. 260–261).

44. Sinclair, *Brass,* p. 26.

45. Sinclair, *Brass,* p. 39.

46. Sinclair, *LFE,* p. 202.

47. *LFE,* p. 253, ellipsis added.

48. *LFE,* pp. 312–315.

49. See Ray Ginger, *Altgeld's America: The Lincoln Ideal versus Changing Realities* (New York: Funk and Wagnalls, 1958), p. 100, for the historical background to this episode.

50. The serialized version of the novel contains many more uses of the word "jungle" than the revised text, as editor DeGruson remarks (*LFE,* pp. xxv–xxvi), but even the later version often evokes the jungle indirectly, with the help of wild beasts and the like.

STEVEN ROSENDALE

In Search of Left Ecology's Usable Past: The Jungle, *Social Change, and the Class Character of Environmental Impairment*

When it comes to genius, to beauty, dignity, and true power of mind, I cannot see that there is any chance for them to survive in the insane hurly-burly of metropolitan life. If I wanted qualities such as these in human beings, I would surely transfer them to a different environment. And maybe that is what Providence was planning for me to understand and to do in the world. At any rate, it is what I am trying to do, and is my final reaction to the great metropolis of Mammon.

—Upton Sinclair, *American Outpost*

As the immigrant Jurgis Rudkus and his family peer out of their train windows on their journey to Chicago in the second chapter of Upton Sinclair's *The Jungle*, the landscape undergoes a remarkable transformation. An hour before they reach the city, the Rudkuses get their first inkling of the possible nature of that change, becoming dimly aware of "perplexing changes in the atmosphere." The air around them is increasingly polluted by an "elemental odor, raw and crude . . . rich, almost rancid, sensual, and strong" (20). Although they are divided in their feelings about this odor, other elements of the environment clearly dismay the immigrants as the train carries them nearer to Chicago. For mile after mile, they witness an increasingly dense "desolate procession" of "ugly and dirty little wooden

From *The Greening of Literary Scholarship: Literature, Theory, and the Environment*, edited by Steven Rosendale, pp. 59–76.

buildings," all the same, punctuated only by the occasional "filthy creek" or "great factory . . . darkening the air and making filthy the earth beneath." Gradually, as Jurgis's group stares out at the view speeding by their train, its natural elements appear increasingly drained of vigor and beauty. Colors are bleached from the visible landscape. Everything in sight becomes "dingier": the grass seems to "grow less green," the fields become "parched and yellow," the landscape progressively more "hideous and bare."

When the group detrains at their new home, Packingtown, the transformation of the landscape is apparently complete. There remains, it seems, no vestige of real greenery, no trace of unaltered, nonhuman nature. In its place, industry has remade the entire environment in its own image. The "elemental" atmosphere that first signaled the approach to the stockyards, for example, turns out to be a product of the rendering-house smokestacks, which simulate a variety of other natural forces as well. They manufacture the region's weather signs—the "vast clouds" that dominate the sky. Alternatively, their smoke is described as an oily "river" and as a "self-impelled" geological force, since it appears to have come from "the center of the world . . . where the fires of the ages still smoulder." Even the soil upon which the houses of the district sit is a by-product of manufacture: it is "made land," the original soil having been excavated and turned to brick, and the hole from the excavation refilled "by using it as a dumping-ground for the city's garbage" (20). As evening falls on the immigrants' first day in Chicago, the only relic of the natural outside that is left is the remote sun, and it is ignored as the immigrant couple survey the horizon: "Jurgis and Ona were not thinking of the sunset . . . their backs were turned to it, and all their thoughts were on Packingtown, which they could see so plainly in the distance. The line of buildings stood clearcut and black against the sky; here and there out of the mass rose the great chimneys, with the river of smoke streaming away to the end of the world" (24).

Metonymically extending "to the end of the world," the Packingtown environment has supplanted not a few particular features of nature but nature itself. Throughout the novel, Jurgis, his wife, Ona, and the narrator will continue to refer to Packingtown as a "wilderness," a "wild," "unsettled country," and the like. Soon after the immigrants' arrival in Chicago, a sound seeps into their frame of awareness, and the procession of similes the narrator provides for it suggests that the by-products of industry have encompassed the entire environment to the farthest horizon: "it was like the murmuring of bees in the spring, the whisperings of the forest . . . the rumblings of a world in motion." The same point is driven home by the narrator's comment that the narrow roads between the houses "resembled streets less than they did a miniature topographical map of a continent," with no pavements but rather miniature "mountains and valleys and rivers, gullies and ditches," with oceanic "great hollows full of stinking green water" (21).

The Rudkus family has, of course, entered the jungle, an encompassing simulacrum of nature to which Sinclair referred in an early version of the novel as the "wilderness of civilization."[1] Although Packingtown initially holds out the promise of a good life for the immigrants (on his first night in Packingtown the factories strike the optimistic Jurgis as a sublime "vision of power"), this hope is quickly gainsaid by the obviously noxious features of the industrial environment itself, a place that increasingly appears bewildering and uninhabitable to the immigrants. Some emphasis upon the crowding and monotony of the urban landscape might be expected in any tale of country folk moving to the city, but Sinclair devotes a full fifteen paragraphs to his initial description of the locale, commencing a critical view of the industrial simulation of nature that is sustained throughout the novel.

Surely one of American literature's great treatments of the environmental consequences of industrial production, *The Jungle* has nevertheless never been taken seriously as a novel with important environmental implications, a failing that this essay seeks to correct. The lack of ecocritical attention to *The Jungle* (and indeed, to the larger Left literary tradition in the United States) can be traced to several sources, the most important of which is a mistaken tendency among ecocritics to confuse the complex and necessary project of developing eco-conscious critical values with a simplistic rejection of "interhuman" concerns like urban social life and class politics. For some ecocritics, the critical focus on such interhuman concerns has simply failed to provide an environmentally acceptable set of critical values, offering instead just another version of what Glen A. Love has called literary studies' "narrowly anthropocentric view of what is consequential in life" (229). "We must break through our preoccupation," Love writes, "with mediating between only human issues, the belief that, as Warwick Fox puts it, 'all will become ecologically well with the world if we just put this or that interhuman concern first'" (227).

The anthropocentrism-busting emphasis in ecocriticism has carried with it a corresponding rejection of traditional notions of politics, including the class critiques of capitalism that so interested the Left in the twentieth century. In the face of global environmental degradation, Theodore Roszak contends, both capitalist and socialist economies resolve into a global and univocally malignant economic "style" that renders even the most basic issues of social justice moot: "We have an economic style whose dynamism is too great, too fast, too reckless for the ecological systems that must absorb its impact. It makes no difference to those systems if the oil spills, the pesticides, the radioactive wastes, the industrial toxins they must cleanse are socialist or capitalist in origin; the ecological damage is not mitigated in the least if it is perpetrated by a 'good society' that shares its wealth fairly and provides the finest welfare programs for its citizens" (33).

Roszak's point is, of course, well taken. Both of the contemporary major modes of economic organization have produced environmental damage on a massive scale, and that damage carries no marker of its political origin. In theory and in history itself, both capitalism and socialism have been driven by a commitment to unlimited production, a similar faith in the power of technology to improve human life, and a virtually identical tendency to hide the environmental costs of production.

The prominence of such ideas in the emerging ecocritical canon explains ecocriticism's failure to examine the environmental implications of Left texts like *The Jungle*. For Sinclair's text is, of course, intensely focused upon interhuman concerns. In contradistinction to the wide array of wilderness-oriented texts already firmly ensconced in the ecocritical canon, *The Jungle* is set in landscapes entirely remade by human industry and agriculture. Despite the novel's extended ruminations on the victimage of stock animals (Sinclair was a vegetarian at the time of the novel's publication), this sympathy is ultimately an anthropomorphism meant to symbolize and accentuate the emphasis on human misery. Indeed, the major political effect of the novel—the passage of federal food purity laws—had nothing to do with the treatment of animals or any other part of nonhuman nature. In fact, the entire novel appears to be focused upon "narrowly anthropocentric" issues: class struggle, the possibility of individual and family success within a complex and predetermined economic structure, and the effect of ward corruption and national politics upon working-class life. Despite Sinclair's obvious interest in describing the environmental consequences of production, environmentally minded readers are likely to object even to Sinclair's central metaphor—the jungle—which often uncritically seems to reinforce an antipathy toward nature itself. The narrative, for instance, unquestioningly describes Jurgis's exploiting economic superiors as "wild-beast powers of nature" and "ravening wolves that tear and rend and destroy" (167, 301).

Nevertheless, there are compelling reasons for reexamining novels like *The Jungle* for their ecocritical potential. A growing body of ecocritical thought has begun to suggest that the simple dichotomy of "interhuman" and "environmental" concerns that has grounded ecocriticism's general failure to address literatures of class and of urban life may itself be part of our environmental problem. As Wendell Berry argued more than two decades ago in *The Unsettling of America*, even the central concept of "environment" suppresses the possibility of a mutualistic relation that might otherwise guide our lived relationship with nonhuman nature: "Once we see our place, our part of the world, as *surrounding* us, we have already made a profound division between it and ourselves. We have given up the understanding—dropped it out of our language and so out of our thought—that we and our country create one another, depend on one another, are literally part of one another . . . and so cannot possibly flourish alone; that, therefore, our culture must be our response to our place, our culture and our place are images of each other" (22).

In a similar vein, Michael Pollan has persuasively argued in "The Idea of a Garden" that the notion of "wilderness" upon which much environmental activism is grounded must now be recognized as a concept with increasingly limited utility, precisely because it rigidly divides nature from human culture and economy: "Essentially, we have divided our country in two, between the kingdom of wilderness, which rules about 8 percent, and the kingdom of the market, which rules the rest. . . . Useful as [the wilderness idea] has been in helping us protect the sacred 8 percent, it nevertheless has failed to prevent us from doing a great deal of damage to the remaining 92 percent. The old idea may have taught us how to worship nature, but it didn't tell us how to live with her. It told us more than we needed to know about virginity and rape, and almost nothing about marriage" (425).

This kind of suspicion regarding environmentalism's reliance on the foundational dichotomy of nature and human culture suggests the need to return to Roszak's notion of the supersession of social justice issues by environmental ones ("ecological damage is not mitigated in the least if it is perpetrated by a 'good society'") with a new and more critical eye. We might, of course, reverse Roszak's formulation, observing that the traditional class-oriented, interhuman concerns that occupy Left novels like *The Jungle* are themselves not "mitigated in the least" if that oppression is perpetrated by a society that has redressed ecological disaster and developed sustainable modes of production. But the deeper point is the absurdity of conceptualizing "environmental" and "interhuman" concerns in isolation from each other, as Berry's proposition that our place and our culture mirror one another suggests.

A number of political theorists have begun an effort to frankly reassess the environmental legacy and potential of the Left in order to move beyond red-green dichotomies and style a politics that addresses human and environmental exploitation in the "kingdom of the market" that comprises the bulk of the American landscape. As Kate Soper has argued: "just as socialism can only hope to remain a radical and benign pressure for social change by assuming an ecological dimension, so the ecological concern will remain largely ineffective (and certainly incapable of reversing the current trends in the manner required) if it is not associated in a very integral way with many traditional socialist demands, such as assaulting the global stranglehold of multinational capital" (82). Integrating environmental concerns and Left-materialist political theory will surely entail a radical revision of some of the most basic assumptions that the Left has cherished. The Left, for example, will need to rethink its production-based notion of social "progress." Whereas Marxism has traditionally regarded the technological basis of production (even under capitalism) as neutral, it must now revise its model of the transition to socialism to account for the necessity of transforming (rather than simply remanaging) the technological basis of production itself.

Concurrent with these efforts to rewrite Left politics in green is an effort to recover lost theoretical precedents for the necessary changes. The last few years have seen a burgeoning of scholarship reconsidering the underemphasized ecological potential of key concepts in Marxism: alienation, the critical theory of production, the notion of natural limits, and so on (see Ted Benton, *The Greening of Marxism*). This effort at theoretical recovery and revision strives to make areas of conceptual consonance between Left and green thought more visible. Both traditions might, for example, find common ground in their shared rejection of the preeminence of money profits over other values and in their common objection to the hiding of environmental and human costs that accompany the production of commodities.

Although "Left ecology" may be thought to have a recoverable theoretical past, there has been very little work done to discover whether a red-green synthesis might possess a cultural past that may prove valuable for contemporary environmentalism. William Empson linked the radical novels of proletarian experience and revolt produced in the first four decades of the twentieth century to the pastoral tradition, but his observation was never developed by subsequent critics. This critical lacuna is curious, for environment often emerges as a rather obvious controlling figure in a surprising number of American radical novels, which frequently compress their critiques of the social milieu into images of place: *The Jungle*, *Industrial Valley*, *Daughter of Earth*, *Parched Earth*, *Land of Plenty*, *USA*, *From the Kingdom of Necessity*, and so on. More than just an emphasis on "setting," these titles point to the American literary Left's curiously strong interest in the idea of nature and in the environmental consequences of industrial production under capitalism.

The full potential of an ecocritical approach to the Left tradition in American literature is too large a subject for this essay, but an analysis of Sinclair's *The Jungle* might serve as a token of the contributions Left literatures can make to ecocriticism and vice versa. If *The Jungle* is narrowly anthropocentric, it is also a text profoundly concerned with the relation of nature and human life: how the immigrant experience in industrial cities recapitulated and gave the lie to dominant ideologies about American pioneering, how economic classes experience the environmental damages consequent to production, how natural forces express themselves in class society, and finally, how the notion of uncorrupted nature itself might be reclaimed as a liberatory idea in a class society.

The main contribution of Sinclair's novel—its articulation of class and environmental concerns—was strikingly manifest in his intellectual development, as it was in the careers of a number of writers on the American Left.[2] Most Sinclair biographies stress the alternation of Sinclair's childhood care between his impoverished parents and a set of wealthy relatives as a formative influence on his intense interest in social class (for example, Floyd Dell, *Upton Sinclair*, 16–32). Although it is less frequently noticed, Sinclair's class experience was also closely linked to a pattern of alternation between urban and relatively natural settings. Through his adolescence, Sinclair's family depended on the graciousness of a wealthy aunt who ensconced the family in a Virginia country retreat and in a rustic Adirondack camp; when his father could get a few months' work in New York, Sinclair would return to the bedbugs and economic uncertainty suffered by "the tribe of city nomads, a product of the new age" (Sinclair, *American Outpost*, 22). Thus alternation of geographical environments became associated with an acute awareness of class difference, with the country and mountain existence striking him mainly as an arena of fulfillment and leisure, while urban life figured as an arena of struggle and poverty. His account of city life is full of dangerous episodes (Sinclair reports, "I was able to reckon up fourteen times that I had missed death by a hair's breadth") that obviously shaped the young boy. The city life presented a vision of harsh natural selection for Sinclair, turning out hundreds of thousands of children onto the street "to develop their bodies and their wits," for "in a rough general way, those who get caught by street-cars and motor-cars and trucks are those who are not quite so quick in their escape-reactions" (24). Usually, such emphases on natural selection support a monistic materialism in which the city life is depicted as equally subject to natural law as the wild, but for Sinclair the class connotations of the urban and the wild preserve an inverted dualism: life in nature, for Sinclair, paradoxically seemed to *escape* the harshest applications of natural law that obtained in the city.

Later in his adolescence, this identification of poverty and the urban, privilege and the rural or wild, was incorporated into Sinclair's career as a writer as well. The despised work at which Sinclair began his career at the age of sixteen—cranking out potboilers and jokes for a meager living while at City College—was expressly an aspect of urban life for the young writer, while major turning points in his development of a more "serious" literary career were associated with nature, the rural, or the wild. One Christmas holiday at his rich uncle's home, Sinclair set out to read his uncle's entire library of unopened leather-bound "classics" in the frenzied course of two weeks. As would become typical of his thought in later years, Sinclair described his appropriation of the literary value of the books by recourse to the environmental metaphor: "Some poet said to a rich man," Sinclair writes, "'You own the land and I own the landscape.' To my kind uncle I said: 'You own the books and I own the literature'" (75).

The aesthetic claim to literature and landscape alike are merged in Sinclair's recollection of his conversion to the literary career. Following his reading frenzy, the young writer had a rapturous hallucination in an open park, wherein he received his literary calling. The sublime experience was repeated, Sinclair reports, many times, often "associated with music and poetry, but still more frequently with natural beauty": winter nights in Central Park, a summer night in the Adirondacks, twilight in the "far wilds of Ontario." The strangeness of the experience drove Sinclair, as it were, deeper into the woods, since, as he admits, "I wanted to be free to behave like a lunatic, and yet not have anybody think me one." After an embarrassing episode when a young girl came upon him while in his rapture, he "became a haunter of mountain-tops and of deep forests, the only safe places" (78).

When he felt ready to forsake potboilers for his first "serious" novel, a romance called *Springtime and Harvest*, Sinclair found it necessary to wait until spring was "far enough advanced so [he] could go to the country." "My one desire," he writes, "was to be alone; far away, somewhere in a forest, where the winds of ecstasy might sweep through my spirit." Building a rude cabin on the shore of an isolated lake, the author lived a summer in this "Fairy Glen" a life after the pattern of Thoreau at Walden, observing the "daily miracle" of sunrise and feeling a special kinship with "the great winds that lashed the forest trees" (91). The retreat would serve to solace him again in the throes of his first, unsuccessful marriage, but the more general association of urban environments with want (and hack writing), and of natural settings with material and spiritual fulfillment (as well as "literature"), persisted.[3]

For Sinclair, then, environment and class were inextricably linked, an association that continued to characterize his thought as he shifted from romantic idealist to "proletarian writer" during the writing of *The Jungle*.[4] In an inversion of his usual practice, Sinclair suspended his dislike of city poverty and voluntarily immersed himself for seven weeks in the brutal world of Chicago's meatpacking district, taking meals at a nearby settlement house and moving about the harrowing slaughtering lines disguised in ragged clothes and carrying a lunch pail to gather his facts. The central metaphor Sinclair developed for the staggeringly horrific proletarian district he had observed—the jungle, or "wilderness of civilization"—represented both an outgrowth and a development of his experience with class difference and its correspondence with the contrast of natural and citified environments.

Although nearly all the criticism of *The Jungle* understands its title metaphor as part of the novel's "naturalism," it would be a mistake to assume that Sinclair's jungle metaphor describes a universally deterministic condition. In fact, nothing could be further from the truth, for the jungle, whether embodied in Packingtown itself or, later in the novel, in the agricultural countryside through which Jurgis tramps, is a specifically proletarian wilderness. Sinclair is at pains throughout the text to demonstrate that the industrial environment, which appears to Jurgis as a terrifying wilderness, is not experienced universally but only by members of a particular class under a particular economic regime. While begging for food during a period of unemployment, for example, Jurgis is befriended by the drunken son of a capitalist family. The young man, whom Jurgis learns to call "Master Freddie," gives Jurgis $100, and Jurgis quickly finds himself invited to supper at the family mansion. The house, just a short distance from Packingtown, astounds Jurgis with its display of riches and presents a stunning contrast to the scenes of environmental degradation that surround the novel's laboring characters. While the Rudkuses live (and die) amid the filthy streams and "made land," the wealth they create while laboring in the stockyards allows Master Freddie a private reserve on the lakefront. When he arrives at the address with his drunken host, Jurgis can only perceive the vast estate, which takes up a city block, as an element of nature itself—an "enormous granite pile." Inside, the decor also recalls a privileged relation with nature, as Jurgis walks through gleaming stone halls. "From the walls strange shapes loomed out . . . wonderful and mysterious-looking in the half-light, purple and red and golden, like sunset glimmers in a shadowy forest," Sinclair writes: apparently the "nature" in which Freddie lives has none of the threatening overtones of Jurgis's jungle (234–235).

Although this idea is hardly presented in sophisticated terms in *The Jungle*, the novel does provide a strong literary illustration of one of the Left's strongest critiques of environmentalism's claim to social neutrality. As Hans Enzensberger argues in "A Critique of Political Ecology," environmental impairment has long had a class character. In a description that uncannily recalls Sinclair's portrait of Packingtown, he writes:

> Industrialization made whole towns and areas of the countryside uninhabitable as long as 150 years ago. The environmental conditions at places of work, that is to say, in the English factories and pits, were—as innumerable documents demonstrate—dangerous to life. There was infernal noise. The air people breathed was polluted with explosive and poisonous gases, as well as with carcinogenic matter and particles that were highly contaminated with bacteria. The smell was unimaginable. In the labor process contagious

> poisons of all kinds were used. The workers' diet was bad. Food was adulterated. Safety measures were non-existent or were ignored. The overcrowding in the working-class quarters was notorious. (24)

Despite the apparent nature of these environmental problems, Enzensberger notes, "it occurred to no one to draw pessimistic conclusions about the future of industrialization from these facts." Not even the emergence of environmentalism in the twentieth century would adequately address this class experience of environmental damage. Environmentalism itself, he contends, is a class concern that emerged in part because of the rising cost of isolating oneself from increasingly universal environmental decline. "The ecological movement," Enzensberger asserts, "has only come into being since the districts that the bourgeoisie inhabit have been exposed to those environmental burdens that industrialization brings with it" (25). If Enzensberger's assessment of environmentalism's unacknowledged class character is even partially right, as I think it is, attention to texts like *The Jungle* might begin to provide a necessary class dimension to the project of environmental criticism.

The failure to address the specifically class character of the jungle world has led to a second error in the critical consensus about the novel that an ecocritical perspective can correct—the astoundingly uniform disparagement of the novel as an aesthetic flop that fails to execute consistently the naturalistic implications of its environmental emphasis. For virtually all critics who have written about *The Jungle*, the novel's major structural flaw surfaces in its division into three fairly distinct sections marked off by changes in the story's settings: the initial naturalistic account of the Rudkus family's destruction by economic forces within Packingtown itself, an episode in which Jurgis leaves Packingtown for a summer on the tramp, and the final chapters, in which Jurgis returns to Packingtown, undergoes a sudden conversion to socialism, and is present during a number of lengthy declamations about the Cooperative Commonwealth. Although critics have uniformly praised the uncompromising depiction of the Rudkuses' grinding existence among the Packingtown proletariat, they have also with very few exceptions disparaged the supposed disruption of the story's organic development by the later sections. Walter Fuller Taylor's treatment of *The Jungle* in *Literary History of the United States* praises the "cumulative power" developed by Sinclair's lurid description of the jungle world, which "little in Zola or Dostoevski surpasses," but also complains that the "fierce partisanship" of the novel's later chapters "estops it from being the fine naturalistic novel implied by some of its philosophical premises" (997). Harvey Swados asserts that "*The Jungle* must renew its hold on the imaginations of an entirely new generation of readers," but nevertheless Swados concedes that "the more we examine a work like *The Jungle*, the more difficult it is to defend its specifically literary merits." "No one could deny that structurally it is a broken-backed book," he continues, "with most of the intensity concentrated in the first two-thirds, which are concerned with the struggle of the immigrants to sustain themselves in Packingtown, and most of the propaganda concentrated in the last third, after the dissolution of Jurgis Rudkus's family and during his conversion to socialism." A critical perspective attuned to the ecological resonance of Sinclair's novel, however, can suggest a thoroughly different view, contesting the remarkably consistent critical consensus about the novel's structural flaws on three major points.

As the discussion above has indicated, Sinclair's fusion of class and environmental concerns ought to seriously challenge the assumptions about Sinclair's commitment to universal determinism that clearly underlie the critique of the novel's supposed structural flaws. Environmental ruin and bestial struggle are the rule in Packingtown, but there are those who live outside the determined landscape—a fact that logically allows the possibility of individual or class ascendance or escape from the jungle.

Moreover, although critics have seen Sinclair's intense interest in environmental description as simply an indication of determinism, the novel also quite evidently manifests a deep interest in the significance of the original nature that the industrial simulation has replaced. Although, as we have seen, the initial description of Packingtown suggests that the industrial perversion has entirely supplanted nature, in fact Sinclair peppers his narration with observations about recalcitrant scraps of nature that have resisted incorporation into the industrial simulation. For example, Sinclair's narrator pauses during the notorious hog-butchering passage long enough to note an exception to the dingy brown weeds (mixtures of pollution and organic life, Sinclair indicates) that otherwise appear to be the only plant life in the district ("of other verdure there is none," he remarks in the serial version of the novel, "for nothing will grow in the smoke" [Sinclair, *Lost Edition*, 39]). "In front of Brown's General Office building," Sinclair notes, "there grows a tiny plot of grass, and this, you may learn, is the only bit of green thing in Packingtown" (38). Comparing the little lawn to the anguished protests of the slaughtered hogs (and, by extension, to the protests of the exploited workers), Sinclair's narrator partially displaces the deterministic implications of his environment with what is essentially an issue of space: "in what can resistance be embodied?" or, in the environmental idiom of the novel, "what basis—literally, what ground—is there for opposition to destructive capitalism?" As Sinclair will eventually suggest, the answer to this question is that resistance—and renewal—must be embodied in a class-conscious proletariat but also in the environment itself. Redress for the proletariat and the environment go hand-in-hand, and the process of Jurgis's conscious move toward socialism begins, appropriately enough, away from Packingtown. While spending a season on the tramp, Jurgis begins to experience a less adulterated nature as a source of potential restoration. In an extended pastoral idyll that is usually understood as introducing the initial structural flaw in the novel, Jurgis enjoys the pleasures of summer as the land itself provides food, cleanliness, open space, rest, and even recreation. In a poignant episode, he bathes in a small spring, and as the accumulated grime of his industrial labors begins to wash away, he splashes about "like a very boy in his glee." Nature itself, that is, affords Jurgis a material and an aesthetic experience that the industrial simulation of nature cannot. In addition to restoring Jurgis's humanity, the countryside affords him enough respite that he can evaluate his Packingtown experience with some clarity and begin to imagine a better life: as Jurgis argues with a farmer about hiring practices, the reader is aware that his experience of the countryside has begun his progress toward class consciousness. A positive "nature" and improvement of the lot of the proletariat are intimately linked in Sinclair's narrative.

This association between the restorative powers of nature and working-class ascendancy comes to fruition in the novel's closing chapters, a fact that should substantially alter the entrenched critique of the novel's supposed structural problems. Of course, the respite the countryside provides is seasonal, and Jurgis eventually is forced to return to Packingtown, where he is again subject to the degenerative forces of the industrial environment. After suffering a number of setbacks, Jurgis's body, once the guarantor of his employability, deteriorates. Just as all signs seem to point to his destruction, he happens upon an orator whose words effect Jurgis's conversion to socialism. The speaker's case against capitalism uses the customary environmental idiom of *The Jungle*, criticizing capitalism as a perverse simulation of nature. Of the capitalist class itself, he rages: "Their life is a contest among themselves for supremacy in ostentation and recklessness, the toil and anguish of the nations, the sweat and tears and blood of the human race! It is all theirs—it comes to them; just as all the springs pour into streamlets, and the streamlets into rivers, and the rivers into the ocean—so, automatically and inevitably, all the wealth of society comes to them. . . . The whole of society is in their grip, the whole labor of the world lies at their mercy—and like fierce wolves they rend and destroy, like ravening vultures they devour and tear!" (301).

"Images of nature" ecocritics are likely to be offended by this characterization of wolves, but it would be well to remember that the image occurs in the context of a critique of the *simulation* of nature in Packingtown, in which "nature" is entirely reduced to the predatory behavior of the capitalist. Jurgis's conversion comes immediately, and following on the positive connotations of nature developed in the tramping episodes, his reaction to the speaker is described as an encounter with a wilderness more genuine than the jungle with which he is so familiar: it occurs to him that seeing the speaker is "like coming suddenly upon some wild sight of nature—a mountain forest lashed by a tempest, a ship tossed about upon a stormy sea" (296). The episode and the chapters that follow are a favorite target of naturalist critics, who charge that they introduce a radical disjunction from the stylistic and philosophical elements that comprise the early sections of the text. Granville Hicks placed *The Jungle* in the mainstream of his "great tradition" of democratic-spirited American literature but faulted Sinclair for committing a "sin against the art of the novel: failure to assimilate the material he so wisely accumulates" with the socialist message of the final section (*Great Tradition* 203). Walter Rideout also suggested that the powerful vision of the jungle world is wasted by this sudden turn, in the novel's final chapters, from naturalistic fiction to "another kind of statement altogether." The naturalistic description of Jurgis's victimization is far more creatively realized than is his existence as a socialist: "the reader cannot exist imaginatively in Jurgis's converted state even if willing, for Jurgis hardly exists himself. What it means to be a Socialist is given, not through the rich disorder of felt experience, but in such arbitrarily codified forms as political speeches, an essay on Party personalities, or the long conversation in monologues about the Cooperative Commonwealth which comprises most of the book's final chapter." "While the capitalist damnation, the destruction of the immigrants, has been proven almost upon the reader's pulses . . . the Socialist salvation, after its initial impact, is intellectualized" (34).

Even the most enthusiastic reader of *The Jungle* would recognize the accuracy of Rideout's description of the final chapters, which are indeed "another kind of statement altogether." But while virtually all critics have heretofore understood this abrupt shift as an aesthetic failing, a critical perspective attuned to emerging Left ecology might find something altogether more admirable in it.

The political optimism of the novel's ending, in which a crowd of socialist workers roar in exultation over positive election results, "CHICAGO WILL BE OURS!" seems (as does most of the explicit political rhetoric in the novel's final chapters) to conceive of capitalism simply as a property relationship rather than as a mode of production: the solution to the workers' problems consists in a transfer of ownership, so to speak, of the city's industries. But as Rossana Rossanda notes, capitalism "cannot simply be done away with by dispossessing private capitalists, even when this expropriation makes it possible in practice to render that part of surplus value available for other purposes than accumulation. The socialist revolution cannot be understood as a transfer of ownership leading to a more just distribution of wealth while other relationships remain alienated and reified. On the contrary, it must lead to totally revolutionized relationships between men and between men and things—that is to say, it must revolutionize the whole social production of their lives" (36).

In fact, Sinclair's environmental focus in *The Jungle* tends to teach just such a lesson: throughout the text, Sinclair has been at pains to describe the environmental consequences of capitalist industry not simply as the result of bad management or accumulation but as an integral feature of the productive process itself. Although a socialist takeover might result in a redistribution of the wealth created by production, there is no provision in the socialist theory propounded in *The Jungle*'s closing pages for a revision of the mode of production, which would ostensibly continue its devastation of the environment under new management. Thus the political optimism that follows Jurgis's conversion is more than a stylistic break in the novel: it is a conceptual contradiction of a more serious nature. If the mode of production is itself despoiling, as the bulk of the novel suggests, it is difficult to imagine how the situation of the workers will be improved through the kind of appropriation proposed by the novel's finale—without, that is, a substantial revision of the technical basis of production itself.

The passage describing Jurgis's conversion consistently mediates this tension through environmental metaphor. As Jurgis responds to the orator's vision, it seems as if his socialist life cannot occur upon the same solid ground as his wage-slavery. The narration depicts his transformation into a socialist as a series of catastrophic events that alter the landscape itself, an "unfolding of vistas before him, a breaking of the ground beneath him." The sky, too, "seemed to split" above Jurgis, as the words of the speaker impress Jurgis as a "crashing of thunder in his soul," the emotions stirred within him, as a "flood." "It was," the narrator explains, "a most wonderful experience to him—an almost supernatural experience." Like the "wild sight of nature" that the speaker recalls, the setting of Jurgis's new life must be imagined as a nature no longer devastated by production. From the natural wilderness setting of an imaginary mountaintop, Jurgis at last gains a useful perspective on the jungle in which he has been immersed: "It was like encountering an inhabitant of the fourth dimension of space, a being who was free from all one's own limitations. For four years, now, Jurgis had been wandering and blundering in the depths of a wilderness; and here, suddenly, a hand reached down and seized him, and lifted him out of it, and set him upon a mountain top, from which he could survey it all—could see the paths from which he had wandered, the morasses into which he had stumbled, the hiding places from which the beasts of prey had fallen upon him" (311).

Although the passage is meant to convey optimism about Jurgis's new condition, it also tends to undermine the note of the here-and-now effectivity of socialism upon which the text ends. To say that Sinclair must imagine Jurgis's socialism as occurring in nature is also to recognize Sinclair's inability to imagine a fulfilling life for his protagonist within the industrial landscape that the socialists propose to expropriate. The novel has so successfully given the picture of the city wilderness that the transition to socialism can't be imagined convincingly except in figural terms that apocalyptically erase the environmental consequences of the productive mode the socialists are about to seize.

Thus while Rideout and others have belittled the abstract, imaginative, and intellectualized nature of Sinclair's attempt to represent Jurgis's converted life, critics with an interest in the environmental implications of literary texts might usefully understand the novel's close as a logical continuation of Sinclair's interest in the connections between environmental and class politics. If, as I suggested earlier, a text like *The Jungle* can furnish ecocriticism with a much-needed class emphasis, an ecocritical perspective can itself offer much to Left theory and criticism by discerning the way in which Sinclair's novel embeds within an apparent formal flaw the need for the left to recognize the non-neutrality of the technological basis of production.

While it is doubtful that Sinclair had anything so sophisticated in mind as the creation of a literary form uniquely capable of articulating this simple political ecology, in fact that is just what he created. While the structural "break" in his novel may not satisfy the accustomed aesthetic standards of literary criticism, it does a fine job of highlighting a basic contradiction between the technological progressivism of socialist thought and the environmental evidence about industrial production. Despite nearly a century of criticism to the contrary, neither the picture of the social world nor the form of *The Jungle* itself is incoherent, flawed, or outworn. Rather, the novel is ambivalent—intently focused upon both the hope of social change and the necessity of revising production's environmental consequences. In a time when the split between environmentalism and anthropocentric social concerns is so easily accepted as an apriority of critical thought, even Sinclair's relatively simplistic attempt to maintain a connection between the two provides a relevant literary model, a usable cultural past upon which Left ecological criticism may be built.

Notes

1. This was Sinclair's original title for the pivotal eighteenth chapter of the serial novel published in the *Appeal to Reason*, which is conveniently available in *The Lost First Edition of Upton Sinclair's* The Jungle, ed. Gene DeGruson (Atlanta: St. Luke's, 1988). Unless noted, all references to *The Jungle* are from the standard Doubleday edition of 1906.

2. In addition to Sinclair, an unusual proportion of writers on the American Left pursued their political-literary agendas while maintaining an interest in nature writing and the outdoors. Robert Cantwell wrote the 1934 strike novel *The Land of Plenty*—one of the central texts of the American proletarian tradition—while also writing feature stories for outdoors magazines. Cantwell went on to write a fine biography of naturalist Alexander Wilson. Noted Marxist critic Granville Hicks, who edited the Communist journal *New Masses* from 1934 to 1938, was also interested in the political possibilities of rural, regional life and economy, subjects he explored in *Small Town*. Hicks later wrote a utopian novel, *The First to Awaken*, which featured productively restrained, regionally planned, environmentally sustainable economies. The figure with whom most environmental thinkers are likely to be familiar is Left sociologist Scott Nearing, who wrote a number of radical novels and socialist treatises but who is primarily known for his long-term sustainable living experiment, detailed in the back-to-nature bible *The Good Life*.

3. Sinclair's *The Journal of Arthur Stirling*, a fictional suicide diary of a misunderstood and neglected literary genius, was written on the Raquette River in the Adirondacks. Another work, *Prince Hagan*, explored the wilderness-literature association more directly, casting the poet-protagonist as a Thoreauvian hero who retreats to the rustic discomforts of life in the woods for spiritual and artistic rejuvenation.

4. Although this term is usually associated with the Communist and fellow-traveling writers of the 1930s, it was a term Sinclair used to refer to himself.

J. MICHAEL DUVALL

Processes of Elimination: Progressive-Era Hygienic Ideology, Waste, and Upton Sinclair's The Jungle

Disappointed that *The Jungle* did not result in a ground-swell of socialist sentiment, Upton Sinclair famously evaluated his best-known novel as a kind of failure. "I aimed at the public's heart," he wrote, "and by accident hit them in the stomach."[1] Yet no one could doubt that Sinclair aimed at the public's heart, given *The Jungle*'s sentimentality, but the idea that he hit the public in the stomach *by accident* obviously overstates the case. More likely, Sinclair aimed at the public's stomach, but hoped that the blow would cause moral outrage and a lasting change in the public's heart. He was following a venerable recipe for fomenting moral judgment: begin with your basic jeremiad, ladle in liberal amounts of the filthy and the revolting, and stir.[2]

As William Ian Miller affirms in *The Anatomy of Disgust*, Sinclair's gambit is right on target. Disgust and moral judgment are nearly always wrapped up together, for "except for the highest-toned discourses of moral philosophers, moral judgment seems almost to demand the idiom of disgust. *That makes me sick! What revolting behavior! You give me the creeps!*"[3] Miller's illustration of how disgust surfaces in expressions of moral judgment highlights that disgust is encoded *bodily*. This is evidenced in the adjectives "sick" and "revolting" and the noun "the creeps," all three quite visceral in their tone and implications.

Invoking the disgusting is but one way in which *The Jungle* enlists the body, in this case, the bodies of readers themselves. Reading Sinclair's novel

From *American Studies* 43, no. 3 (Fall 2002): 29–56.

as cultural critique, in what follows, I explore the idea of the body in Progressive Era hygienic ideology, a context within which Sinclair not only worked as a novelist but also as a health reformer.[4] I develop a theory of how waste works in a capitalist system under the auspices of a certain way of thinking about and through the body, demonstrating how Sinclair's novel simultaneously criticizes and codifies these processes of elimination. When I refer to "the body" in the singular, as I will throughout this essay, I am speaking of an abstraction within Progressive Era hygienic ideology and thinking, especially as it addresses the processes of digestion, and not a generalized or universal concept such as could include all actual bodies. I take it as a given, as Karen Sánchez-Eppler has observed in relation to antebellum reform discourses of abolition and feminism, that a "universal, and so, incorporeal" understanding of persons, as one finds in any ideological construction of embodiment, will inevitably collide with the "fleshy specificity of embodied identities."[5] This essay endeavors, in part, to map out just such a collision.

In trying to make his readers sick, to revolt them, Sinclair became the muckiest of muckrakers. Theodore Roosevelt had coined that term the same year *The Jungle* appeared as a novel[6] to describe what he thought a dangerous, excessive journalistic practice. Like Bunyan's man with the muck-rake, to Roosevelt, some journalists could see only the filth and nothing of the good that they could easily glimpse if only they turned their gaze upward. In contrast, for Sinclair, the muck-rake serves as an essential tool toward social change; exposing the sordid would lead to change. A heaven might be made on earth, but only if first the churned-up disgust of the populace takes hold and motivates real and substantial (that is, socialist) change in the here and now. Thus did Sinclair hope to hit the heart by going through the stomach.[7]

Soon after the novel was published, Finley Peter Dunne satirized its attack through his Irish comic philosopher/barkeep, Mr. Dooley. He tells a tale of President Roosevelt's reaction. While reading through the novel over a "light breakfast" at the White House, Roosevelt, according to Dooley, "suddenly rose from the table, an cryin': 'I'm pizened,' begun throwing sausages out iv th' window."[8] Were it not for journalistic propriety, Dunne might just as well have depicted Teddy's hurling his sausages out the window in the way we euphemistically mean by *hurling* today: vomiting, that is. I adduce Mr. Dooley's fictional report here not only for its considerable entertainment value[9], but also because it foregrounds an imperative of the body which is foremost in Sinclair's novel—while there is a range of things which can be taken into the body as nourishment, what is filthy, dirty, and/or polluting must resolutely remain outside the body. The consequence of not maintaining such a boundary is poisoning, a dissolution of the body from the inside out.

Perhaps Dunne seized on Roosevelt because it was public knowledge that reading Sinclair's book had rejuvenated the president's commitment to strong food-protection legislation. Roosevelt was particularly concerned with what the proper bodily maintenance of individuals would mean for the body of the nation as a whole, an extrapolation of what the robustness of his own body had meant for his own life.[10] Thus Dunne's choice of the nation's president as victim of foul sausage also signals a broader context as well: impurity in food not only affects individual bodies, but also ravages the body politic itself, the nation as an aggregate of the bodies of its citizens. Via this nested construction of bodies, individual and national, a threat of dissolution to the body of the president at breakfast in the White House is also, via synecdoche, a threat to the body of the nation itself.

Sinclair's appeal to the sickening, then, gains its authority and force not only through the significant office that disgust holds in the moral appeal, but also because it taps into a generalized idea of the nation as a body. This has special resonance with a popular discourse about health contemporary with *The Jungle* and composed of a collection of fads revolving around the maintenance of the digestive process, especially the scientific chewing theories of Horace Fletcher. This discourse, a manifestation of hygienic ideology, relies on demarcating the body's boundaries along the lines of purity, holding to an ideal of the "*clean and proper*" body, as Julia Kristeva puts it.[11] This resides especially in controlling and monitoring input (ingestion) and output (excretion).

Ingestion, excretion, and what happens in between—the processes of the digestive system—connect in a narrative track running through *The Jungle*, making available to Sinclair what I call an "alimentary logic" for a critique of capitalist production. Deriving energy from the hygienic ideology undergirding popular digestive health fads, especially Fletcher's chewing theory, which presents a convergence of biologistic and mechanistic thinking in the idea of "efficiency," the novel's narrative collapses the distinction between body and machine. The novel instates a slaughterhouse machine penetrated by the operations of the body, becoming a monstrous "alimentary machine" that ingests its workers, extracts and assimilates their labor, and finally excretes their spent bodies.

Jurgis Rudkus, the novel's central character, undergoes the complete digestive process. But while Jurgis can ultimately rise above his condition as a converted brother in the socialist order, the narrative fails to similarly remediate the bodies and lives of others. This happens, I argue, not because other characters fail to join the socialist cause, but rather as a direct result of *The Jungle*'s commitment to thinking through the operations of the body. Employing the very same alimentary logic from which the narrative would rescue Jurgis, the novel eliminates, as agents in the body politic, women and African American laborers, even while striving to articulate a socialism inclusive of all workers. In a kind of constitutive contradiction ultimately pointing to a basic flaw in thinking through the body, the novel wants to stand outside the alimentary machinations of the capitalist organism but apparently can do so only through masking (or perhaps forgetting) its own digestive narrative procedures.

Digestion was much on Sinclair's mind in the years preceding his writing of *The Jungle* in 1905 and immediately following, when he wrote *Good Health, and How We Won It* (1909), co-authored with Michael Williams, and *The Fasting Cure* (1911)[12]—plus numerous articles in such popular magazines as *Cosmopolitan* and *Physical Culture*. With these efforts, Sinclair became a health reformer in a tradition dating back to the Jacksonian era, a period which Ruth Clifford Engs describes as having witnessed the first of three "clean living movements" in the United States.[13] Antebellum dietary reformers such as William Andrus Alcott and Sylvester Graham promoted healthy eating and living as the highest of callings and of national importance. Speaking with the same zeal amid the "second clean living movement" (1880–1920, according to Engs[14]), Sinclair's health reform writings joined in a broad Progressivist culture that responded to a rapidly changing America. Health reform at this time, especially in urban environments, employed a wide array of ameliorations for what seemed to be ailing the nation:

> Physical culture, birth control, diet, and the concept of the "whole man" began to be emphasized, beginning in the 1890s. A crusade to regulate food, patent medicines, and the elimination of "narcotic addictions" arose in the first two decades of the twentieth century. Public-health reforms, such as sanitation, and crusades against specific diseases, such as tuberculosis, gained momentum during the first decade of the century. All these issues together culminated in one of the most widespread reform eras in the history of the nation.[15]

In both of Sinclair's health books, the cultural and the personal come together. As an entry into their specific agendas, each book gives a thumbnail sketch of the poor state of Sinclair's young adult body in his early days as a novelist—general problems with health, ranging from a seminal case of "a new and fashionable ailment called 'la grippe' [influenza]" while in college[16] to chronic dyspepsia that began while he was working on his first novel, *Springtime and Harvest* (1901), and worsened as he finished his second, *The Journal of Arthur Stirling* (1903).[17] Tellingly, Sinclair describes the state of his body in these years as in a crashing nosedive:

> Gradually, . . . I was forced to realize that I was losing that find [*sic*] robustness which enabled me to say that I had not had a day's sickness in fourteen years. I found that I caught cold very easily—though I always attributed it to some unwonted draught or exposure. I found that I was in for tonsillitis once or twice every winter. And now and then, after some particularly exhausting labor, I would find it hard to get to sleep. Also, I had to visit the dentist more frequently, and I noticed, to my great perplexity, that my hair was falling out. So I went on, until at last I was on the verge of a nervous breakdown, and had to drop everything and go away and try to rest.

As one might expect, given Sinclair's good old-fashioned narrative of decline and salvation (which is the stuff of health-reformer testimony), having tried many a doctor and finding no help, a fortunate and life-changing accident awaited the supplicant at his lowest moment: "That was my situation when I stumbled upon an article in the *Contemporary Review*, telling of the experiments of a gentleman named Horace Fletcher. . . . This article came to me as one of the greatest discoveries of my life."[18]

Fletcher, a widely read, charismatic health reformer at the turn of the twentieth century, promoted, as part of a general philosophy of life, a gospel of scientific chewing.[19] Perhaps the greatest testimony to his popularity in his time is his having left us an eponymous verb for vigorous chewing, "to fletcherize."[20] In brief, Fletcher argued that people do not chew their food thoroughly enough, the result of which is that the rest of the alimentary track has to take on a burden for which, according to Fletcher, it was not designed. Thorough chewing resulted in the liquidification of solids, which could then be swallowed, which, in turn, occurred just at the right moment automatically by means of an irresistible impulse that Fletcher called "Nature's Food Filter."[21] Any excess fibrous material or "bulk" left in the mouth afterwards would need to be spit out, such material thought by Fletcher to be unnecessary to the body and so, dangerous.[22] In this way, the best that food has to offer could be assimilated readily, with no overwork on the part of the body.[23]

Improperly masticated material, on the other hand, would lie in the gut and putrefy as the direct result of the influx of bacteria that becomes necessary to deal with such matter. This in turn would lead to "auto-intoxication," or a self-poisoning from within, manifesting itself in a general malaise and a host of related health problems. Just as surely as spoiled meat could poison the unknowing consumer, such as Mr. Dooley's Roosevelt, even fresh foods improperly chewed could result in a form of self-poisoning. Correct the mistake of insufficient mastication, however, and one banishes auto-intoxication and lays claim to a surplus of energy, strength, and vigor.

It would be tempting to reduce Fletcher to the rank of mere quack, where he would join the likes of uber-reformer John Harvey Kellogg, so humorously satirized in T. Coraghessan Boyle's *The Road to Wellville.*[24] The same kind of criticism has been leveled at Sinclair. William Bloodworth classifies Sinclair's health reform writings in the early twentieth century as "part of an undercurrent of bizarre interests (including various kinds of psychic phenomena) that have little obvious relationship to Sinclair's political and social views." Moreover, Bloodworth finds that for his purposes, "this 'spookology,' a term used by some of Sinclair's friends to describe such interests," apart from "reveal[ing] the breadth of the author's concerns and shed[ding] some interesting light on his personality," "includes little worthwhile writing and deserves little attention.[25]

Reducing either Sinclair or Fletcher's health-reform writings to a sort of cultural froth that has little to say about politics and society, however, would be a mistake. While these writings appear to be thin and ephemeral, they resound with Progressive Era culture and ideology.[26] As James C. Whorton, in his study of Fletcher, argues:

> When any health crusader's popularity is lazily explained by nothing more complex than human credulity, he is reduced to the status of a mere aberration, a figure whose illusions are idiopathic rather than symptomatic of his intellectual and social environment. Instead, health reform movements must be understood as hygienic ideologies, idea systems which identify correct personal hygiene as the necessary foundation for most, even all, human progress, and which invite acceptance by incorporating both certain universal feelings about man and nature, and the popular values and anxieties peculiar to distinct eras.[27]

In adopting Fletcherism and in engaging with health reform efforts, Sinclair had much more than simply his own health and well being at stake. Similarly, it would also be fair to expect in *The Jungle* an obvious engagement with not only socialist ideology, but also hygienic ideology.

As Whorton keenly observes, hygienic thought systems figure forth a certain vision of nature. But to summon "nature" is also to summon "culture," intentionally or not; neither concept proves capable of being thought in isolation from the other. For Fletcher and other reformers, the body and its processes are "natural," and yet Fletcher's understanding of these processes is also shot through with reference to man-made machinery. So serviceable does he find this way of thinking that he devotes nearly ten pages of *The New Glutton* to an extended analogy between the body and a "modern electric power plant," assigning both the former and latter to the category of "energy-creating machines."[28]

Thinking of the body through the machine is nothing new, of course. As Bryan S. Turner observes, the mechanistic model of the human body goes as far back as Descartes's *Discourse on Method*, which avers that "the body, not requiring a soul, can function like a machine according to mechanical laws."[29] The Progressive Era, however, marks an inflection of Cartesian thinking through industrial capitalist organization, making for a new way of understanding the body. The body in the Progressive Era, then, is not simply "like a machine," but more specifically like an industrial capitalist machine. As Cynthia Comacchio explains:

> The contemporary industrial system ... became the central metaphor of the body. Just as social science borrowed from medicine to convey its images of social malaise, medicine increasingly appropriated an industrial vocabulary to conceptualize bodily health. Depicted variously as a machine, a motor, a factory in itself, the human body absorbed industrial symbolism. Industrialization dramatically reconfigured such earlier mechanistic versions as the "animal-machine" of the seventeenth-century Cartesian discourse and LeMettrie's preliminary "man-machine" theories from the mid-18th century.[30]

This convergence of the body and the machine at the turn of the twentieth century is further examined in Mark Seltzer's landmark study of American literary naturalism, *Bodies and Machines*. Seltzer suggests that what surfaces here are both ways of thinking about bodies and machines and a generalized anxiety about their inter-relationship. Seltzer attends especially to "the *relays* articulated between the life process and the machine process: the invention of systematic and scientific management and the work of human engineering, and the practices and discourses that manage to 'coordinate' the body and the machine." What he isolates as "the American body-machine complex" resides in "a double discourse of the natural and technological" that exposes a "shifting line between the natural and the technological in machine culture."[31]

What is of particular import in this nexus between the "natural and the technological," or put another way, between the natural and the cultural, is how efficiency serves as a linchpin concept holding the two systems together. "Efficiency," of course, strikes us most immediately as a way of thinking about systems of production, as the main subject of the discourse of scientific management and Taylorism.[32] It is well to note that Sinclair, despite his opposition to capitalist economics, like Edward Bellamy before him, held efficiency of production and organization in great reverence.[33] This is apparent in the narrator's attitude toward the slaughter process in *The Jungle*, in which revulsion for what happens when workers are caught up in slaughterhouse machinery is tempered by a genuine fascination for the meat-packing process. He views the slaughter process, "pork-making by machinery, pork-making by applied mathematics," with spectatorial rapture: "it was all so business-like that one watched it fascinated."[34] He speaks in adulatory tones of "wonderful" machines, both in the slaughterhouse (44) and later in the novel, when in the harvester plant (238).[35] Moreover, in the year following the publication of *The Jungle*, Sinclair himself would take his narrator's fascination for systems of efficient production to a higher level of generality. In *The Industrial Republic*, he praises the development of the trust as a signal of the very ripeness of time for the rise of a socialist reorganization of the economy.[36] Redirected from the goal of accumulating wealth for a very few, efficiency could provide the capacity for meeting the needs of everyone. What Bloodworth observes of the closing sections of *The Jungle*, then, fairly characterizes Sinclair's general teleology of history and the place of efficiency within it: "the industrial jungle gives way to a garden of technological delight."[37]

What the writings of health reformers in general and Fletcher in particular throw into relief is the degree to which efficiency was a concept to be *discovered* in nature and in the human body itself. In other words, it was not only associated with machinery and business. Whorton notes that, like scientific management experts, health reformers too talked of "efficiency," putting it through "hygienic conjuring," by using the terms of what he calls a "financial concept" (but what is perhaps better thought more broadly as an "economic" one) to describe and evaluate the processes of the body: "deposits of food and rest" and "withdrawals of exertion and self-neglect," with "wise management yield[ing] efficiency of operation."[38] "Hygienic conjuring," however, may be an overstatement. It seems to suggest a concerted effort to bend efficiency to fit within the mold of health reform, when in the case of Fletcher, at least, there is no need for such an interpretative move—efficiency is a *fait accompli* of nature, clearly visible when one attends to the *sine qua non* of efficiency-thinking: the elimination of waste.

If we maintain our end of the bargain, according to Fletcher, the human body wastes nothing. This is made obvious to us, Fletcher notes, in excretion, whose products, according to a chapter in *The New Glutton* entitled "Tell-tale Excreta" (which follows on the heels of his human body/power plant analogy), can be read as signs of the system's health: "there is no knowledge so valuable in its relation to health as that which enables one to read health bulletins by means of the excreta."[39] As Whorton notes, Fletcher thought initially that the proper maintenance of digestion at entry would result in no excretion whatsoever: "ideally, it would appear, there should be no excreta to tell tales," proper chewing and swallowing having eliminated at the source anything not capable of complete absorption.[40]

In practice, though, and for obvious reasons, Fletcher eventually moved away from the notion of the no-waste human body. He adopted the next best thing, however. The properly functioning body would produce only a small, dry, and inoffensive remainder every "six, eight, or ten days" and not daily, as some thought proper.[41] Such excreta, to Fletcher's mind, were not unlike the dusty remains of the spent coal used in generating electricity, leading him to tern excrement "economic digestion-ash":

> The economic digestion-ash forms in pillular shape and when released these are massed together, having become so bunched by considerable retention in the rectum. There is no stench, no evidence of putrid bacterial decomposition, only the odour of warmth, like warm earth or "hot biscuit." Test samples of excreta, kept for more than five years, remain inoffensive, dry up, gradually disintegrate and are lost.[42]

Thus, the body, like a machine, operates on a knowable and predictable input/output model. Garbage in—garbage out. Like an efficiency expert, Fletcher studied the body/machine's output with great scrutiny in order to evaluate the input and to lay hold of the greatest efficiency of "movement," so to speak. That Fletcher articulates this understanding of the body, couched in terms like "economic digestion-ash" and reinforced through recourse to industrial machinery, at the same time as the armature of scientific management is being wound suggests a deeper matrix of thinking about how "systems" operate. If scientific management had made incisive observations about efficiency in machinery and in human organization, it was because these were already felt in some deep way to be laws of nature itself. Under the apotheosis of Fletcher, the body looked like not only a machine, but also the perfect Progressive Era industrial machine—lean, clean, and super-efficient.

It was precisely this kind of body that Sinclair wanted for himself. As he puts it in a recollected dialogue with the doctor he visited for his first bout of "*la grippe*": "I want to get as much out of my body and mind as I can."[43] Furthermore, not only did Sinclair *desire* such personal bodily efficiency, but he also believed it entirely within the realm of human possibility. *The Jungle* manifests this in a character who has brought his body to a state of perfection through careful self-management. Dr. Nicholas Schliemann, spokesman for socialism, has broken down the needs of his body to its basic elements and knows exactly how to soldier these resources toward abundant health. Besides his hirsuteness (a sign perhaps of his virility and vigor) and his status as ex-professor of Philosophy (no slouch in the thinking department, either), his keen body management is the first thing we learn about him in the novel: "He studied the composition of foodstuffs, and knew exactly how many proteins and carbohydrates his body needed; and by scientific chewing he said that he tripled the value of all he ate, so that it cost him eleven cents a day" (395). A master of nutrition, economy, and management, Schliemann serves as the precursor for the man that might be. Sinclair held on to such optimism for quite some time after *The Jungle*, as is evident in *The Fasting Cure*[44], which opens with the following appeal:

> PERFECT HEALTH!
>
> Have you any conception of what the phrase means? Can you form any image of what would be your feeling if every organ in your body were functioning perfectly?[45]

The hygienic ideology that saw the human being as perfectible, like the properly-managed machine, meshed well with Sinclair's socialist ideology. Both engaged in a utopic sensibility and optimism.

Against this Schliemannesque body of the future is projected the stunted and used-up worker body of the present in *The Jungle*. The novel's critique of capitalism owes much of its energy and direction to the body-machine matrix made available to Sinclair in turn-of-the-century hygienic ideology. Moreover, Sinclair's narrative, as through a camera obscura, flips the relation between body and machine latent in Progressive Era hygienic ideology and manifest in Fletcher's work. The novel's narrative does not explore the idea that bodies are like machines but instead presents the idea of a machine that is like a body, figuring the slaughterhouse under capitalism as taking on the digestive nature of a living animal-ingesting, assimilating, and excreting.

As an entry point into *The Jungle*'s machine/body, Mark Seltzer's work provides at least one compelling avenue. The "radical and intimate *coupling* of bodies and machines," he notes, can occur on a number of fronts, including centrally, "the linked problems of production and reproduction," for which the naturalist novel works out "a counter-model of generation that incorporates and 'manages' these . . . problems."[46] Certainly an anxiety over reproduction and production describes *The Jungle* quite well, and though not a through-and-through naturalist novel, it does make central use of the naturalist narrative of breakdown and decline. Working out of Seltzer's description of the "Naturalist Machine," Scott Derrick has keenly observed that production and reproduction in *The Jungle* precipitate a crisis in male authority, represented especially in the horrific birth of Ona's second child and more generally in scenes of enclosure which serve to entrap men in figurative wombs.[47]

To adduce an example of such entrapment not used by Derrick, we can clearly see such a figuration at work, but we can also begin to see how the Seltzerian account of the linking of body and the machine could be expanded. Speaking of the men on the killing beds, the narrator notes that, "there was not even a place where a man could wash his hands, and the men ate as much raw blood as food at dinner time. When they were at work they could not even wipe off their faces . . ." Replete with imagery redolent of life and death, the passage closes with a simile in which the narrator implies the infantilization of the male worker, made obvious in their "helpless" bodies covered in blood, stillborn, yet powerless even as such to escape their horrific womb: "they were as helpless as newly-born babies . . ." (123).

So far this reading falls squarely in line with Derrick's account of male entrapment within a figurative womb. If, however, we turn our attention to the lines immediately preceding this passage, it becomes clear that there is more to this particular moment, and more to the novel in general, than such a reading might suggest: "the men who worked on the killing beds would come to reek with foulness, so that you could smell one of them fifty feet away; there was simply no such thing as keeping decent, the most careful man gave it up in the end, and wallowed in uncleanliness" (123). If we read both quotations, as the novel encourages us to, in terms of the body, we can begin to see that the "radical and intimate *coupling*" of body and machine in Sinclair's novel lies not solely in the realm of (re)productivity, but also in the idea and reality of waste, its processing, and its elimination, although the two are clearly linked. Thus the men within the machinery of the packing system become not only infants, the bloody products of a female body, but also feces, their stench so potent as to be apparent to strangers at a great distance.

The two types of bodily ejectamenta can be categorized, as Julia Kristeva suggests in *Powers of Horror*, under two headings: "while they always relate to corporeal orifices as to so many landmarks parceling-constituting the body's territory, polluting objects fall, schematically, into two types: excremental and menstrual.[48] This taxonomy, in turn, informs the larger process of abjection, by which bodies and subjects begin to take shape through the elimination of what is for the subject the radically "not me" (2), that which refuses to be assimilated by the body and/or the subject:

> These body fluids, this defilement, this shit are what life withstands, hardly and with difficulty, on the part of death. There, I am at the border of my condition as a living being. My body extricates itself, as being alive, from that border. Such wastes drop so that I might

> live, until, from loss to loss, nothing remains in me and my entire body falls beyond the limit—*cadere* [Latin—"to fall"], cadaver."[49]

Elimination as such continuously structures bodies and subjects. Furthermore, that which is eliminated as abject, "lies there, quite close, but it cannot be assimilated,"[50] threatening terrible disruption and dissipation even as it underwrites the very existence of bodies and subjects.

With this in mind, slaughterhouse production in the novel begins to look as much like a digestive process as it does like machine-disciplined work. As a machine, the slaughterhouse becomes an "alimentary machine." The slaughterhouse, like the digestive track, presents not an assembly, but rather a disassembly line. Hogs and cattle enter at its highest elevation and are carried by their own weight "through all the processes necessary to make them into pork" or beef (42), enabled along the way by great wheels, pulleys, trucks, and so forth, the machinery of the disassembly line.

Aside from this cursory comparison, the novel's narrator also portrays the slaughter process with a distinctly organic, digestive overtone, continually describing the openings through which flow the remainders, entrails and other items, as "holes," calling up biologistic imagery of sphinctered passages from one section of the digestive canal to the next. The severed head of a hog falls and vanishes "through a hole in the floor" (46); "through various yawning holes there slipped to the floor below—to one room hams, to another forequarters, to another sides of pork" (47); blood from slaughtered cattle is shoveled "through holes," their rolled-up skins "tumbled . . . through one of the inevitable holes in the floor" (49). In the various chambers below, the further work of processing and making meat into marketable products occurs.

This is comparable to the body's work of assimilation, in which it absorbs nutriment through breaking down complex foodstuffs. Assimilation, in line with the word's etymology, "makes it the same" as the body. That which it cannot absorb is ultimately ejected, in some form or other, from the system. The packing system, likewise, works through the same basic process: breaking down animals and assimilating them, but assimilating them to the order of the saleable commodity. The dream of the packers is, of course, to assimilate the entire animal to saleable products—to use everything but the squeal.

But the drive for perfected assimilation in the alimentary machine of the packinghouse, in which "no tiniest particle of organic matter [is] wasted . . ." (50), presents a bizarre body indeed. Rather than a canal, which assumes a single-directed stream of matter, the flow of waste in the packinghouse continuously folds back on itself, literally "recycling"[51] in an effort to reclaim all organic matter that might be assimilated to the order of the commodity. Thus, applying the word "waste" to any matter within the packinghouse makes little sense. On their initial tour of the packinghouse, Jurgis's family visits the floor below the killing beds, "where the various waste materials were treated" (47), but the very definition of the blood and guts of the slaughter as "waste" does not hold. In their "treatment" or processing, these items become usable, suggesting that "waste" is not much more than a temporary appellation, a temporary conceptual place-holder for that which might be assimilated in the future.

"Waste" describes items that have exited the system completely, but even marking whether matter has "left the system" becomes difficult in *The Jungle*. The most striking example here is the story of "Bubbly Creek," a "blind" arm of the Chicago River so named for the "filth" and "drainage of the square mile of packinghouses" that stays in its depths "forever and a day," producing "bubbles of carbonic acid gas," which "burst" on the water's surface, leaving "rings two or three feet wide" (115).

The packing system, however, ultimately encloses even this "open sewer." The narrator tells of how "an ingenious stranger" began raking the filthy scum off the surface of the water in order to turn it into lard;

> then the packers took the cue, and got out an injunction to stop him, and afterwards gathered it themselves. The banks of "Bubbly Creek" are plastered thick with hairs, and this also the packers gather and clean. (115)

The Chicago River itself becomes an extension of the alimentary machine of the packing system, the water's surface a means to congeal lard-making material, the banks a screening system to trap valuable animal hair. As with the guts and blood swept into the holes in the killing bed floor for further processing below, Bubbly Creek also indicates that "waste" is only ever a temporary condition of matter as inassimilable.

That said, however, there is one end product of the alimentary machine which ultimately falls beyond the limit of the packing system and is eventually ejected: the used body of the immigrant worker. Workers are forced to leave work in the packing system for a variety of reasons, which can mostly be subsumed under the category of the breakdown, or even disassembly, of the body under the weight of the work process. In this way, they often come off as failed parts of a vast machine, an inevitability of machinery itself. Thus, the narrator notes of Jurgis:

> In the beginning he had been strong, and he had gotten a job the first day; but now he was second-hand, a damaged article, so to speak, and they did not want him. They had got the best out of

> him—they had worn him out, with their speeding-up and their carelessness, and now they had thrown him away! (149)

"Flung aside, like a bit of trash" (192), Jurgis joins the ranks of those who were once proud "cogs" in the "marvelous machine" (41), but now are just the "worn-out parts of the great merciless packing machine" (150).

In keeping with the penetration of the body into the machine, however, the narrative does not represent Jurgis's breakdown solely in mechanistic language. Rather, what Jurgis has undergone in the packing system is a "process of elimination." This becomes all the more evident once he enters work at the fertilizer plant, the only place where he can get a job after having becoming injured on the killing floor. The narrator gives us a catalog of the ways in which Jurgis becomes, literally, a "fertilizer man." Six times more potent than that of the killing-bed worker, "the odour of a fertilizer-man would scare any ordinary visitor at a hundred yards . . ." (120). Discolored by the penetration of the brown constituent elements of fertilizer into his skin, mouth, and ears, Jurgis, after his first day of work in the fertilizer mill, begins to look "like a brown ghost at twilight—from hair to shoes he became the color of the building and everything in it . . ." (156). At the dinner table, "he smelt so that he made all the food at the table taste [*sic*], and set the whole family to vomiting; for himself, it was three days before he could keep anything upon his stomach—he might wash his hands, and use a knife and fork, but were not his mouth and throat filled with the poison?" (157). Jurgis becomes the excremental abject, the packing house system, like a body, having ingested and processed him, assimilating his labor.

The machine in *The Jungle*, then, is emphatically like a body, but, as I have noted above, it is also a perverse one. In its folding back on itself, its reintegrating of waste matter and its processing of and excreting of the bodies of laborers, two systems have come together, resulting from the penetration of the operations of the body into the industrial machine of the packing system. As recuperation, *The Jungle* wishes to pull these two systems apart, to rescue the body from the mouth of the machine, in essence restoring a "clean and proper" body. This same process, it is worth noting, can also be seen from the other side; not only does socialism rescue the body from the machine, it also recovers the machine from "the body," where, under capitalism, it has come to take on the contours of a digesting, organic being. This is the essential separation (see below) that must occur in order to restore a kind of purity to the economic system and to its relation to its subjects.

The Jungle's narrative grows out of a fertile crossing between socialist and hygienic ideology. Quite suggestive itself on an etymological level, hygiene is defined as the practice or science of preserving and promoting good health, but there is also a related and strong idea of "cleanliness" and "purity." As I mention above, Sinclair deliberately sought to disgust his readers by exposing them to the unclean and impure, and he gained much from this, although in the end he felt that he gained too little. What generates the reaction of disgust is the sense of an unsavory mixing having occurred. Things that should have remained separate, notably various kinds of waste and meat meant for human consumption, were mixed together, polluting what should have been healthful and beneficial. As repugnant as were the conditions of the packing plants, however, the novel appears to want to generate a still deeper level of disgust, a revulsion with the extent to which capitalism has allowed what Mark Seltzer has referred to in a different context as the "miscegenation of nature and culture" (125). The Pure Food and Drug Act of 1906, propelled in no small part by the controversy that *The Jungle* stirred up,[52] cannot go far enough in relation to the real problem as encapsulated by the novel because capitalist structure, the novel suggests, is itself fundamentally impure and unclean. The legislation can only be an *ad hoc* solution, since as the novel seeks to make clear, the real problem is an improper relation between the economic at large and the body.

For Sinclair, democratic organization of the means of production will return the fullness of the individual, a return of previously exploited and expropriated labor and a re-integration of the previously dis-integrated body. What is hoped for in the novel's articulations of a socialist world view, primarily in its last four chapters, is no less than a total *conversion*—a qualitative shift from the previous capitalist organization to an economy that addresses need alone. Such is the theory bandied about by the novel's card-carrying socialists. In practice, however, the only conversion that seems to take place in the novel is the quasi-religious one of Jurgis from the dregs of society to member of the socialist brotherhood. Sinclair's narrative, though, does not provide for an all-encompassing system.

Indeed, the novel calls for certain key *separations* along the lines of gender and race,[53] where people are sloughed off, set aside, or entirely eliminated as agents from the body politic. Furthermore, the narrative suggests that qualitative conversions, such as that of Jurgis to socialism, absolutely require such separations.

To say that Jurgis's is the only conversion in *The Jungle*, though, is to miss something significant in the novel about the status of conversion under capitalism. One of the key criticisms of the meat packing industry in the novel is that it relies too much on conversion. The packers' very fortune rested on the margin provided by converting waste in a traditional butcher shop into saleable products, which in the estimation of meat-packing giant, Philip Armour, was all to the benefit of the consumer.[54] Sinclair would probably not have argued otherwise when it came to such useful materials as buttons, fertilizer, and glue. It is the conversion of what should *remain* waste into edible products that bothers Sinclair and so nauseates the public.

A series of "miracles of chemistry" are performed in these conversions, in which the packers are capable of "giving to any sort of meat, fresh or salted, whole or chopped, any colour and any flavour, and any odour they chose" (162). But some conversions go beyond even the purview of chemistry, seeming to partake of the magical, transformative powers of alchemy:

> They were regular alchemists at Durham's; they advertised a mushroom catsup, and the men who made it did not know what a mushroom looked like. They advertised "potted chicken",—and it was like the boarding-house soup of the comic papers, through which a chicken had walked with rubbers on. Perhaps they had a secret process for making chickens chemically—who knows? said Jurgis's friends; the things that went into the mixture were tripe, and the fat of pork, and beef suet, and hearts of beef, and finally the waste ends of veal, when they had any. (117–18)

Even Jurgis's trip through the fertilizer mill tends toward a conversion so incredible as to merit comparison between his stench and the pure power of radioactive elements, only recently discovered by the Curies and others: "as it was, he could be compared with nothing known to men, save that newest discovery of the savants, a substance which emits energy for an unlimited time, without being itself in the least diminished in power" (157).

These and other such conversions that violate a sense of "the real," not to mention the healthful, serve as examples of "false" conversions in the novel. They are opposed to the "true" conversion of Jurgis into a socialist and, by extension, the true conversion of capitalist into socialist production. Jurgis's conversion, essentially religious in nature, compares with the "alchemical" transformations taking place within the packing system, which essentially turn waste into profit, base matter into gold. Like Emma Lazarus's "wretched refuse" in the sonnet which since 1902 has graced the base of the Statue of Liberty, Jurgis, the "brown ghost" and broken "cog" of *The Jungle*, passes through a "golden door."[55]

Instructive here are the many attempts in the period to convert garbage into profit.[56] One of these particularly worth looking at more closely for its use of the alchemical sensibility of conversion is a 1902 investment pamphlet, *The Garbage Question*, which provides a striking turn-of-the-century illustration of this sudden conversion of value.[57] In its cover illustration, refuse poured from a garbage cart enters a mill and appears again underneath as a vast sack of gold coins. The site of conversion from polluting material into gold is a device labeled USGR Co. (United States Garbage Reduction Company), the company in which the brochure asks readers to invest. The Day System, named after the brochure's author, Albert C. Day, processes the wastes from other systems—domestic,[58] agricultural, industrial—promising to produce no waste itself. Whether as tin cans sorted from the incoming garbage, livestock feed reduced from it, or brick formed from incinerator ashes, the former waste reenters the world of use value. The Day System eliminates all waste."[59]

Day couches this reclamation in terms of purification. The dross that enters the Day System by means of conveyors, an appalling amalgam that includes "infected rubbish, dangerous sputum, and human excreta" is reduced and purified into wholesome, useful products for the consumer.[60] As in the slaughterhouse, the Day System is not so much an assembly line as a disassembly line, the end of which is the return to purity. Such is the dream of the totally efficient system.

Of course, at base the Day pamphlet represents little more than a slick marketing brochure, an attempt to gather (or bilk) capital from investors by appealing both to a social conscience and a keen business sense. Not surprisingly, the dream of the wasteless system of garbage reduction is inconsistent with the reality of such turn-of-the-century efforts. As Rathje and Murphy note in their recent study on the archaeology of garbage, such reduction plants "emitted nauseating odors as well as a black liquid runoff that polluted nearby watercourses."[61]

And yet the alchemical sensibility here is quite powerful, representing a utopian optimism in the machine's ability to convert loss into gain, to close the loop of production and circumvent the very law of entropy. Ultimately, though, the impossibility of alchemy makes its narrative a fundamentally religious one. Such is Jurgis's conversion from wasted and broken laborer to comrade in the socialist cause, a conversion that is a problem in the narrative of the novel because it ruptures what can be seen as a naturalist tendency toward decline. I want to focus on the extent to which the alchemical/religious conversion of Jurgis, not unlike the miracles of the Day system, is *not* conversion without loss or remainder. Rather, in *The Jungle*, the movement of Jurgis into a socialist fullness of being demands loss, requiring the separation from and wasting of the bodies and agency of women and blacks.

Scott Derrick observes of *The Jungle* that the very "desire of the text," acting out of a deep anxiety about masculine authority, enacts Jurgis's separation from his family and especially from femininity.[62] That separation also constitutes a detachment from strong female characters in the novel, especially Marija. As Martha Banta argues, the novel's narrative structure makes the world of political action solely the world of the collectivity of men, leaving the female characters powerless and without agency. Thus, "the women who appear during the first half of the novel are wiped out as human agents long before Jurgis has his place usurped by the nameless voice crying, 'Organize! Organize!'"[63] Women become a means to an end, and when the end is reached they disappear.

This tendency toward the separation from women is encapsulated in the very scene of Jurgis's conversion, which takes place, and perhaps could only take place, through a woman as an intermediary. Having dozed off at a socialist rally, at which he is only present as a respite from the harsh weather outside, Jurgis is awakened by "a voice in his ear—a woman's voice, gentle and sweet—'If you would try to listen, comrade, perhaps you would be interested'" (357). Jurgis responds by slowly coming to and turning his focus on the woman who had spoken to him. What he sees there puzzles him at first, but it eventually makes him turn his attention to the speaker on which she is transfixed.

> She sat as one turned to stone, her hands clenched tightly in her lap, so tightly that he could see the cords standing out in her wrists. There was a look of excitement upon her face, of tense effort, as of one struggling mightily, or witnessing a struggle. There was a faint quivering of her nostrils; and now and then she would moisten her lips with feverish haste. Her bosom rose and fell as she breathed, and her excitement seemed to mount higher and higher, and then to sink away again, like a boat tossing upon ocean surges. (358)

After witnessing the woman's quasi-orgasmic response to the speaker, it occurs to Jurgis to turn his attention there, too. This is shortly attended by his own epiphanic, if not an also orgasmic moment, characterized variously as "vistas" unfolding before him, the ground breaking, feeling "suddenly a mere man no longer," "a flood of emotion" surging "up in him" (366). This woman, so vital an intermediary at the central moment of Jurgis's life and the plot of the novel, however, ultimately disappears from the narrative, without the slightest comment. She might perhaps be seen as a kind of singular *deus ex machina* if it were not for the thoroughgoing pattern already established in the narrative concerning women. The novel uses up its female characters, and once they have served their purpose they simply disappear, occasionally reappearing on the margins, as does Marija in the house of prostitution, as a remainder.

But if strong and important women like Marija represent a gross remainder by the end of *The Jungle*, African Americans fare even worse. Barring their irruption into the story line in the appearance of Southern blacks as strikebreakers just two chapters before Jurgis's conversion, the novel features few, if any, black people in Chicago. Sinclair depicts strikebreakers, like the packers, as another opposition to organized labor, but in doing so he neatly bifurcates the union and the strikebreakers racially. Interestingly, such a racial division is not borne in the historical record of the 1904 strikes in Chicago, on which Sinclair bases the strike in the novel. According to James Barrett, labor unions in Chicago sought to be inclusive by skill, gender, and ethnicity as well as race.[64] Barrett cites John R. Commons, an early social historian, "who viewed the strike firsthand" and commented that "'perhaps the fact of greatest social significance . . . is that the strike of 1904 was not merely a strike of skilled labor for the unskilled, but was a strike of Americanized Irish, Germans, and Bohemians in behalf of Slovaks, Poles, Lithuanians, and Negroes.'"[65] While racial and ethnic tensions were a factor in unions at the time, Sinclair nonetheless provides a frightening representation of black strikebreakers and erases blacks from labor politics.

Blacks, along with "the lowest foreigners," as the narrator puts it, "had been attracted" to the stockyards "more by the prospect of disorder than by the big wages" (322). According to the narrator, "the 'Union Stockyards' were never a pleasant place, but now they were not only a collection of slaughterhouses, but also the camping place of an army of fifteen or twenty thousand human beasts" (328). As if the work stoppage were not itself chaos enough, Sinclair's blacks inaugurate a veritable "saturnalia of debauchery-scenes such as never before had been witnessed in America," "hell . . . let loose in the yards":

> any night in the big open space in front of Brown's, one might see brawny Negroes stripped to the waist and pounding each other for money, while a howling throng of three or four thousand surged about, men and women, young white girls from the country rubbing elbows with big buck Negroes with daggers in their boots, while rows of wooly heads peered down from every window of the surrounding factories. (328)

The sense of disorder for the narrator grows out of a catalog of sinful and dangerous behaviors. But at its heart lies a tapping into fears of miscegenation, transmitted in only slightly veiled language—"young white girls from the country rubbing elbows with big buck Negroes"—suggesting profound contamination and pollution. Worse than any of the novel's better-known descriptions of the pollution rife in the meat packing industry, this association of black males and white females threatens to pollute in the most disturbing of ways: "the nameless diseases of vice were soon rife; and this where food was being handled which was sent out to every corner of the civilized world" (328).[66]

While he does so *ad infinitum* (or even *ad nauseam*) on behalf of Jurgis, the narrator fails to bemoan these blacks' status as eventual rubbish, objects to be used to break a strike and then cast off. Rather, the narrator seems to endorse the idea of the black workers as a kind of pollution, material frighteningly out of place[67] in the stockyards of the North. Or perhaps a more apt description would be that blacks serve in the narrative as the category of the abject, which is precisely in line with the body politic metaphor.[68] Having been cordoned off from the rest of the narrative, blacks suddenly disrupt it in the strike scene, bringing not only chaos, but also the threat of an uncontainable contamination, figuratively, of course, but also literally in the food that goes out of the plant to the nation and the world. Once returned to their proper place outside the narrative, geographically "the South,"[69] with the ending of the strike and the return of the non-black union workers, however, Sinclair can freely articulate his socialist narrative vision. Sinclair's body politic constitutes its identity along the line of an essential separation—the redeemed and pure Jurgis only exists because the impure has been submerged.

In the strike scene, the very urgency of the strike as a problem for organized labor, then, turns on the threat of who is breaking the strike even more so than the threat of the packing trust itself. The trust is exploitative of (white, lower-class) labor, but for Sinclair this arrangement maintains some sense of order, perhaps because, for all its faults, the trust represents the future. But this is not to say that Sinclair's treatment of blacks, or women, for that matter, in the context of a socialist agenda is unusual. As James Barrett observes, to expect anything else from him would have been asking too much, for Sinclair, despite his own brushes with privation, cut his teeth in a genteel tradition of reform that provided little intimate contact with members of the working class he sought to champion:

> His Socialist party was the party of middle-class professional reformers, radical intellectuals, populist farmers, and Christian socialists—legitimate heirs of America's nineteenth-century radical reform tradition, the most recent generation of rebels against industrial capitalism's debasement of traditional American values.[70]

That appeal to traditional American values ultimately had little to do with advancing a party that included women and blacks in any real way.

It would be easy to tally this under the category of racism and misogyny, but that is not my intent. Instead I argue that this very exigency arises as a result of Sinclair's adoption of a certain way of thinking through "the body." Turn-of-the-century hygienic ideology, in a rapprochement with efficiency thinking, made available a perfectible human body, characterized in Fletcher's iteration of it as a body that emits practically no waste. A true case of utopian dreaming, such a body, totally self-enclosed, stands alongside the perpetual motion machine in its optimism for circumventing the very laws of thermodynamics. Such a body, then, is also a practical impossibility.

Moreover, this progressive body *requires* the retrograde body as its alibi. In stark contrast to the progressive body, *The Jungle* presents, in the alimentary machine of the capitalist slaughterhouse and the worker bodies that it digests, a retrograde, even atavistic body that serves as a potent critique of capitalism. And yet, *The Jungle*, in its very effort to stand outside the perverse body of the alimentary machine in order to make it visible, also engages in a similar digestive operation. In producing Jurgis the socialist, the novel finds it necessary to use up and "eliminate" others. As surely as Jurgis is ground-up and expelled in order to produce the packers' meat products and profit, blacks and women undergo a similar operation in the narrative of Jurgis's rise. Once Sinclair opens the tap on digestive thinking, there's no turning it off. The very operations against which the novel mounts its struggle, then, turn out to be essential to its own narrative. *The Jungle*, too, is an alimentary machine.

At his utopian best, Sinclair dreams of closing off open systems, as did many of his contemporaries. Fletcher promised that the natural processes of the body could be marshaled toward perfect assimilation of food, resulting in a superabundance of energy and practically no waste. Similarly, efficiency thinking promised a perfected manufacturing process by curtailing "wasted" time and effort. Promises, promises. Instead, what becomes apparent in Sinclair's narrative is that the linear necessity captured in the example of a real and stinking digestive system disrupts the utopian closed system. Implying a canal open not only at the "top," but at the "bottom" as well, processes of elimination make possible, continuously condition, and threaten the idea of a perfected factory, a perfected human body, and even a perfected nation.

Nauseating the nation, *The Jungle* rudely demonstrated that the meat packers had been feeding the body politic God-knows-what for God-knows-how-long. Yet Sinclair was not the first to mobilize a sense of the digesting body politic under the threat of what it was unknowingly eating. That model had been established when Sinclair was still in short pants, and did not at that time refer to threats from the food supply, per se, but rather, the more abstract threats to the digestive body politic from immigration. In 1885, Social Gospel leader Josiah Strong warned that immigration had so glutted the nation that America must either "digest or die." Undoing a body metaphor for cultural assimilation that he borrows from Henry Ward Beecher, Strong cautions that, when it comes to immigration, we are what we eat:

> Mr. Beecher once said, "When the lion eats an ox, the ox becomes lion, not the lion, ox." The illustration would be very neat if it only illustrated. The lion happily has an instinct controlled by an unfailing law which determines what, and when, and how much he shall eat. If that instinct should fail, and he should some day eat a badly-diseased ox, or should very much over-eat, we might have on our hands a very sick lion. I can even conceive that under such conditions the ignoble ox might slay the king of beasts. Foreigners are not coming to the United States in answer to any appetite of ours, controlled by a unfailing moral or political instinct. They naturally consult their own interests in coming, not ours. The lion, without being consulted as to time, quantity or quality, is having the food thrust down his throat, and his only alternative is, digest or die.[71]

"Digest or die," Strong's reworking of Beecher's body politic metaphor curiously suggests a body with no apparent means of purging itself of unfit matter. It must, without an outlet, simply bloat and maintain the corrupting matter which has been forced into it, eventually to be poisoned and to disintegrate from the inside out. Like Sinclair's alimentary machine, it folds back on itself, instead of eliminating pollutants, re-incorporating them, or seeking to, into its being. Or, from another angle, the self-enclosed Lion is not unlike Fletcher's most idealist thinking on the no-waste human body. That Strong's insistence on the metaphor stops short of carrying through to the bitter end, as it were, is perhaps nothing more than a simple matter of propriety. But it could also just as easily be a fundamental problem in applying the body metaphor to the nation. The difficulty is that the real Lion is not an enclosed system, vomiting or excreting as necessary removes the unassimilable, and there will always be the unassimilable which must be expelled.

On this score, the nation cannot very well be seen as a body. One might even surmise, given this, that the central purpose behind Strong's extension of Beecher's metaphor is to push it to the breaking point. But Strong, it appears, is equally committed to the notion of a digesting body politic. In his chapter on the perils of religion and public education, which argues against private religious schools, he strongly asserts the digesting body politic figure:

> Democracy necessitates the public school. Important as is the school to any civilized people, it is exceptionally so to us, for in the United States the common school has a function which is peculiar, viz., to Americanize the children of immigrants. The public school is the principal digestive organ of the body politic. By means of it the children of strange and dissimilar races which come to us are, in one generation, assimilated and made Americans.[72]

Assimilation for Strong means here just what it means elsewhere, to make the same: "it is the heterogeneous character of our population (especially in cities) which threatens the integrity of our public school system and at the same time renders it supremely important to maintain that integrity."[73] The social body, then, demands homogeneity, and so its alimentary canal must not simply pass the heterogeneous through (and out), but must somehow convert the alien material and absorb it.[74]

Strong's reworking of Beecher's lion metaphor, alongside the various bodies invoked in Sinclair's *The Jungle*, suggests a turning, by the closing years of the nineteenth century, toward an emphasis on digestive processes for understanding a wide range of complex and increasingly general systems, from the human body to the nation itself. Sinclair, to mix a metaphor, had put his finger on something important in *The Jungle*. When these various digesting bodies come into operation or surface in Progressive Era reform literature, they point toward the idea of a "core truth" about human beings. It is a profoundly democratic, if ultimately ambivalent observation: the human "heart" may vary, but the one thing we all share is a digestive system that works in the same way for all people. At least that was the idea. Sinclair's effort to disgust the populace, then, appeals to the universal "truth" of digestion. Yet the processes of elimination that attend that truth amply suggest that Sinclair's outcry against and solution for class-exclusion in capitalist America bases itself on still-deeper exclusions along the lines of race and gender.

Notes

1. Upton Sinclair, "What Life Means to Me," *Cosmopolitan* 41 (October 1906): 594.

2. Although new editions of *The Jungle* emerge every couple of years (the latest one, edited by Clare Virginia Eby, was issued in 2002 [Norton Critical Editions. New York: Norton, 2002]), relatively little criticism on the book has appeared recently. Witness to the thinness of the field is a collection of previously published interpretations (1975–1997) of the novel that has just come out (Harold Bloom, ed., *Upton Sinclair's The Jungle: Modern Critical Interpretations* (Philadelphia: Chelsea House, 2002). While Bloom's collection features notable essays by Michael Brewster Folsom and Scott Derrick (which I cite in the original below), it seems "padded"

with sections reprinted from biographical studies of Sinclair and editorial commentary to two of the novel's innumerable paperback editions. (Also worth mentioning here is that the collection omits notes from the authors' original pieces.)

Bloom's dismissive introduction to the collection (which ruminates on "inadequate literature," "period pieces," and "bad books" [1]) reiterates the double gesture of recognition and repulsion that has animated the literary-critical take on *The Jungle* for most of the last century. While critics without exception bow to the historical import of the novel, for the most part, they become squeamish about its "failure" as art. Fortunately, efforts such as Folsom and Derrick's, which I have found particularly suggestive for my approach to the novel, rise above the art versus propaganda dialectic. Folsom understands the narrative structure of the novel as conditioned by its process of composition and publication, the points of contact between the author's aim and the audience to which he was reaching out ("Upton Sinclair's Escape from *The Jungle*: The Narrative Strategy and Suppressed Conclusion of America's First Proletarian Novel," *Prospects* 4 [1979]: 237–266). Derrick observes some of the gender and body dynamics that subtend the novel's narrative structure ("What a Beating Feels Like: Authorship, Dissolution, and Masculinity in Sinclair's *The Jungle*," *Studies in American Fiction* 23 [1995]: 85–100).

Biographical and critical studies of the life and work of Sinclair worth reading include R. N. Mookerjee, *Art for Social Justice: The Major Novels of Upton Sinclair* (Metuchen. N.J.: Scarecrow Press, 1988); William A. Bloodworth, *Upton Sinclair* (Boston: Twayne, 1977); and Jon A. Yoder, *Upton Sinclair* (New York: Frederick Ungar, 1975).

3. William Ian Miller, *The Anatomy of Disgust* (Cambridge: Harvard University Press, 1997): xi.

4. See William G. Little's *The Waste Fix: Seizures of the Sacred from Upton Sinclair to* The Sopranos, Literary Criticism and Cultural Studies: Outstanding Dissertations (New York: Routledge, 2002) for a different treatment of the relation between Sinclair as novelist and health reformer and concepts of the wasting body.

5. Karen Sánchez-Eppler, *Touching Liberty: Abolition. Feminism, and the Politics of the Body* (Berkeley: University of California Press, 1993): 1.

6. James Harvey Young notes that while it is thought that Roosevelt was directing his harangue at David Graham Phillips, who had written about corruption in the Senate, Sinclair's work could not have been very far from Roosevelt's mind when he constructed the speech ("The Pig that Fell into the Privy: Upton Sinclair's *The Jungle* and the Meat Inspection Amendments of 1906," *Bulletin of the History of Medicine* 59 [1985]: 471).

7. Emory Elliott is precisely on the mark when he says that, "as is often the case with jokes," Sinclair's "seeming flip remark" to the effect of having missed the heart and hit the stomach instead, "contains more truths than are immediately apparent: it speaks directly to the purpose, techniques, and results of the novel" ("Afterward to *The Jungle*" in Bloom, *Upton Sinclair's The Jungle*, 89). At least two other critics have flipped Sinclair's joke on its head. William Bloodworth, who seeks to understand the relationship between Sinclair's health writings and his reform fiction (if incompletely, to my mind), suggests that "Sinclair apparently felt that the way to a reader's heart was through his stomach" ("From *The Jungle* to *The Fasting Cure*: Upton Sinclair on American Food," *Journal of American Culture* 2 [1979]: 447).

Michael Brewster Folsom, who effectively analyses the composition and rhetoric of the novel, makes the case in relation to Sinclair's horrific representations of black strike-breakers, which i will come to at the end of this article. A direct appeal to the polite white reader's worst racist imaginings, "the vision of [a] brute sexual threat to white womanhood" in the form of black "scabs" has Folsom exclaiming: "clearly, Sinclair did not 'accidentally' hit his reader's stomach; he aimed straight at it!" ("Upton Sinclair's Escape," 261).

8. F. P. Dunne, "Mr. Dooley on the Food We Eat," *Colliers* (23 June 1906): 15.

9. This particular scene goes on to reach great heights of absurdity. Many sausages flew out the window, but

> Th' ninth wan sthruck Sinitor Biv'ridge on th' head an' made him a blond. It bounced off, exploded, an' blew a leg off a secret service agent, an' th' scattered fragments desthroyed a handsome row iv ol' oak trees. Sinitor Biv'ridge rushed in, thinkin' that th' Prisidint was bein' assassynated be his devoted followers in th' Sinit, an' discovered Tiddy engaged in a hand-to-hand conflict with a potted ham. Th' Sinitor fr'm Injyanny, with few well-directed wurruds, put out th' fuse an' rendered th' missle harmless. (*Ibid.*, 15)

10. See, for instance, Roosevelt's *The Strenuous Life* (New York: The Century Co., 1900; Bartleby.com <http://www.bartleby.com/58/>, 27 Nov. 2001).

11. Julia Kristeva, *Powers of Horror: An Essay on Abjection*, trans. Leon S. Roudiez (New York: Columbia University Press, 1982): 108.

12. Upton Sinclair and Michael Williams, *Good Health and How We Won It* (New York: Frederick A. Stokes, 1909); Upton Sinclair, *The Fasting Cure* (New York: Mitchell Kennerley, 1911). It should be noted that while Williams collaborated with Sinclair on *Good Health*, the introduction, from which I cite hereafter, was penned by Sinclair. For a treatment of the fasting movement which *The Fasting Cure* joins, see R. Marie Griffith, "Apostles of Abstinence: Fasting and Masculinity during the Progressive Era," *American Quarterly* 52 (2000): 599–638.

13. Ruth Clifford Engs, *Clean Living Movements: American Cycles of Health Reform* (Westport, CT: Praeger, 2000). See also James C. Whorton, *Crusaders for Fitness: The History of American Health Reformers* (Princeton: Princeton University Press, 1982) and, for a lighter approach, Ronald M. Deutsch, *The Nuts among the Berries* (New York: Ballantine, 1967).

14. Engs, *Clean Living*, 101–102.

15. *Ibid.*, 102.

16. Sinclair and Williams, *Good Health*, 1.

17. Sinclair, *The Fasting Cure*, 14.

18. Sinclair and Williams, *Good Health*, 3–44.

19. Fletcher's influence was wide-spread, among both common people and the intelligentsia. Among his more famous devotees was Henry James. See chapter two, entitled "Waste Products," of Tim Armstrong's *Modernism, Technology and the Body* (Cambridge: Cambridge University Press, 1998) for an interesting reading of James's revision of his novels for the New York edition. Armstrong suggests that James's revision process shows a marked influence from Fletcher's chewing theory, surfacing especially in the prefaces in a penchant for masticatory figures. James, also,

as it turns out, had corresponded with Sinclair about Horace Fletcher (Sinclair, *My Lifetime in Letters* [Columbia: University of Missouri Press, 1960]: 31–32).

20. Sinclair and Williams attribute the word to John Harvey Kellogg, "after the analogy of 'pasteurizing'," *Good Health*, 49–50.

21. Horace Fletcher, *The New Glutton or Epicure* (New York: Frederick A. Stokes, 1912): 8. Fletcher's 1912 text provides a summary of his thinking on digestion dating from the late 1890s, when he began publishing articles in the popular press. Fletcher's books largely consist of material gleaned from materials he printed earlier in popular periodicals.

22. This was a point of contention between Fletcher and John Harvey Kellogg, the chief diet reformer of the period. While he had adopted Fletcher's chewing philosophy wholeheartedly and without reservation for patients at his Battle Creek sanitarium, Kellogg put a premium on "regularity," and found the assistance of fibrous material to this end to be indispensable. James C. Whorton notes that both reformers were after the same thing—purity of the body: "Kellogg shared Fletcher's loathing of internal filth. . . ." Their opposed attitudes toward fiber merely represented two different means of approaching the same goal: Kellogg would have a regularly swept system, Fletcher a system that would not need sweeping since nothing untoward would enter it in the first place ("'Physiologic Optimism': Horace Fletcher and Hygienic Ideology in Progressive America," *Bulletin of the History of Medicine* 55 [1981]: 83).

23. Jaime Osterman Alves has pointed out to me an analog to Fletcher in our contemporary popular culture: the Juice Man, whose infomercials for a juicing system and philosophy of eating frequently appear on late-night television and cable shopping channels. In essence, his claim is the same as Fletcher's: the juicer extracts what is best from food, making it ever so easily available for assimilation, and at the same time saving the internal organs the trouble of breaking the food down.

24. T. Coraghessan Boyle, *The Road to Wellville* (New York: Penguin, 1993).

25. William Bloodworth, *Upton Sinclair* (Boston: Twayne, 1977): 70–71.

26. Fletcher himself was after much more than change in the eating habits of Americans. His theory of chewing was but one, albeit significant, part of a larger social reform effort. Whorton points out that Fletcher was much concerned late in his life that his legacy not be reduced to his chewing theory: "He complained repeatedly during his later years that this popular conception of his work was a simplification which detracted from his complete program. Careful chewing of food was the major element—but only one element—of a philosophy designed to stimulate mental, moral and social progress, in addition to physical improvement" (Whorton, "Physiologic Optimism," 59).

27. *Ibid.*, 60.

28. Fletcher, *The New Glutton*. 133, 136.

29. Bryan S. Turner, *Regulating Bodies: Essays in Medical Sociology* (London: Routledge, 1992): 182.

30. Cynthia Comacchio, "Mechanomorphosis: Science, Management, and 'Human Machinery' in Industrial Canada, 1900–45," *Labour/Le Travail* 41 (1998): 38.

31. Mark Seltzer, *Bodies and Machines* (New York: Routledge, 1992): 3–4.

32. Although I make much in this analysis of the role of efficiency-thinking in relation to Progressivism, this does not imply that the two are coextensive

concepts. Taylorism represents but one pronounced thread in the web of Progressivism. Nor should Taylor himself be seen as the singular progenitor of the discipline and technologies of scientific management. As a recent biography puts it, "he was no genius in the way Einstein or Picasso were. Rather, he took fragments of thought and practice drifting through the nineteenth century and directed them down one tight channel, focused them, packaged them, sold them as a single idea—and projected it into the twentieth century" (Robert Kanigel, *The One Best Way: Frederick Winslow Taylor and the Enigma of Efficiency* [New York: Viking, 1997]: 19).

There have been many good studies of efficiency and scientific management and American culture and literature. Among these are Martha Banta's *Taylored Lives: Narrative Productions in the Age of Taylor, Veblen, and Ford* (Chicago: University of Chicago Press, 1993) and Cecilia Tichi's *Shifting Gears: Technology. Literature, Culture in Modernist America* (Chapel Hill: University of North Carolina Press, 1987).

33. As Michael Brewster Folsom observes, Sinclair's *Mammonart* (1925), his analysis of the relationship between literature and society, takes special pains to differentiate the socialist *Looking Backward* of Edward Bellamy from the socialist *News from Nowhere* of William Morris precisely along the lines of efficiency thinking, which, interestingly, also serves to encapsulate for Sinclair what is "American" about Bellamy:

> Explaining his differences with William Morris on the matter of art and industry, [Sinclair] noted that *News from Nowhere* is a reply to *Looking Backward*, which Morris "did not like, . . . because Bellamy was an American, and had organized and systematized everything." Sinclair was pleased to identify himself with things organized, systematized, and, thus, American: "I am a Socialist who believes in machinery, and has no interest in any world that does not develop machine power to the greatest extent." (242)

34. Upton Sinclair, *The Jungle* (New York: Penguin, 1985): 44. All subsequent page numbers are cited parenthetically in the text.

35. Folsom aptly characterizes Sinclair as captivated by the "efficiency and power—even the beauty—of men and machines organized together in an essentially ugly (but necessary) business" ("Upton Sinclair's Escape," 242). Sinclair was not alone in his appreciation of efficient production models. The stunning efficiency of the meat packing system, according to James Barrett, in the introduction to his edition of *The Jungle*, captivated "economists and other professionals" of the time: "'it would be difficult to find another industry where division of labor has been so ingeniously and microscopically worked out,' pioneer labor historian John R. Commons observed in 1905. 'The animal has been surveyed and laid off like a map'" (quoted in James R. Barrett, ed., *The Jungle*, by Upton Sinclair [Urbana: University of Illinois Press, 1988], xv). A model of efficiency which both predates and informs Henry Ford's assembly line, the packer's "division of labor and . . . introduction of a 'disassembly line' had made meat packing the most modern industry in the economy, at least so far as the organization of the labor process was concerned" (*Ibid.*, xv).

36. In *The Industrial Republic*, Sinclair is incredulous at the suggestion of destroying the trusts:

> But surely we must destroy the trusts! You say. *Why* must we destroy the trusts? The trusts are marvelous industrial machines, of power the like of which was never known in the world before: they are the last and most wonderful of the products of civilisation [sic]—and we must destroy them! (Sinclair, *The Industrial Republic: A Study of the America of Ten Years Hence* [1907; reprint, Westport: Hyperion, 1976], 47.)

37. Bloodworth, *Upton Sinclair*. 63.
38. Whorton, "'Physiologic Optimism,'" 62.
39. Fletcher, *The New Glutton*, 142.
40. Whorton, "'Physiologic Optimism,'" 69.
41. Fletcher, *The New Glutton*, 146.
42. Fletcher goes on to relate a rather strange story in evidence of his claim. It concerns a writer under observation for his nutritional and excretory habits while plying his trade. He lives on a modest diet of "a glass of milk with a trace of coffee, and corn 'gems,' four of which he consumed" a day, and in really hot weather, the occasional glass of lemonade. Yet he produces an enormous amount of work:

> That such an amount of work, with the maintenance of perfect health, could be accomplished on such a small quantity of food can be accounted for only on the assumption of a complete assimilation of the ingested material. As the degree of combustion is indicated by the ashes left, so the completeness of digestion is to be measured by the amount and character of the intestinal excreta. A conclusive demonstration of thorough digestion in Mr.——'s case was afforded me. There had, under the *regime* above mentioned, been no evacuation of the bowels for eight days. At the end of this period he informed me that the rectum was about to evacuate, though the material he was sure could not be of a large amount. Squatting upon the floor of the room, without any perceptible effort he passed into the hollow of his hand the contents of the rectum. This was done to demonstrate human normal cleanliness and inoffensiveness; neither stain nor odour remaining, either in the rectum or in the hand. The excreta were in the form of nearly round ball, varying in size from a small marble to a plum. These were greenish-brown in colour, of firm consistence, and covered over with a thin layer of mucous; *but there was no more odour to it than there is to a hot biscuit.* (*The New Glutton*, 148–50)

43. Sinclair and Williams, *Good Health*, 2. Looking back on his life from the vantage of some fifty years later, Sinclair says of another of his health inclinations, his off-and-on vegetarianism, that he never engaged in it on the ethical principle that to eat animals is wrong, but rather that: "Most of my life I was looking for a diet that would permit me to overwork with impunity" (Sinclair, *My Lifetime in Letters*, 24). But despite this more cynical take on the matter, encapsulated in the idea that there can be "overwork," Sinclair had internalized during the years surrounding *The Jungle*, as did Fletcher, the notion of a nearly endless capacity for work in the properly-run human body.
44. By the time of *The Fasting Cure*, Sinclair had moved away from being a thoroughgoing Fletcherite. He is clear as to the debt, however, that he owed him:

> All the physicians I had known were men who tried to cure me when I fell sick, but here was a man who was studying how to stay well. I have to find fault with Mr. Fletcher's system, and so I must make clear at the outset how much I owe to it. It set me upon the right track—it showed me the goal, even if it did not lead me to it. (*Fasting Cure*, 15)

45. *Ibid.*, 9.
46. Seltzer, *Bodies and Machines*, 5.
47. Derrick, "What a Beating," 88.
48. Kristeva, *Powers of Horror*, 71.
49. *Ibid.*, 3.
50. *Ibid.*, 1.
51. As Susan Strasser points out, the origin of the word "recycling" does not lie, as one might think, in the environmental movements of the 1970s, but rather, as the *OED* points out, emerged in the context of production, specifically in the oil industry, in which "partially refined petroleum [was] sent through the refining cycle again to reduce waste" (Strasser, *Waste and Want: A Social History of Trash* [New York: Metropolitan Books, 1999], 72).
52. See Young, "The Pig that Fell into the Privy." Young details the significant impact of *The Jungle* on the legislation and examines the conflicted relationship between Sinclair and Theodore Roosevelt. Although they worked together initially, ultimately neither one had much patience for the other's methods and politics. See also Jon A. Yoder, *Upton Sinclair* (New York: Frederick Ungar, 1975): 41–44.
53. William Bloodworth notes a kind of separation, too, in the near-erasure of Jurgis's experience as worker in his conversion to socialism. To some extent, this is an effect of the narrative's religious tendency. As the novel comes to a close, it falls hack, not unlike its model in Stowe, on a religious structure. This grafting of a religious ending on to a plot of naturalist tendencies, however, presents a problem of proportions. As Bloodworth puts it:

> In the sequence of naturalistically depicted episodes preceding Jurgis's emotional conversion, Sinclair does not imply that the workers' own experiences will result in practical political action. The life of Jurgis Rudkus offers little foundation for radical politics. Sinclair's proletarians move directly from their naive dreams of success to degradation and anomie. In this way *The Jungle* suggests that the American working class at its lowest level is a vulnerable and easily destroyed culture. (Bloodworth, *Upton Sinclair*, 62)

Moreover, Jurgis's conversion, noticeably Protestant in nature, requires a radical break from his previous life. "The rhetorical technique by which Jurgis enters the Socialist movement," Bloodworth notes, "is that of Protestant evangelicalism. Little about it is proletarian; in fact, it depends largely on a rejection—a purging—of the proletarian experiences that came before it." And this rejection is attended with a feeling of guilt for his past (*Ibid.*, 63). Furthermore, what also stands to be lost here is the collective proletarian experiences of Jurgis's family, without whom he never could have survived after his injury on the killing bed. Granted, Jurgis does make some use of his past in his service as a kind of authentic exhibit brought in to testify informally to conditions in the packing plants in Tommy Hinds's discussions with cattlemen from out West. But by and large. Jurgis's previous experiences seem to just fall away as a kind of useless appendage to the new man.

54. As historian William Cronon notes, since the packers could not undersell the traditional butcher and still turn a profit on dressed beef alone, they turned their efforts to converting "waste" into commodities:

> Only by selling by-products could the packers turn this losing transaction into a profitable one. Indeed, the income from such sales was crucial to enabling the packers to lower dressed beef prices far below those of ordinary butchers. As Swift and Armour saw it, they earned their profits on the margin largely from things that butchers threw away. (Cronon, *Nature's Metropolis: Chicago and the Great West* [New York: Norton, 19911: 252)

Indeed, waste, or that which would ordinarily go to waste, came to be the central means of profit for the packers, made available through an economy of scale. Philip Armour, who, in Cronon's view "had built his empire on waste" (253), extolled the virtue of such as only possible at the present historical moment of systemization and efficiency:

> "There was a time," remembered Philip Armour at the end of the century, "when many parts of cattle were wasted, and the health of the city injured by the refuse. Now, by adopting the best known methods, nothing is wasted, and buttons, fertilizer, glue, and other things are made cheaper and better for the world in general, out of material that was before a waste and a menace." (quoted in Cronon, 250)

The crowning achievement of the system of the slaughterhouse, and the same might be said of the science of efficiency in general, is that, in the words of the immigrants' volunteer slaughterhouse tour guide near *The Jungle*'s beginning, "'they don't waste anything here'" (42).

55. Emma Lazarus, "The New Colossus" (*Sonnet Central* <http://www.sonnets.org/lazarus.htm#100> 25 July 2001): 12, 14.

56. The recycling trade really took off at the turn of the twentieth century. Strasser points out that scavengers had long been the main conduit for the collection and re-sale of refuse, but that the end of the nineteenth century saw the rise of an organized trade in waste, replete with its own weekly publication, *The Waste Trade Journal*, which began publication in 1905. Jacob Riis confirms this shift toward organization in *How the Other Half Lives*, where he recounts the organization of Italian immigrant under the auspices of a "padrone":

> The discovery was made by earlier explorers that there is money in New York's ash-barrel, but it was left to the genius of the padrone to develop the full resources of the mine that has become the exclusive preserve of the Italian immigrant. (Riis, *How the Other Half Lives: Studies Among the Tenements of New York*. ed. David Leviatin [Boston: Bedford, 1996]: 93)

57. Albert C. Day, *The Garbage Question: A Profitable Solution* (n.p.: American Underwriting Company, 1902).

58. The brochure begins with the line, "the fortunes of the future will be made from the crumbs that fall from the world's table" (*Ibid.*, 1).

59. Moreover, the USGR seeks to make use of all the world's garbage in such a way. The pamphlet calls for a kind of sanitation imperialism that continues the project of Manifest Destiny in the economic field.

60. *Ibid.*, 4.

61. William Rathje and Cullen Murphy, *Rubbish!: The Archaeology of Garbage* (New York: HarperCollins. 1992): 175–76.

62. Derrick, "What a Beating," 89.

63. Banta, *Taylored Lives*, 183, 184.

64. Barrett, Introduction, *The Jungle*, xxii. William M. Tuttle, Jr. offers a similar view of the composition of the union at the time of the 1904 strike: "racial jealousies and antagonisms crumbled . . . as the unskilled enthusiastically joined the union because of dissatisfaction with the prevailing wage, . . . and blacks joined as well as whites" (*Race Riot: Chicago in the Red Summer of 1919* [New York: Antheneum]: 116). Tuttle, however, also demonstrates that while "many of the 500 black workers in the Chicago yards" joined the Amalgamated Meat Cutters and Butcher Workmen (*Ibid.*, 116), this remarkable moment of solidarity was but that, a moment. The larger frame of events surrounding Chicago meat-packing strikes since the 1894 strike, when the packers began to make it a practice to bring in blacks to break strikes, had already dictated a conflation of the categories of race and "scab." By the end of the 1904 strike, "the words 'Negro' and 'scab' were . . . synonymous in the minds of numerous white stockyards workers; and, lest they forget, racist labor officials and politicians were present to remind them" (*Ibid.*, 119).

65. Barrett, Introduction, *The Jungle*, xxiii.

66. Sandra Gunning ties Sinclair's use of the black male as contaminant and contaminator to the black rapist myth, which served a role even in progressive writing: "the black rapist would become a staple of metaphor for social disorder and injustice, even for many white writers dedicated to changing the status quo." In the strike scene in *The Jungle*, "the figure of corrupting black male presence is made to validate class protest. . . ." (*Race, Rape, and Lynching: the Red Record of American Literature, 1890–1912*. [New York: Oxford University Press, 1996]: 24).

67. The idea that pollution boils down to "matter out of place" is most commonly associated with Mary Douglas, whose *Purity and Danger: An Analysis of the Concepts of Pollution and Taboo* (1996. Routledge: London, 1996), out of this time-worn definition of pollution, develops a complex anthropological theory about what counts as pollution and what pollution means in different cultural contexts.

68. Iris Marion Young has observed that abjection as a process works well as a descriptive framework for fears of "the other," including a generalized xenophobia, phobia experienced in the context of racism and ableism and homophobia (*Justice and the Politics of Difference* [Princeton: Princeton University Press, 1990]).

69. Houston A. Baker, Jr. and Dana D. Nelson in their preface to a recent special issue of *American Literature* observe that the ambiguous and free-floating geographical, yet largely conceptual, region known as "the South" serves a central role in figuring the nation through abjection. I would argue that Sinclair's politics are also imbricated in just this fashion: "'We the people' have of course never been whole; . . . 'our wholeness' has long been constructed through the abjected regional

Other, 'The South'" (Houston A. Baker, Jr. and Dana D. Nelson, "Preface: Violence, the Body, and 'The South,'" *American Literature* 73 [2001]: 236). Baker and Nelson point out that this becomes especially apparent when one considers the oxymoronic formulation "Civil War," which hides the decidedly uncivil failure to remark the death and dismemberment of the "scores of thousand who were not on the muster rolls—such as blacks trying to leave plantations and both blacks and whites who died as a result of guerilla actions":

> Thus "The South" is thick with civily disappeared history, the history of indigenous, black, Latino, and Asian laborers and their families, their joys and suffering largely effaced in this history of the Civil, under the mark of "The South" (*Ibid.*, 236).

70. Barrett, Introduction, *The Jungle*, xxiv.

71. Josiah Strong, *Our Country: Its Possible Future and Its Present Crisis* (Rev. ed; New York: Baker & Taylor, 1891): 61. Strong first published this text in 1885 and published the second edition (from which I cite) after the 1890 census, incorporating some of the new census figures in the text, particularly when discussing immigration.

72. *Ibid.*, 92.

73. *Ibid.*, 89.

74. In my dissertation, I argue that Strong's self-enclosed body metaphor for understanding the nation gains some of its power precisely by submerging or repressing the question of elimination (J. Michael Duvall, "Processes of Elimination: Waste and Wasting in American Literature at the Turn of the Twentieth Century" [Ph.D. diss., University of Maryland, 2003]). Elimination resurfaces in the well-worn trope of the immigrant-as-garbage, or "wretched refuse" as Emma Lazarus, in a recuperative mode, has it in "The New Colossus" (Lazarus, 12).

ORM ØVERLAND

The Jungle: *From Lithuanian Peasant to American Socialist*

1. The Novel as History

Upton Sinclair's *The Jungle* has been controversial since its first publication. Then, as well as later, controversy focused on the novel's politics and the veracity of its account of industrial practices and labor conditions in the meatpacking industry. Responding to a reviewer in *The Independent*, who had concluded that the novel was "almost surely exaggerated as to facts," Sinclair declared it all true and based on his own experience and observations, "not merely in substance, but in detail, and in the smallest detail." Indeed, "so true that students may go to it, as they would a work of reference." When the veracity of *The Jungle* has remained an issue, the author must shoulder much of the responsibility. His accounts of the making of the novel are about his research while he downplays his literary contribution: "there are many men who know how to construct a novel better than 'The Jungle' is constructed; but they do not know anything about the stockyards workers, and they do not care to know."[1] In his *Autobiography* (1962) Sinclair makes a strange statement: "I had my data and knew the story I meant to tell, but I had no characters."[2] Clearly, he is not using "story" in a novelist's sense of the word, where character is the essence, but as a journalist speaks of having a good news story.

Many were convinced. To Van Wyck Brooks, who did not think it a verv good book, "The story was a nightmare and all quite true,—it was never

From *American Literary Realism, 1870–1910* 37, no. 1 (Fall 2004): 1–23.

disproved in any part."[3] Two historians who have considered the veracity of *The Jungle* are particularly well qualified to pass judgment and have strangely disparate judgments. Within a year of each other, in 1986 and 1987, historians Louise Carroll Wade and James R. Barrett published books on Chicago's stockyards at the turn of the nineteenth century and then presented two radically divergent studies of Sinclair's novel.[4] Their differences as readers of *The Jungle* may be due to their different focuses as historians. Wade was primarily interested in the remarkable growth of an industry and Barrett in the lives and conditions of the workers. Their titles—*Chicago's Pride* and *Work and Community in the Jungle*—speak of how different may be the value judgments of professional historians.

In her article on the novel, Wade is primarily concerned that students will get "a fundamentally flawed picture of urban immigrant industrial life in early twentieth century America." She concludes, "Turn of the century evidence buttressed by recent scholarship exposes the many ways in which Sinclair loaded the dice to convince readers that packinghouse workers led heart-breaking lives in a capitalist jungle. In the process he distorted the truth about the packers and their product and about immigrant workers and their community."[5] Barrett has studied the same historical facts with the same care and the same regard for truth. Yet his view of the historical value of *The Jungle* is far more positive than Wade's. Indeed, he implies a criticism of some aspects of her work:

> . . . Sinclair understood something many of the industry's scholars have missed—that while this labor process was a miracle of rationality from a manager's perspective, those who performed the work often experienced it very differently. Thus Sinclair's descriptions of this labor process may be read both for the detail they provide about the organization of work in the nation's first assembly-line industry and also for the insight they offer into the *experience* of mass-production work. . . .

Both Barrett and Wade, however, agree about one weakness in Sinclair's account as history. Wade observes that "most immigrants were not passive victims of exploitation," and, with reference to Barrett and others, she points to the successful efforts of the Packingtown workers to improve their conditions through the American Federation of Labor. What is missing, in Barrett's view (as in blade's), is "the immigrants' own efforts to build stable communities in the midst of this jungle'" through their secular and religious ethnic organizations and through trade unions. To Barrett, however, an awareness of what is missing in Sinclair's text is as important as what is present for our understanding of the novel and its relation to its ideological and social context.[6]

The main reason for the difference in Barrett and Wade's evaluation of *The Jungle*—as history and as literature—may be that their readings are based on very different assumptions about time and genre. Barrett reads the novel as a text of its time while Wade regards Sinclair as a "historical novelist" and asks "Does *The Jungle* have value as historical fiction?"[7] Sinclair had just completed his Civil War novel *Manassas* (1904) when he began work on *The Jungle* and was surely conscious of the difference between the two literary endeavors. In *The Jungle*, the narrator does not have a historical or retrospective point of view. The novel itself is part of the history we read in it. If we wish to read *The Jungle* as a documentary exposé of social conditions in Packingtown at the beginning of the twentieth century, we must do this with an awareness of the radically different points of view of then and now. Nor is the documentary necessarily an objective genre.

Sinclair insisted he was telling the truth and there is no reason to doubt his sincerity. His editors at the socialist weekly *The Appeal to Reason*, where a version of his novel was first serialized, and his editors at Doubleday, Page, who had the facts investigated to their own satisfaction, all believed that the facts in the fiction were true.[8] As Ronald Gottesman has observed, reviewers were sharply divided in their views: liberals took the novel as truth while conservatives criticized it as a collection of pernicious lies.[9] Without necessarily arguing with Wade's carefully documented demonstration of how she sees and interprets the facts in a very different light than did Sinclair, one may nevertheless conclude that his novel documents how these facts appeared to a contemporary novelist and to many of his contemporary readers.

We see the past as a prelude to our own time; those who lived in the past saw it without our benefit of hindsight. To many, the turn of the nineteenth century was a period of crisis with either chaos or radical change as possible outcomes. This sense of a society in crisis may be seen in the popularity of fictional accounts of doomsday predictions as well as of utopian solutions. Edward Bellamy's *Looking Backward: 2000–1887* (1888), Ignatius Donnelly's *Caesar's Column: A Story of the Twentieth Century* (1891), Frederick Upham Adams' *President John Smith: The Stary of a Peaceful Revolution* (1897), and Jack London's *The Iron Heel* (1908) are some well known instances of the genre.[10] We know how things turned out, so our perceptions of the period are necessarily different from those of contemporary observers, for whom these fictions were potential futures projected from a troubled present. When Eugene Debs, the perennial presidential candidate of the Socialist Party, first read *The Jungle*, it was as a participant in a society in the throes of radical change: "The pulse of the proletarian revolution throbs in these pages. It is a novel of the impending crisis, and will prove a powerful factor in precipitating it."[11] To him the novel was more about making the future than about writing history.

When Sinclair wrote *The Jungle*, he was a recent convert to Marxism and had a convert's faith in historical necessity. There is a sense of the inevitable socialist victory on the verge of happening in the concluding shout in the novel. In 1907, in *The Industrial Republic*, Sinclair had "prophesied socialism in America in the year 1913; instead," he wryly comments in his *Autobiography*, "we had two world wars and the Russian Revolution."[12] Our knowledge of history after 1906 makes our reading of the concluding sentence, "CHICAGO WILL BE OURS!" different from the readings of contemporaries for whom the victory of the Socialist Party appeared to be inevitable. They may seem to have been naively optimistic, but Barrett reminds us that predictions of a socialist victory at the polls "appear less fantastic viewed from the perspective of the early . . . twentieth century."[13]

The value of *The Jungle* as history cannot be separated from its value as a novel. As a novel it relates to its time and place in ways that are different from the ways historians such as Wade and Barrett make use of sources to acquire a sense of the workings of the meat industry in the nineteenth century. As June Howard exhorts in her study of American literary naturalism, "The search for the real must give way to a search for the historical." When she explains that "Naturalism does not provide a window into reality," her discussion may be a useful reminder in the study of most narrative genres: "Rather it reveals history indirectly in revealing *itself*—in the significant absences silhouetted by its narratives, in the ideology invoked by the very program that proclaims a transparent access to the real, in its transmutation of content into form and form into content."[14] To read *The Jungle* today as it was read in 1906 is impossible. To read it in history with an awareness of this impossibility must be part of the critical endeavor.

2. Subtext: "From Lithuania to the Chicago Stockyards"

This reading of *The Jungle* is informed by a text that suggested both theme and structure to the author. Sinclair never acknowledged help from Ernest Poole, a writer and journalist who covered the stockyard strike in 1904.[15] In his memoirs, Poole remembers Sinclair as "a lad in a wide-brimmed hat, with loose-flowing tie and a wonderful warm expansive smile. . . . He already had a man digging for 'the inside dope' on conditions in the Yards, and I gave him some tips on where to get more, and the color that he wanted." Poole had written articles in favor of the strikers, and for both facts and "color" he evidently gave him his text, "From Lithuania to the Chicago Stockyards—an Autobiography by Antanas Kaztauskis." It had just appeared in the *Independent* and in 1906 was collected in Hamilton Holt's *The Life Stories of Undistinguished Americans as Told by Themselves.*[16]

Poole's memory failed him when he wrote in his memoirs that he had put "the whole case for the strikers into one brief narrative of a Lithuanian." The story summarized in his memoirs is of misery and defeat, whereas the one in the *Independent* is of success. Indeed, his memory of his own story may have been influenced by Sinclair's novel. Poole remembers explaining to an agent of the President that "He's not one man; he's forty thousand. You'll find him all around the Yards."[17] Antanas Kaztauskis may be a composite character, but not in the degree suggested by Poole's rhetorical figure of "forty thousand." The sketch in the *Independent* rings true as the story of an individual immigrant. For Sinclair, his meeting with Poole was as lucky a source of inspiration as was his chance coming upon a Lithuanian wedding party when "wandering about 'back of the yards' one Sunday afternoon."[18] Barrett suggests that Poole's story "probably helped to shape the character of Jurgis Rudkus."[19] I believe that it gave shape to the novel itself. The case for a close relationship, however, must be made in the reading. Sinclair's papers from before 1907 were destroyed by the fire at Helicon Hall, a utopian colony organized by the author.[20]

Poole's story is the story of an immigrant. It begins one winter evening on a farm in Lithuania, where the young Antanas is fully at home with his parents and siblings in his peasant environment. The economy is pre-industrial; they tan their own cowhides and a traveling shoemaker makes "there into boots." The shoemaker has a son in Chicago and he also brings stories of the United States and smuggled newspapers.[21] Antanas gets his vision of America as well as warnings from the shoemaker: there are "man-wolves" there as in Russia, men who "are grabbing all the good things—the oil and coal and meat and everything." But America is "where they can choose their own kind of God—where they can learn to read and write, and talk, and think like men—and have good things!" From a Lithuanian Chicago newspaper the shoemaker reads the stirring words of the Declaration of Independence (translated back into English for our benefit): "We know these are true things—that all men are born free and equal—that God gives them rights which no man can take away—that among these rights are life, liberty and the getting of happiness" (8–10).

Antanas eventually follows the advice of the shoemaker—"That boy must go to America!"—and in Chicago he soon learns two important lessons, to be quicker than in Lithuania and to recognize "grafters." He boards with "three Lithuanians, who knew my father's sisters at home" and they laugh at his notion of "the getting of happiness" and explain that in America "What you need is money" (13). Clearly he must find a new basis for his life in the

New World. The ways of the pre-industrial peasant society will not work here. His Lithuanian-American guides take him on a tour of the stockyards:

> [W]e stopped on the bridge and looked into the river out there. It was so full of grease and dirt and sticks and boxes that it looked like a big, wide, dirty street, except in some places, where it boiled up. It made me sick to look at it. When I looked away I could see on one side some big fields full of holes, and these were the city dumps. On the other side were the stockyards, with twenty tall slaughterhouse chimneys. The wind blew a big smell from them to us. Then we walked on between the yards and the dumps and all the houses looked bad and poor. In our house my room was in the basement. I lay down on the floor with three other men and the air was rotten. (15)

The account of Antanas' tour is quite similar to the description of Ona and Jurgis' first evening walk in Chicago in *The Jungle* and both are followed by the protagonists' determination to get a job. At the slaughterhouse Antanas gets his first lesson in graft: "We went to the doors of one big slaughter house. There was a crowd of about 200 men waiting there for a job." A "special policeman" comes out and selects a few workers and the others are chased away by other police. He learns that the "special policeman" expects to be paid, gives him $5 the next morning, and is among those who are asked to enter (15). At work he is told that the entire business is organized "so as to save everything and make money." As another Lithuanian worker explains, "They get all the blood out of those cattle and all the work out of us men." But Antanas is soon out of work, probably because "some other man had paid for my job." He also learns about the hazards of buying a home on the installment plan: "I found that many Lithuanians had been beaten this way." A coming election gives him a new opportunity. A Lithuanian saloonkeeper is Republican boss of the district and gets him involved in corrupt politics. With his political connections he gets a job in a slaughterhouse owned by a "big politician" (17). "Then I felt that I was getting in beside the game" (18). But competition for work gets tougher as immigrants keep coming in increasing numbers: "The employers in the yard liked this, because those sharp foremen are inventing new machines and the work is easier to learn, and so these slow Lithuanians and even green girls can learn to do it, and then the Americans and Germans and Irish are put out and the employer saves money, because the Lithuanians work cheaper." The first union local he joins is controlled by a corrupt saloonkeeper who takes them out on strike: "We met twice a day in his saloon and spent all of our money on drinks, and then the strike was over. I got out of this union after that" (19).

From this point the two stories diverge. Jurgis eventually finds his home in the Socialist Party; Antanas discovers the value of the Chicago Federation of Labor where the swearing-in is much like a religious ceremony:

> The night I joined the Cattle Butchers' Union I was led into the room by a negro member. With me were Bohemians, Germans and Poles, and Mike Donnelly, the President, is an Irishman. . . . We swore to be loyal to our union above everything else except the country, the city and the State—to be faithful to each other—to protect the women-workers—to do our best to understand the history of the labor movement, and to do all we could to help it on. (20)

The Union takes a place in his life that earlier had been filled by the Church. Antanas says that when his baby child was old enough to begin school, he would send him to a public school rather than to a Lithuanian Roman Catholic one, where "two priests . . . teach only in Lithuanian from prayer books," because the public school teachers "belong to the Teachers' Labor Union, which . . . belongs to our Chicago Federation of Labor" (19).[22] The Union is also his portal into the America envisioned by the shoemaker: "No man knows what it means to be sure of his job unless he has been fired like I was once without any reason being given. . . . You must get money to live well, and to get money you must combine. I cannot bargain alone with the Beef Trust. I tried it and it does not work" (20).

This story of an immigrant is of a passage from a secure Old World identity, through the loss of identity, and to the achievement of a new identity. It begins with an identity formed by a European peasant society. It then takes the immigrant through a difficult intermediary stage after he has lost faith in the validity of the old ways in his confrontations with industrial and capitalist Chicago. He tries various ways of belonging—ethnic nostalgia (17), corrupt employers, corrupt politics and corrupt unions—that prove unsatisfactory and leave him empty and disillusioned. Eventually, the Cattle Butcher's Union of Lithuanians, Negroes, Bohemians, Germans, Poles, and Irish becomes his new home, giving him a security from the "man-wolves" that even the tight family bonds of the old homeland could not provide. His new father figure is Mike Donnelly, President of the multiethnic Cattle Butchers' Union. His identity is that of an organized American. worker who owes all to the Chicago Federation of Labor; he studies labor history rather than prayer books. Solidarity, "to be faithful to each other," is his faith. The version of Antanas's story in the *Independent* concludes with his wish that the "ugly shoemaker" could come to Chicago: "He would make a good walking delegate."[23]

Poole's story of Antanas is much like Sinclair's story of Jurgis Rudkus but with two major differences. Antanas never experiences the depths of despair of Jurgis before he sees the light. This difference may be one of genres: the realism of the "autobiography" and the melodramatic naturalism of the novel. The other difference is political. Antanas acquires his education and his identity through the Cattle Butcher's Union, a local of the American Federation of Labor. Implied in his levelheaded statement, "I cannot bargain alone with the Beef Trust," is a belief in the efficacy of the solidarity of labor within the existing system. To the socialist author *The Jungle*, however, "bread and butter" unions represented a band-aid solution to the fatal disease of capitalism. With religious fervor, Jurgis at the end of the novel looks forward to a new social order rather than merely to improved working conditions.

3. Thesis: The Education of an American Socialist

The Jungle begins *in medias res*. Not until chapter seven does the chronological story catch up with the wedding with which the novel opens. The first chapter may not seem essential to the narrative. Indeed, with minor revisions in the second and seventh chapters, the story of Jurgis Rudkus could have been told without it. But this would change the structure of the novel and, consequently, make a central theme peripheral. Strangely, this is how some critics have interpreted the novel.[24] The opening chapter is one of the most poignant sketches in American literature of a common experience of immigration: the loss of a culture in all its complexities—including language—and the acquisition of poorly understood fragments of a new one.

Sinclair makes music speak of the loss of a culture. The music of the Lithuanian immigrants celebrating a wedding in "the rear-room of a saloon in that part of Chicago known as 'back of the yards'" (4) is not glorified, nor is the fiddler sentimentalized as an undiscovered Paganini:

> His notes are never true, and his fiddle buzzes on the low ones and squeaks and scratches on the high; but these things they heed no more than they heed the dirt and noise and squalor about them—it is out of this material that they have to build their lives, with it that they have to utter their souls. And this is their utterance; merry and boisterous, or mournful and wailing, or passionate and rebellious, this music is their music, music of home. (8)

As it gets late, however, the music of home is exchanged for a fragment of "an American tune . . . they have picked up on the streets; all seem to know the words of it—or, at any rate, the first line of it, which they hum to themselves, over and over again without rest: 'In the good old summer time—in the good old summer time! In the good old summer time—in the good old summer time!'" (19). Jane Addams, in a lecture at the University of Chicago in 1904, spoke of this negative acculturation process as "the American process of elimination," an encouraged, even enforced Americanization where the important thing was not so much what you acquired as what you forgot.[25] The immigrant experience of loss and displacement is at the center of Oscar Handlin's now classic narrative of immigration in American history, *The Uprooted* (1951). For Handlin, as for Sinclair, an important aspect of the drama of immigration was the incongruous meeting of nineteenth-century European peasant cultures with a tvventieth-century American urban capitalist and industrial society.

The hosts have done their best to have the wedding feast, the *veselija*, "in due form, and after the best home traditions" (3). Tradition requires a wedding speech by the father of the groom. It was usual, we are told, to take such a speech from a book, "but in his youthful days Dede Antanas used to be a scholar. . . . Now it is understood that he has composed an original speech of congratulation and benediction, and this is one of the events of' the day" (19).[26] But traditions from "the forests of Lithuania" are not easily transplanted "in the stock-yards district of Chicago" ()) and there are signs that the traditions of home are surrendering to new ways. When the dance begins, "Most of them prefer the 'two-step,' especially the young, with whom it is the fashion. The older people have dances from home, strange and complicated steps which they execute with grave solemnity" (11). The dance draws the narrator's attention to how people are dressed: Many older people "wear clothing reminiscent in some detail of home-an embroidered waistcoat or stomacher, or a gayly colored handkerchief, or a coat with large cuffs and fancy buttons. All these things are carefully avoided by the young, most of whom have learned to speak English and to affect the latest style of clothing" (11).

But a culture is more than its folklore; it is what makes a community more than a mere society. A new family is the responsibility of all and the *veselija* is an occasion to contribute to a sum that will pay for the feast and ensure the newlyweds a good start: "The *veselija* is a compact, a compact not expressed, but therefore only the more binding upon all. Every one's share was different—and yet every one knew perfectly well what his share was, and strove to give a little more. Now, however, since they had come to the new country, all of this was changing . . ." (15). Most guests sneak off without paying. But while the old rules no longer apply for the guests, a new set of rules applies for the young couple; there is no way to avoid the saloonkeeper's "frightful bill," for he "stood in with all the big politics men in the district; and when you had once found out what it meant to get into trouble with such people, you would know enough to pay what you were told to pay and shut up" (16). The old compact has been broken and the new does not favor the weak. The groom, Jurgis Rudkus, is undaunted: "1 will work harder." And Ona, his teenage bride, has trust in her "husband who could solve all problems, and who was so big and strong!" (17–18). Jurgis' father and Ona's stepmother, Elzbieta, had insisted on the *veselija* because they feared that the "journey to a new country might somehow undermine the old home virtues of their children." But these virtues offer no more protection than does the plaster "babe of Bethlehem" Elzbieta buys for fifty cents when they go to mass on their first Sunday in Chicago (64).

Neither ethnic nor American institutions are presented as pillars of support. The owner of the saloon is also a Lithuanian, a local boss backed by "the big politics men in the district" and not by a constituency of fellow-immigrants. Another influential fellow ethnic is the corrupt agent who "proved a scoundrel, and got them into a trap with some officials, and cost them a good deal of their precious money" (24). The local Lithuanian Roman Catholic Church, with priests who speak their language, sells them gimcracks they can ill afford and opposes the public schools (44). Jurgis is not given much reason to trust fellow immigrants or ethnic institutions. Sinclair's omissions of the impact of the immigrants' own institutions on their lives, criticized by Wade and Barrett, appears deliberate. In his descent into the abyss, however, Jurgis is involved with two American institutions, politics and unions, and the first chapter warns that they are not to be trusted either. The "big politics men" figure as a threat, and if Jurgis read the signs above the saloon door he would know that the place to which he owes so much money is a "Union Headquarters" (4). More may be learned from the pages of this chapter; it should be read carefully. Before Sinclair, no Anglo-American writer had expressed such an intuitive insight into the loss of language and culture experienced by many immigrants.

The Jungle has a structure of movements from one basis for a confident identity, through a tough educational process, to a basis for a new confident identity: from confidence in muscle to confidence in understanding, from confidence in self to confidence in solidarity, from the community values of a local peasant culture to those of an international Socialism, from a dream of a glorious America to the visionary advent of a new America, and from an ethnic nuclear family to a multi-ethnic family of socialists. The focus throughout is on the education of Jurgis.[27] *The Jungle* is a Bildungsroman but with a twist: this young man's education does not lead him into his society but to an understanding of the need to change this society. It is certainly not a historical novel, looking back on a period of social change and the passing of an old order and the coming of a new, as Georg Lukâcs described the historical novels of Scott.[28] It is a novel of a contemporary society but also of a future society ensured by the inevitable Socialist victory and the consequent passing of the present order and the advent of a new. While it thus has a dialectic movement similar to that which Lukács saw in Scott, it also has much in common with the many utopian and dystopiian novels of the turn of the nineteenth century. Written in a decade with the then highest rate of immigration, it is an immigrant novel.[29] Class, however, is a more important identifier than ethnicity, as it was for many in a period of class struggle unequalled in American history: it is also a working-class novel.

Many read *The Jungle* as a naturalist novel, and in the present reading, too, it is a naturalist novel—up to a certain point. My understanding of literary naturalism is informed by Charles Child Walcutt, whose 1953 *American Literary Naturalism* remains a valuable contribution, and June Howard, whose *Form and History in American Literary Naturalism* (1985) has further deepened our understanding of naturalism as a genre. To read *The Jungle* as a novel of the education of the reader as well as of the protagonist both affirms Walcutt's analysis of literary naturalism and shows that Sinclair's novel departs from the norms of this genre.[30] To Eric Homberger, *The Jungle* a radical novel.[31] The quality of his reading demonstrates that this may be a useful label, but the concept of "radical" may require that the present-day reader responds politically to the conclusion of the novel in ways that the present reading tries to avoid: radical in 1906 pray not be radical a century later.

Readings that apply the restrictions of a single gene to the interpretation of a complex work of fiction will necessarily miss the significance of aspects that are not only considered foreign but counter to the genre. Similarly, readings that seek confirmation of a present-day understanding of the past of a novel may close our eyes to ways in which a work of fiction is a part of and not an interpretation of the past we try to understand. What follows is a reading of *The Jungle* as a naturalist, utopian, and didactic immigrant and working class Bildungsroman with a radical twist.

4. History as a Novel

Chronologically, the story of *The Jungle* begins with the second chapter and the presentation of the families of Ona and Jurgis. Jurgis is strong and confident: "He could not even imagine how it would feel to be beaten." He is proud of his physical strength: "Do you want me to believe that with these arms . . . people will ever let me starve?" Moreover, he is naïve, "a boy from the country" (21). One does not have to be a student of classical tragedy to realize that a character introduced in this manner has bad trouble in store.

His confidence is not only in himself but also in America, where, "rich or poor, a man was free" (23). His immigrant faith in America colors all he sets. After moving into their first miserable lodgings, Jurgis and Ona go sightseeing among the garbage dumps, the "great hollows full of stinking green water," the swarms of flies and the "fetid odor" of their new neighborhood. What they see, however, is their vision of America: in the twilight of sunset, Packingtown "seemed a dream of wonder, with its tale of hurnan energy, of things being done, of employment for thousands upon thousands of men, of opportunity and freedom, of life and love and joy" (30). Jurgis' confidence is boosted by the apparent ease with which he gets a job the very next day, so when he and the others go on a guided tour, he has a "sense of pride. Had he not just gotten a job, and become a sharer in all this activity; a cog in this marvelous machine?" (33). At the center are the cattle, driven by horseback riders with "long whips." Both machine and whip are central metaphors and serve to measure the education of the hero. Neither the whip nor the inexorable fate of the animals, whose passage strikes the narrator as "a very river of death," suggests "metaphors of human destiny" to Jurgis, who "thought only of the wonderful efficiency of it all" (33–34). Their guide makes sarcastic remarks, but to Jurgis it is "like a wonderful poem" (37). On his first day at work, wading in "streaming hot blood" and in an "almost overpowering" stench, his "whole soul was dancing with joy" (42).

His faith makes failure seem impossible and Jurgis "grew more confident every hour, more certain of his mastership" (49). He "did not mind" the grueling tempo of his job—"the first time that he had ever had anything to do which took all he had in him . . . he rather enjoyed it" (56). He has no patience with the union's talk of solidarity or workers' rights, concepts as strange to his Old World experience as to his American dream: "Jurgis had not studied the books, and he would not have known how to pronounce 'laissez faire'; but he had been round the world enough to know that a man has to shift for himself in it, and that if he gets the worst of it, there is no-body to listen to him holler" (57).

There are warnings. Three unsuccessful teachers stand out; Lithuanian immigrants like their student. The first, their guide Jokubas, is a shopkeeper and sees the world from a liberal, middle-class point of view; he "understood all the pitfalls of this new world, and could explain all of its mysteries" (26). In spite of the obvious irony, it is evident that Jokubas has a limited insight not yet available to Jurgis. He is proud of Packingtown but cautions his admiring tourists that there was much that the packers did not allow them to see (34). To the admiring Jurgis "it seemed almost profanity to speak about the place as did Jokubas, skeptically; it was a thing as tremendous as the universe" (41).

His two other instructors speak from a socialist, working-class point of view. The first is a fellow worker, Tamoszius, who plays the fiddle at the wedding and who "would go out with a couple of other men and a soapbox, and shout himself hoarse on a street corner Saturday nights" (250).[32] He explains the system of graft to Jurgis, how "from top to bottom the place was simply a seething cauldron of jealousies and hatreds; there was no loyalty or decency anywhere about it, there was no place in it where a man counted for anything against a dollar." But Jurgis "could not bring himself to believe in such things": his friend was "simply another of the grumblers. . . . Then, too, he was a puny little chap" who "had been left behind in the race" (59). There is nothing puny, however, about his third teacher, Grandmother Majauszkiene, who "was a socialist, or some such strange thing; another son of hers was working in the mines of Siberia, and the old lady herself had made speeches in her time, which made her seem all the more terrible to her present auditors." She not only explains how workers are cheated when they believe they have bought a house, but gives Jurgis her views on corrupt unions and police and the collusion of both with the Democratic Party machine. But Jurgis has a long way to go before he is ready for the lessons of a Socialist. At this point he only makes his usual answer. "I will work harder" (69). He has to acquire experience before he can appreciate theory. The workers who regard him with suspicion when he asks questions have a point when they say, "Never mind, you stay here and see for yourself" (57).

After the wedding Jurgis is no longer quite so ignorant—"He had learned the ways of things about him now"—but his understanding is negative: there is no social contract in the New World but "a war of each against all." His new creed is, "You did not give feasts to other people, you waited for them to give feasts to you." He believes "that he understood it" (73–74), but this is disillusionment rather than insight. And he still has faith in his ability to survive. Moreover, he has his humanities; his responsibility for his family and his love for Ona acquire new depth and meaning when he becomes a father.

As difficulties mount, Jurgis realizes that the survival of his family depends on him alone. When the first winter storm stalls the streetcars, "the soul of Jurgis rose up within him like a sleeping lion," and Jurgis triumphs. He more or less carries his wife and one of the children to work: "foot by foot he drove his way, and when at last he came to Durham's he was staggering and almost blind. . . . When it was over, the soul of Jurgis was a song, for he later met the enemy and conquered, and felt himself the master of his fate" (110). As the reader will expect, Jurgis now falls "into his trap" (111). Indeed, it is from this point that naturalist metaphors begin to pile up. As long as Jurgis is strong and able to control his immediate environment, hardships may be dealt with even if at great cost. When he becomes weak it is another matter entirely. After an accident, the company doctor sends him home with the message that "he had probably laid himself up for months by his folly" (111). He is now but "a damaged article . . . and they did not want him. They had got the best out of him—they had worn him out . . . and now they had thrown him away!" He has become one of the many "worn-out parts of the great merciless packing machine" (120).

Now begins Jurgis' descent into the depths of depravity. No longer do he and his wife harbor hope for the future. Their fate, the narrator insists, is a tragedy:

> It was not less tragic because it was so sordid, because that it had to do with wages and grocery bills and rents. They had dreamed of freedom; of a chance to look about them and learn something; to be decent and clean, to see their child grow up to be strong. And now it was all gone—it would never be! They had played the game and they had lost. (133)

As their humanity wanes, the place that had seemed "a dream of wonder" becomes a jungle. At night Ona lies awake, "afraid of the beating of her own heart, fronting the blood-red eyes of the old primeval terror of life" (133). Jurgis rages at his wife, who "was visibly going to pieces," deplores his marriage, and then gazes at her "as helpless as a wounded animal" (135–36). When he learns that she has been seduced by her boss, Connor, he rushes off like a raging animal, "breathing hoarsely, like a wounded bull," then waits, "crouching as if for a spring," and, when he finds Connor, fights "like a tiger" (147–48). In jail, his thoughts "lashed him like whips upon his naked back" and he paced "up and down his cell like a wild beast" (154).

When Jurgis is released, he tracks down his family only to see Ona die giving birth to their stillborn child. In his cell he had pondered on his fate: "He was of no consequence—he was flung aside, like a bit of trash, the carcass of some animal." Those responsible he identifies vaguely but vehemently as "they": "That was their law, that was their justice!" But even though this was "the beginning of his rebellion, of his outlawry and his unbelief," he is still too ignorant to identify his enemy: "He had no wit to trace back the social crime to its far sources—he could not say that it was the thing men have called 'the system' that was crushing him to the earth" (155–56). Jurgis is a man sorely in need of education.

He takes five consecutive courses in how to get along with the "system": reform, dropping out, crime, politics and unions.[33] His first lesson in the efficacy of reform is in a factory "to which philanthropists and reformers pointed with pride." Its technology is advanced and "it had some thought for its employees": a restaurant with low prices, a reading room and separate facilities for men and women. This workplace seemed "a kind of a heaven" (192), but on his ninth day he is informed that "his department of the harvester works would be closed until further notice!" (195). The laws of supply and demand are as unrelenting here as with the Beef Trust. "One more bandage had been torn from his eyes, one more pitfall was revealed to him! Of what help was kindness and decency on the part of employers—when they could not keep a job for him, when there were more harvesting machines made than the world was able to buy" (196). Another reformer soon comes to his rescue, a young idealistic settlement worker who learns of the sad fate of the family and writes "a letter that Jurgis was to take to a gentleman who was superintendent in" a steel mill (199) .This time it is not supply and demand but fate that intervenes—and behind fate is, of course, "the system" that reformers are not willing to touch. Jurgis' son drowns in one of the many and deep puddles in the streets and Jurgis is inconsolable. He turns his back on his former life and on responsibility for anyone or anything but himself:

> He had been a fool, a fool! He had wasted his life, he had wrecked himself, with his accursed weakness; and now he was done with it—he would tear it out of him, root and branch! There should be no more tears and no more tenderness; he had had enough of them—they had sold him into slavery! Now he was going to be free, to tear off his shackles, to rise up and fight. (206)

Now Jurgis begins to live outside society and—in a variety of ways—outside the law.

Survival as a tramp proves not so difficult. His health returns, "all his lost youthful vigor, his joy and power that he had mourned and forgotten!" (211). Freedom means satisfying his thirst for alcohol as well as his sexual desires, but neither brings much happiness: "Jurgis could not help being made miserable by his conscience. It was the ghost that would not down" (213). The sight of a baby awakes such strong emotions that "the tomb of memory was rent open" (214). Fall brings him back to Chicago with survival uppermost in his mind: "he meant to save himself in this fight" (266). The dropout's passive response to adversity is not adequate to Jurgis' as yet dimly perceived needs.

In jail again, he meets an acquaintance who introduces him first to violent crime and then to politics, "the high-class criminal world of Chicago. The city, which was owned by an oligarchy of businessmen, being nominally ruled by the people, a huge army of graft was necessary for the purpose of effecting the transfer of power" (244). Jurgis is soon involved in this high class of crime and this time around he acquires a better understanding of politics than when he had sold his vote for a couple of dollars. Working for the Democratic boss, Scully, he poses as a Republican, gets a job in a packing plant, and takes part in a scam campaign, learning to make rise of "the extra bung holes of the campaign barrel" to fill his own pockets (254).

Identified as a Republican, however, Jurgis is no longer useful in politics after the election and Scully suggests that he stay in his job at the plant and not go out with the union on strike. In his earlier life, Jurgis had once placed his faith in the union and the union had also been his first introduction to corrupt politics. He does not realize that the man behind the union, Scully was also the one who made sure that he paid his debt to the saloonkeeper, nor does he know that Scully had made a fortune on the housing scam and the environment of which he and his family have been victims. Now, mastering the art of scabbing and union busting as he has that of politics, he is a true henchman in the system that governs Packingtown. It would seem that Jurgis has entered the "vision of power" that he so admired on his first evening walk in Chicago. However, his education has not only thoroughly demystified Packingtown, it has utterly changed the tale it initially had presented to him "of opportunity and freedom, of life and love and joy." Opportunity is to help himself to money from the campaign barrel and freedom is to move with ease from Republican to Democrat, from union member to scab, wherever the higher bid may be. In this tale there is neither love nor joy, nor the loyalty that was the mainstay in his battle for his family. His education has not only prepared him for entry into Packingtown society but has made him acceptable to its arbiters—the very men responsible for the loss of his home and the deaths of his wife and son. Had the novel concluded with his initiation this would have been in keeping with the formal structure of the Bildungsroman—but not with its ethos. Clearly, this is not a society the reader would be happy to see the hero enter.

To win such a world is to lose your soul, and Jurgis has come close to losing his. He has become much like his old enemy, Connor, who again enters the story as his nemesis just when Jurgis' future as one of Scully's henchmen seems secure. Jurgis' emotions are not quite dead and "a blind frenzy seized him" (268). Again he beats him up and again he is thrown in jail. His bail costs him all his savings. "Poor Jurgis was now an outcast and a tramp once more" (271). Now, however, his situation is worse because he understands more and has memories of the time when he "had been of the elect, through whom the country is governed—when he had had a bung in the campaign-barrel for his own!" (340).

Jurgis is not yet ready for the course that will give him understanding. He has become the human equivalent of a rogue elephant. He has no ties with family, friends or, indeed, society. By chance he comes upon Ona's cousin, Marija, now a prostitute and a morphine addict. It is thematically and structurally fitting that she, the character who enters the novel in its second sentence, shouldering the responsibility for the wedding feast, now reawakens his awareness of responsibilities, family ties, and love. In her degradation, she is still the mainstay of the remnant of the family, giving them her earnings. Marija, too, has taken courses in the workings of the system and she absolves Jurgis of all guilt: "You did your best—the job was too much for us. . . . We were too ignorant—that was the trouble. We didn't stand any chance. If I'd known what I know now we'd have won out" (281). Jurgis' meeting with Marija and her revelations bring him to a critical point in his life: emotions that "had become strangers" to his soul are "far-off and shadowy. . . . Their voices would die, and never again would he hear them—and so the last faint spark of manhood in his soul would flicker out" (282–83).

His salvation may be in what is left of his family, and he is on his way to reunite with his mother-in-law when he passes a lecture hall where the night before he had fallen asleep and been thrown out as a bum from a Republican rally. Jurgis enters the crowded hall once more and finds a seat in the back where he can rest. This time, instead of a policeman's voice he hears "a woman's voice, gentle and sweet, 'If you would try to listen, comrade, perhaps you would be interested'" (289). Beaten, but ready for home, Jurgis has acquired as much of an education as his courses could offer and is ready for his final lesson.

Jurgis has been exposed to Socialism before. When exhorted by Grandmother Majauszkiene, he still had the mentality of a peasant and could not appreciate her analysis of their situation. When Tamoszius had tried to explain things to him, Jurgis had ironically regarded the Socialists as "the enemies of American institutions [because they] could not be bought, and would not combine or make any sort of a 'dicker'" (251)—as did the unions. Now, however, he is ready. In dire need of a family, he is welcomed as a "comrade" by a "young and beautiful" woman in "fine clothes." Jurgis is worn out, emotionally and physically, and is hardly aware of the lecturer's words. His response is sensual, first to the quality of the voice of the young woman and then to how the speaker affects *her*. He wonders, "what could be going on, to affect anyone like that?" And so his attention is directed to the quality of the speaker's voice: "To hear it was to be suddenly arrested, to be gripped, transfixed" (289–90). Only then does he become aware of the speaker's words, and as they begin to come through, it is as if they have a personal message for Jurgis:

> I feel sure that in the crowd that has come to me tonight . . . there will be some one man whom pain and suffering have made desperate, whom some chance vision of wrong and horror has startled and shocked into attention. And to him my words will come like a sudden flash of lightning to one who travels in darkness—revealing the way before him, the perils and the

> obstacles—solving all problems, making all difficulties clear! The scales will fall from his eyes, the shackles will be torn from his limbs, he will leap up with a cry of thankfulness, he will stride forth a free man at last! (292–93)

This is the language of Christian revivals and Jurgis' awakening is religious in nature. When the speaker comes to the end of his peroration, "The audience came to its feet with a yell; men waved their arms, laughing aloud in their excitement. *And Jurgis was with them. . . .*"

There was a falling in of all the pillars of his soul, the sky seemed to split above him—he stood there, with his clenched hands upraised, his eyes bloodshot, and the veins standing out purple in his face, roaring in the voice of a wild beast, frantic, incoherent, maniacal. And when he could shout no more he still stood there, gasping, and whispering hoarsely to himself: "By God! By God! By God!" (297)[34]

He has not understood much but he knows that he has been reborn and that he is free: "He would no longer be the sport of circumstances, he would be a man, with a will and a purpose" (298). He understands that he is not alone, that he is again in a supportive community and that he again has a caring family—and that he must not lose what he has found.[35] And so he dares to approach the speaker, who directs him to a Polish comrade who speaks Lithuanian.

On their arrival, Jurgis and the other Lithuanian immigrants did not know the language of their new land. Gradually, they acquire the rudiments of English, but even at this late point in the novel Jurgis speaks it so poorly that the speaker realizes that he needs someone who can explain socialism in his own language. The choice of a Pole as interpreter may be found aesthetically fitting. Marija opens the novel scolding a coachman in Polish to ensure that the traditional *veselija* is held "after the best home traditions" (5). Now a Pole explains the theory and organization of a new American home in Lithuanian. Jurgis has been able to get along with the English he has picked up from other immigrants and fellow workers but the poor quality of his English may easily be forgotten by the reader since the author, wisely, after a few phrases in the opening pages, renders the Lithuanian speech of the immigrant characters in grammatical English. In the concluding chapters Jurgis says very little. Sinclair could have made him speak in broken English but chose to silence him in the company of so many literate speakers. His inability to speak a literate English does not, of course, indicate lack of understanding or of intelligence.

5. Beyond History

As a Socialist, Jurgis acquires the insight that enables him to break out of the determinism of the naturalist novel—and of history. Walcutt helps us to understand why this is so and why *The Jungle* at this point ceases to be a naturalist novel. Walcutt distinguishes between the naturalist novel's unenlightened main character and its enlightened reader. The naturalist novel is

> a tragedy in which a human being is crushed and destroyed by the operation of forces which he has no power to resist or even understand. . . . And if the victim's lot is sordid, the need for reform is 'proved.' The more helpless the character, the stronger the proof of determinism; and once such a thesis is established the scientist hopes and believes that men will set about trying to control the forces which now control men.[36]

In *The Jungle*, however, not only the reader but the protagonist realizes the need to control these forces. Indeed, Jurgis learns *how* they may be controlled and is assured that they *will be* controlled.

The reader Sinclair had in mind when he wrote his novel may not, as Howard has observed, have been an impoverished and uneducated immgrant.[37] As it is read here, however, the novel bridges what Howard sees as a "chasm" between Jurgis and the reader through empathy: the text encourages the reader to feel and respond with rather than to the protagonist. The novel is explicit about Jurgis' release from determinism: "To Jurgis the packers had been equivalent to fate. Ostrinski showed him that they were the Beef Trust. They were a gigantic combination of capital, which had crushed all opposition, and overthrown the laws of the land, and was preying upon the people" (304–05). Fate cannot be defeated; predators can. That night sleep comes late to Jurgis "for the glory of that joyful vision of the people of Packingtown marching in and taking possession of the Union Stockyards!" (306) To Howard, "the depiction of profound social change, which would propel us from the present into a parallel or a future world and thus into utopian or science fiction, is generically proscribed" in a naturalist novel.[38] In *The Jungle*, however, the protagonist acquires an understanding of profound social change that enables him to break out of the sordid world of facts researched by his author and that propels him to the threshold of utopia. He defeats the fate determined by the facts he has come to understand. The reader's understanding is Jurgis' understanding.

Naturally, there is now a shift in gears. To this point Jurgis has been educated in what *is*; now he is educated in what *is to be*. The future, however ensured it may be, cannot be learned from experience. Jurgis is now exposed to theory, to Marxism, a "science" that explains not only what is but also what *must* become. This is not very promising material for a novelist. *The Jungle*, like

Adventures of Huckleberry Finn, maybe a great book with a weak ending. If so, it is for a very different reason. For while Mark Twain may have shied away from an ending that could have resolved the serious implications of his story, Sinclair has his hero face what he believed was the one way out of the corrupt society into which he had brought his hopeful Lithuanian immigrants.

The last two chapters are often criticized for being exposition rather than narrative. Theology does not have the emotional force of revelation: Jurgis' study of Socialism cannot be made as dramatic as his conversion.[39] Yet study he must. Sinclair did not believe that a socialist future could be achieved through emotional outbursts and violent revolution but at the polls, and this requires an educated Jurgis—not merely an emotionally aroused Jurgis—as well as a great many educated readers. Nevertheless, for a reader less enthusiastic than the protagonist it may be taxing to follow the lectures he so religiously attends. Indeed, if we follow them too closely, we may miss what is at the center of the two concluding chapters: not the lectures but the building of a new community for the protagonist—an alternative to his lost peasant community and an expansion of his Lithuanian family to an international one. The first and the last two chapters of the novel are thus structurally and thematically complementary.[40] And as the story of the opening chapter is rooted in immigration history, that of the two concluding ones is steeped in the history of American Socialism.

Belonging is central to Jurgis' conversion: "And Jurgis was with them." The concluding chapters further explore his initial intuition of fellowship. He finds a new home in the hotel of Tommy Hinds. More important, he gets to know a wide range of socialists, some of them portraits of real-life figures.[41] Schliemann's monologue is indeed long and its aesthetic awkwardness in the last chapter is hardly alleviated by having the character self-consciously joke about it—"That was a lecture" (330). Yet it is the necessary underpinning of the conviction with which Jurgis responds to the concluding promise of a socialist future: "CHICAGO WILL BE OURS!" The first person plural does not only include Jurgis but speaks of a new community and a new way of life for humanity.

Jurgis, the immigrant, did not only lose his old home; he was divested of the identity that had made him comfortable in that home. His new identity as an American Socialist is inseparable from his new home in a socialist fellowship and his conviction that he will also be at home in the future Chicago of that fellowship.[42] The protagonist has experienced the breaking down of his former Lithuanian peasant community and suffered the indignities and the horrors of the capitalist society that took its place before he acquires an understanding of the concluding dialectic movement of history as predicted by Marxism: the victory of his own class and the consequent realization of—utopia!

Most of us cannot share this optimistic vision of the future.[43] We know too much about how Marxist dreams became nightmares. One challenge for a post–twentieth century reader is to appreciate the history in the novel and try to recapture and appreciate the convictions and the faith embodied in the text. Thus to read *The Jungle* in history may, at the beginning of the twenty-first century, be a prerequisite for an aesthetic rather than a political response to the novel, in particular to the utopian promise of its ending.

For me, the first step in recognizing the structure and themes of Sinclair's novel was the shock of recognition on reading Ernest Poole's immigrant narrative. In my reading of *The Jungle*, Poole's text is present as a subtext. This does not mean that the one text depends upon the other. Whatever the sources of his inspiration, Sinclair created a major work of literature as he grappled with making sense of his experience of the life lived by workers in the meat industry in Chicago. Understanding the novel's underlying dialectics, appreciating that it both is and is not a naturalist novel, and reading it as an immigrant Bildungsroman with a radical twist may help its realize that *The Jungle* is a flawed but nevertheless great American novel.

Notes

1. Upton Sinclair, "Is 'The Jungle' True?" *Independent*, 17 May 1906, pp. 1129, 1133. The review he is responding to is in the issue for March 29.

2. Upton Sinclair, *The Autobiography of Upton Sinclair* (New York: Harcourt, Brace & World, 1962), p. 110.

3. Van Wyck Brooks, *The Confident Years* (New York: Dutton, 1952), p. 381.

4. Louise Carroll Wade, *Chicago's Pride: The Stockyards, Packingtown, and Environs in the Nineteenth Century* (Urbana: Univ. of Illinois Press, 1987) and "The Problem with Classroom Use of Upton Sinclair's *The Jungle*" *American Studies* 32 (Fall 1991), 79–101; James R. Barrett, *Work and Community in the Jungle: Chicago's Packinghouse Workers, 1894–1922* (Urbana: Univ. of Illinois Press, 1987) and his introduction and notes to the University of Illinois Press edition of *The Jungle* in 1988. References to the novel in this article are to this edition.

5. Wade, "The Problem," p. 97.

6. Barrett., "Introduction," pp. xv, xix, xx; Wade, "The Problem," pp. 80, 92. As will be demonstrated, however, *The Jungle* has characters who are "not passive victims of exploitation." Both that the main character does not have the necessary understanding to heed their lessons and that the ameliorative program of trade unions is not commensurate to his affliction, are central to the theme of the novel.

7. Wade, "The Problem," pp. 79, 97.

8. On the serialization see Gene DeGruson, ed., *The Lost First Edition by Upton Sinclair's The Jungle* (Memphis: Peachtree, 1988). Ronald Gottesman has studied the assessment at *The Appeal to Reason* and also notes that Doubleday, Page accepted the novel "only after an independent investigation corroborated Sinclair's

allegations." See his "Introduction" to Upton Sinclair, *The Jungle* (New York: Penguin, 1985), pp. xvi-xxi.

9. Gottesman, "Introduction," pp. xxii-xxiii.

10. Bellamy has all social problems solved by 2000; Donnelly spells the disintegration of civil society in the near future; Adams sees the United States healing itself; and London has the socialists defeated by a fascist dictatorship.

11. Eugene Debs in *The Appeal to Reason* (21 July 1906) as quoted in Eric Homberger, *Arnerican Writers and RadicaI Politics, 1900–39: Equivocal Commitments* (London: Macmillan, 1986), p. 51.

12. Sinclair, *Autobiography*, p. 133.

13. Barrett, "Introduction," p. xxvi.

14. June Howard, *Form and History in American Literary Naturalism* (Chapel Hill: Univ. of North Carolina Press, 1985), p. 29.

15. Upton Sinclair, "Is 'The Jungle' True?" *Independent*, 17 May 1906, pp. 1129–33; Sinclair, *Autobiography*, pp. 108–10.

16. Ernest Poole, *The Badge: My Own Story* (New York: Macmillan, 1940), p. 85; William Hard and Ernest Poole, "The Stockyards Strike," *Outlook*, 13 August 1904, pp. 884–89; Poole, "The Meat Strike," *Independent*, 28 July 1904, pp. 179–84; "From Lithuania to the Chicago Stockyards—an Autobiography by Antanas Kaztauskis," *Independent*, 4 August 1904, pp. 241–48; Hamilton Holt, *The Life Stories of Undistinguished Americans as Told by Themselves*, intro. Werner Sollors (New York: Routledge, 1990). References are to the 1990 edition.

17. Poole, *The Bridge*, p. 95, Poole's confusion has confused several scholars. Wade has Poole explaining that Antanas Kaztauskis was not one person but forty thousand and Barrett repeats her claim that Kaztauskis was "in fact, a composite character." Wade, "The Problem," p. 83; Barrett, "Introduction," p. xxxi, n23.

18. Sinclair, *Autobiography*, p. 110.

19. Barrett, "Introduction," p. xxxi, n23.

20. Sinclair, *Autobiography*, pp. 134–35; Floyd Dell, *Upton Sinclair: A Study in Social Protest* (Long Beach, Cal.: George H. Doran, 1927), p. 124.

21. There was a ban on the use of the Latin alphabet in Lithuanian publications between 1864 and 1904. Books and journals were smuggled in from neighboring East Prussia (now the Russian enclave of Kaliningrad).

22. When Jurgis hears about the public schools where children "could go for nothing," the narrator explains that he was yet unaware that "the priestwould object to these schools" (44).

23. Poole, "From Lithuania to the Chicago Stockyards," p. 248.

24. Homberger's reading begins with "the butchery of hogs" (44) and Howard's is chronological, beginning with the immigrants' arrival in Chicago (156). It should not be necessary to observe that literary characters only exist as aspects of a text, and that in this particular text their lives begin in the first chapter.

25. Jane Addams, "Immigration: A Field Neglected by the Scholar," Convocation Address at the University of Chicago, 1904. Published in *The Commons* (,January 1905) and reprinted in Philip Davis, ed., *Immigration and Americanization: Selected Readings* (Boston: Ginn, 1920), pp. 3–22.

26. It should be noted that Antanas, who commands such respect for his learning in an Old World context, is considered useless in Packingtown. Indeed, Jurgis is told, not only here but "everywhere in America" the rule is that there is no use for old people (55).

27. Several critics have missed this point. One is Jacqueline Tavernier-Courbin: "Had Sinclair ended *The Jungle* with chapter 21 and the climax of little Antanas's death, the novel, as an allegory of victimization, would have had a unity of theme and effect infinitely more powerful, without alienating the reader by belaboring themes already dramatized or by presenting socialism as a universal and miraculous panacea" ("*The Call* of *the Wild* and *The Jungle*: Jack London's and Upton Sinclair's Animal and Human Jungles," in *The Cambridge Companion to American Realism and Naturalism*, ed. Donald Pizer (Cambridge: Cambridge Univ. Press, 1995), p. 259.

28. Georg Lukács, *The Histoical Novel* (London: Merlin Press, 1962).

29. The concluding conversion experience of the protagonist may be compared with the conversion experiences that conclude the immigrant autobiographies of Mary Antin (*The Prornised Land*, 1912) and Jacob Riis (*The Making of an American*, 1902).

30. The didactic nature of naturalist fiction is implied by Walcutt in his enlightening discussion of how the author of a fiction controlled by determinism "appeals to the reader's freedom and idealism as he shows that his hero is trapped" (Charles Child Walcutt, *American Literary Naturalism: A Divided Stream* [Minneapolis: Univ. of Minnesota Press, 1956], p. 27).

31. Howard, pp. 156–160; Homberger, pp. 34–58.

32. It may be noted that Tamoszius' socialist faith does not lead him to discard the music of his former homeland.

33. A sixth course may be labeled "Life Among the Aimless Rich." This is chapter 24, about his night with the home-alone spoiled and drunken son of one of the members of the Beef Trust. The implied lesson may be the eventual pointlessness of the wealth amassed at the expense of so many wasted lives, but this is a lesson missed by Jurgis as well as by critics of the novel. Matthew J. Morris sees this encounter as a dramatization of class struggle, which also seems a reasonable reading ("The Two Lives of Jurgis Rudkus," *American Literary Realism*, 29 [Winter 1997], 50–67). Morris has a similar reading of this section of the novel but to him it is the narrator who "tries to show the causes of the earlier suffering" to the reader while I see it as part of the education of Jurgis.

34. David M. Fine has pointed to "the recurrent 'conversion' pattern' in the immigrant labor novels of this period as well as of "the 30's proletarian novel—in which the protagonist is converted to the cause of organized labor" (*The City, the Immigrant, and American Fiction, 1880–1920* [Metuchen: Scarecrow, 1977], p. 75).

35. Central to Sinclair's account of his own conversion experience is also a sense of fellowship: "It was like the falling down of prison walls about my mind; the most amazing discovery, after all these years—that I did not have to carry the whole burden of humanity's future upon my two frail shoulders. . . . The principal fact which the Socialists had to teach me, was the fact that they themselves existed" (Sinclair, *Autobiography*, p. 101).

36. Walcutt, *American Literary Naturalism* p 25. Walcutt does not discus *The Jungle* and this may be because it does not quite fit into his model since the hero escapes from the laws of determinism by sharing in the education given to the reader. L. S. Dembo makes a similar point: "without the specifically socialist conclusion, Jurgis' story would be that of a naturalist man in a naturalist world" (*Detotalized Totalities: Synthesis and Disintegration in Naturalist, Existential, and Socialist Fiction* [Madison: Univ. Of Wisconsin Press, 1989], p. 169).

37. Howard, p. 159. To Howard, "There is no pretense in *The Jungle* that the group Sinclair is writing *about* is the same or even has much in common with the group he is writing *for*."

38. Howard, p. 145.

39. Walter Rideout observes that at this point "Sinclair turns from fiction to another kind of statement," and that "the Socialist salvation, after its initial impact, is intellectualized." To him as to several other critics, "The reader cannot exist imaginatively in Jurgis' converted state even if willing, for Jurgis hardly exists himself" (*The Radical Novel in The United States* 1900–1954 [1956; rpt. New York: Columbia Univ. Press, 1992], pp. 33–36).

40. Michael B. Folsom has pointed to this complementarity, observing that the account of "the Socialist movement in the last chapters provides a contrasting, new, and possible standard of life" ("Upton Sinclair's Escape from *The Jungle*: The Narrative Strategy and Suppressed Conclusion of America's First Proletarian Novel," *Prospects*, 4 [1979], 252).

41. In his notes Barrett has identified these characters.

42. In his enlightening reading of *The Jungle*, Christophe den Tandt highlights the novel's "three types of social structtures: the families of Old World immigrants, the economic machinery of capitalism, and the socialist utopia" (*The Urban Sublime in American Literary Naaturalism* [Urbana: Univ. of Illinois Press, 1998], p. 173).

43. We may, however, be all the more ready to share Sinclair's eschewal of violence as a means to achieve this vision. As Rideout puts it, Sinclair's socialist future "is to be accomplished by the ballot and not by the bullet" (*The Radical Novel*, p. 36).

GIEDRIUS SUBAČIUS

Sinclair's Sources and His Choice of Lithuanian Characters

There are many different considerations concerning Sinclair's decision to select Lithuanians as his protagonists for *The Jungle*.

1. Sinclair's Method of Gathering Material for His Novel

During the course of his very long life Sinclair wrote and spoke many times about the genesis of *The Jungle*, including in his autobiography, which was published in 1962. After the publication of Sinclair's novel *Manassas*, the editor of the socialist newspaper *Appeal to Reason* wrote him an enthusiastic letter and asked him to write something else about "wage slavery." Later Sinclair gave the details of their agreement:

> I answered that I would do it, provided he would stake me. The editor, Fred D. Warren, agreed to advance five hundred dollars for the serial rights of the novel, and I selected the Chicago stockyards as its scene. The recent strike had brought the subject to my thoughts. (Sinclair, 1962, 108–109)

On the basis of this offer, Sinclair decided to investigate the Chicago stockyards—his attention having been attracted by the recent (summer of 1904) strike there.

> So, in October 1904 I set out for Chicago, and for seven weeks lived among the wage slaves of the Beef Trust, as we called it in those days. People used to ask me afterward if I had not spent my life in Chicago, and I answered that if I had done so, I could never have written *The Jungle*; I would have taken for granted things that now hit me a sudden violent blow. (Sinclair, 1962, 109)

In 1906, two years after his stay in Chicago, Sinclair elaborated on his methods of data collection in *The Independent*:

> In the earliest portions of the book, which deal with conditions in Packingtown, I have not invented the smallest detail. Everything that has been there described has, to my own positive knowledge, happened to some one in that neighborhood. And likewise every fact or figure which I have given is absolutely accurate and exact, the result of patient inquiry and investigation. I spent seven weeks in the stockyards district alone, living with the people, meeting them in their homes, in the places where they worked, in their saloons and clubs. During that time I talked with hundreds of workingmen; I talked also with every other class of persons to be found in the district, with bosses and superintendents, with doctors and lawyers and merchants, with saloon keepers and policemen, clergymen and criminals. Everywhere I took note of what they said, testing the statements of one by those of another, and verifying every minutest detail; and afterward, when I came home, I kept up a continual correspondence with many people in Packingtown—in cases which I could name I wrote several letters in order to make sure of a single statement which I was making in the story. (Sinclair, 1906b, 1129–1130)

Fifty-six years later, Sinclair's explanation became much shorter, less strident, with fewer details (in the following quotation from his autobiography he omitted, for example, his conversations with saloon keepers, clergymen, and criminals):

> I sat at night in the homes of workers, foreign-born and native, and they told me their stories, one after one, and I made notes of everything. . . . I went about the district, talking with lawyers, doctors, dentists, nurses, policemen, politicians, real-estate agents—every sort of person. I got my meals at the University Settlement, where I could check my data with the men and women who were

> giving their lives to this neighborhood. When the book appeared, they were a little shocked to find how bad it seemed to the outside world. (Sinclair, 1962, 109)

In a typescript introduction to one of the editions of *The Jungle* that are kept at Lilly library at Indiana University in Bloomington, Sinclair wrote about the author of the novel (I give the first text before its correction): "In the evenings he sat in the workers' homes, asking them questions about their lives and filling notebooks with what they told him." (Sinclair, *Introduction*, 1). Sinclair gave one more explanation to a communist reporter from Lithuania—Albertas Laurinčiukas—who visited Sinclair after his 90th birthday. Laurinčiukas recounted Sinclair's version of the novel's genesis:

> They gave me five hundred dollars and I set up for Chicago. There I got acquainted with the Lithuanian workers. I lived together with them for seven weeks. We became friends. (Laurinčiukas, 1981, 163)

The author's four explanations differ in the number of the details given and in certain nuances. Unlike the first three descriptions, Sinclair made evident to Laurinčiukas that he met many *Lithuanian* workers and made them his friends. From Laurinčiukas's allusion, it might be understood that Sinclair chose Lithuanians *because* he had many Lithuanian friends. But this "last confession" was made in front of a Lithuanian—Sinclair might have especially emphasized the Lithuanian aspect to please his interviewer.

Thus, Sinclair spoke to a variety of people, lived among the workers, and made notes of their stories (his notes were destroyed during the fire of his Helicon Hall house in March of 1907). Yet Sinclair denied that he had selected any particular Lithuanians as his protagonists: "In my literary characters you can find peculiarities of many Lithuanian workers that I met sometime" (Laurinčiukas, 1981, 164). Only one of the main characters—Ona—was a prototype of his wife: "Ona was Corydon [Sinclair's wife], speaking Lithuanian but otherwise unchanged.... Externally, the story had to do with a family of stockyard workers, but internally it was the story of my own family" (Sinclair, 1962, 112). There was no trace of any specific personal reason for Sinclair to select Lithuanians.

2. Immigrants in the Chicago Stockyards

The arrival of Lithuanian immigrants at the stockyards of Chicago was referred to in many contemporary and later publications. For instance, in 1904, in *The Independent*, Ernest Poole described immigrant Chicago laborers as: "The more recent Polish and Slavonian and Lithuanian immigrant men" (Poole, 1904b, 180); "fresh immigrants, Lithuanians, Bohemians, Slavs and Poles" (182); "constant buzz outside of voices in the big outside room speaking in Polish, Lithuanian, Bohemian, Slavic" (183); "notice, which is printed in English, German, Lithuanian, Polish and Bohemian" (184). (At that time *Slavonian* or *Slavic* for Poole and many others might also mean 'Slovak.')

Carrol D. Wright published the report "Influence of Trade Unions on Immigrants," in 1905, where he described immigration in the stockyards: "The Poles began to come into yards in 1886, after the settlement of the strike" (2); "The Bohemians began to affect noticeably the situation in 1894" (2); "In 1895 the Lithuanians began coming in, followed by Slovaks in 1896" (2–3); "Two years ago an enormous influx of Lithuanians, Slovaks, and Russian Poles occurred, swamping the labor market in the yards" (3).

Rick Halpern, in his *Down on the Killing Floor,* also wrote about the immigrants:

> This group of semiskilled workers . . . was dominated by newcomers, most notably Poles, who by 1905 comprised the largest foreign-born group in the packinghouse workforce. The Slovaks and Lithuanians who followed after the turn of the century had a more difficult time adjusting to the industrial setting, in part due to their smaller numbers and, consequently, greater isolation. Unattached and unsettled, isolated by the formidable language barrier, these ethnic groups occupied the lowest space on the social ladder. (Halpern, 1997, 27)

An extensive study of Chicago's Packinghouse workers, *Work and Community in the Jungle,* was published by James R. Barrett in 1990. Barrett demonstrated that from 1900 to 1910 there was an increase in the number of Lithuanian male heads of household in Packingtown from 0.5% to 11.0%, of Poles—from 17.5% to 29.0%, of Slovaks—from 0% to 6.0% (Barrett, 1990, 74, table 5). It was obvious that these ethnic groups were the freshest in the stockyards and therefore living in the worst conditions. This is what Sinclair was looking for. At the same time, other ethnic groups of emigrants were losing their share in Packingtown: Germans had diminished from 34.5% to 16.5%, Irish—from 18.5% to 9.5%, Bohemians—from 18.0% to 13.0% (Barrett, 1990, 74, table 5).

The neighborhood that Sinclair concentrated his attention on in *The Jungle*—the one between Ashland Avenue and Robey (today Damen) Street, west of the stockyards—was predominantly populated by Lithuanians and Poles, according to Barrett and his map No. 2 (Barrett, 1990, 80).

Rabindra Nath Mookerjee wrote: "Of all the immigrant groups, the Lithuanians, who were simple, honest workers believing in 'work and more work,' were the worst sufferers" (Mookerjee, 1988, 42). For certain reasons he was persuaded that Lithuanians suffered the most.

Lithuanian authors, or the authors who had analyzed Lithuanian aspects of *The Jungle*, also discussed this issue. For instance, Alfonsas Šešplaukis believed that Sinclair's selection was "economically oriented" and that "one finds the answer in the sixth chapter" where Sinclair explains: "after a workers' strike the Irish shoved out and their place was taken by Czechs and Poles, and then by Lithuanians and incoming Slavs" (Šešplaukis, 1977, 26). Šešplaukis was familiar with the general plight of immigration in Chicago but did not proceed any further in his analysis.

The Lithuanian author Antanas Musteikis also discussed the Lithuanian characters of *The Jungle*. He did not try to find Sinclair's reasons for selecting the nationality. Musteikis found many arguments to support the thesis that Lithuanian psychological aspects in the book do not agree with reality; in the words of the author they should be included "in the category of real distortions" (Musteikis, 1971, 30). Musteikis concluded that "the Lithuanian attributes of the heroes of *The Jungle* found their place in the novel accidentally" (Musteikis, 1971, 37). Musteikis found many mistakes, inconsistencies, and misrepresentations that, according to him, proved Sinclair's relationship with Lithuanians to be very superficial. Similarly, some "inaccurate" or "erroneous" descriptions of the Lithuanian character were pointed out in Šešplaukis's article (1977, 28, 29). Sinclair was accused of distorting Lithuanian cultural and psychological peculiarities, which could be an indirect signal that he did not research particular aspects of Lithuanian life in Chicago while talking with the "workingmen, . . . with bosses and superintendents, with doctors and lawyers and merchants, with saloon keepers and policemen, clergymen and criminals."

In 1965, in Soviet Lithuania, Antanas Venclova wondered how Sinclair came up with the idea of Lithuanian protagonists:

> Even then, when I was writing my small book about Sinclair and his oeuvre in 1931, I wondered about the circumstances under which the author of *The Jungle* became acquainted with specifically Lithuanian immigrants, how he gathered the material for his novel and how he wrote it. (Venclova, 1965, 160–161)

Venclova published a book about Sinclair's life and oeuvre in 1931 in Lithuania (Venclova, 1931), but he did not discuss the Lithuanian aspects of *The Jungle* there. However, in 1963 Venclova wrote a personal letter to

Upton Sinclair asking about the Lithuanian origin of *The Jungle*. Sinclair had a chance to explain some additional details; but instead he only sent his autobiography and several other books to Venclova and elucidated that "answers to your questions are given in my *Autobiography*" (Venclova, 1965, 161).

Another article about Lithuanian life in *The Jungle* was written by Suk Bong Suh—"Lithuanian Wedding Traditions In Upton Sinclair's *The Jungle*" (later he published the book *Upton Sinclair and The Jungle* in Seoul in 1997, which also encompassed this article as a chapter under the name "The Lithuanian Heroes," 121–133). The author did not unravel the issue either; he merely mentioned that "by the turn of the century Lithuanian immigrants constituted one of the most important ethnic groups in the Chicago Stockyards district, so that it is no wonder that they attracted Sinclair's attention when he visited there in late 1904" (Suh, 1987).

In all, there were four nationalities mentioned most frequently at the time as the newest immigrants in Chicago-Lithuanians along with Poles, Bohemians, and Slovaks. Even those authors who researched the Lithuanian features of *The Jungle* usually gave no explanation regarding what might have been the concrete reasons of Sinclair's selection. Sinclair was well aware of the novelty of these nationalities in Chicago—he spoke about the "newest foreigners—Lithuanians, Poles, Bohemians, Slovaks" in *The Jungle* (*FE* 231; Ch 26; *FE* = *First Edition*, an abbreviation of *The Lost First Edition of Upton Sinclair's The Jungle*, edited by Gene DeGruson in 1988, which is a reprint of the first 1905 newspaper serial; here and further on I shall mostly quote *The Jungle* from this edition, unless I indicate otherwise; when quoted, two figures are usually used: the first one indicates page number and the second indicates the number of a chapter; in certain cases only a page number of *FE* is added to a quoted Lithuanian word).

It seems plausible to assume that since Sinclair had no personal reasons to select Lithuanians (he said that he got acquainted with Lithuanian workers only in Chicago, and Lithuanian scholars claimed Lithuanian attributes found their place in the novel accidentally), he might have chosen a family of laborers of any of those ethnicities.

3. Two Main Lithuanian Sources for *The Jungle*

The overall immigrant panorama did not force Sinclair to select Lithuanians exclusively, although it was an understandable choice—one of several imaginable. Presumably, there were concrete causes for Sinclair to decide on Lithuanians and not on Poles, on Lithuanians and not on Slovaks or Bohemians. Undoubtedly it *could* have been mere chance. . . . In the following pages, however, I shall argue that this chance might have been stimulated by at least two sources: (1) the Lithuanian wedding feast, which Sinclair saw with his own eyes and which he transformed into the first chapter of *The Jungle* and (2) the journalist Ernest Poole's text about a fictional Lithuanian immigrant Antanas Kaztauskis, which could not have escaped Sinclair's attention, along with the advice Poole gave Sinclair.

3.1. The Lithuanian Wedding

Many agree that the Lithuanian wedding was described very realistically in the first chapter of *The Jungle.* Suh compared the traditional Lithuanian wedding to the one described by Sinclair. He found that many Lithuanian traditions depicted in that chapter are convincing. For instance, he claimed that "Sinclair has fully demonstrated the old tradition to serve the guests with abundant food and drinks" (Suh, 1987); also "probably the most important feature of the Lithuanian wedding feast is the songs, music, and dances, and Sinclair has wonderfully portrayed them in the novel" (Suh, 1987). All in all, Suh evaluated the portrayal of Lithuanian immigrant life in the first chapter as very compelling. In addition, Suh inferred that those descriptions "are just byproducts of Sinclair's intention to denounce 'a modern economic system'" (Suh, 1987).

Other authors also assessed the Lithuanian wedding scene as containing nothing inaccurate or unacceptable (Šešplaukis, 1977, 26–29), or nothing that didn't "truly" belong to the Lithuanian culture (Musteikis, 1971, 33). These two Lithuanian authors uncovered no inconsistencies in the opening chapter, which is, according to many scholars the "most Lithuanian" chapter of *The Jungle.* To mention mere linguistic features, where else if not in the wedding could Sinclair have picked up such specific Lithuanian words used in weddings—*veselija* 'wedding' and *aczaviuas* (sic!; <u> instead of <m>) 'thanking'? Scholars ventured to value the Lithuanian features of the wedding episode more than any other in the novel.

As with his description of the way he took notes in Chicago, Sinclair gave several different explanations of how he created the opening wedding scene of the novel. The first account was written following the publication of the book edition of *The Jungle* in 1906:

> No one who knows anything about literature will need to be told that I saw the wedding feast with my own eyes. It was about four o'clock one Sunday afternoon. I had been over to inspect Tom Carey's dump, and had narrowly escaped a clubbing at the hands of a policeman who had been posted there for the express purpose of preventing what I attempted—the taking of a photograph of it. I noticed a crowd in front of a saloon, and I pushed my way in, and behold, there was the opening scene of my story, a gift from the

> gods. I stayed there until seven o'clock; and then I went away and had a little supper, and returned and stayed there until two o'clock in the morning. My habit of working is such that I can carry long scenes about in my memory for days, and then write them down word for word; I seldom write anything about which I really care without having done this for a long period. So I sat there and wrote that whole chapter in my mind—every tiniest detail of it and every emotion of it; I watched the people there and had imagined their lives, and little by little the whole story took shape. Everything which I had previously planned seemed in some miraculous way to fit in with them, and when I came away I was so exhausted that I could scarcely walk; but I knew that I had my whole book. That was two years ago, yet even now I cannot hear a child whistle "In the Good Old Summer-time," without feeling the tears start into my eyes. (Sinclair, 1906b, 1132)

The second account is found in Sinclair's *Autobiography* and it is somewhat similar to the one printed in 1906, although shorter and rephrased anew:

> At the end of the month or more, I had my data and knew the story I meant to tell, but I had no characters. Wandering about 'back of the yards' one Sunday afternoon I saw a wedding party going into the rear room of a saloon. There were several carriages full of people. I stopped to watch, and as they seemed hospitable, I slipped into the room and stood against the wall. There the opening chapter of *The Jungle* began to take form. There were my characters—the bride, the groom, the old mother and father, the boisterous cousin, the children, the three musicians, everybody. I watched them one after another, fitted them into my story, and began to write the scene in my mind, going over it and over, as was my custom. . . . It was two months before I got settled at home and first put pen to paper; but the story stayed, and I wrote down whole paragraphs, whole pages, exactly as I had memorized them. (Sinclair, 1962, 110)

The introduction to an edition of *The Jungle* that was written some forty years after the novel was printed encompassed different details on the rear room of the beer saloon, on several people there who spoke English (first text before correction):

> Towards the end of his stay he chanced to be walking on a Sunday afternoon through the unpaved streets of this vast and depressing slum, when he saw a bridal couple alight from a hack and enter the rear room of a beer saloon. Other persons followed, and the writer joined them. No one appeared to have any objection to his presence, on the contrary they appeared to take it as an honor, and so he sat on a bench by the wall and watched the proceedings of a Lithuanian bridal supper and dance. Several who spoke English explained to him what was going on and answered his questions, and gradually he realized that this was the family he wanted for his story. From four o'clock until close to midnight he sat, making note of every detail and composing in his mind what here appears as the opening chapter of a novel . . . he had trained himself to go over a scene and fix it verbally in his mind and retain it. (Sinclair, *Introduction*, 1–2)

Sinclair wrote one more portrayal of the wedding party around 1965 and again the details were somewhat different, such as the process of getting all the information about the couple and Sinclair's singing in Lithuanian (first text before correction):

> I was going to write a novel and I had everything but the characters. Then late one Sunday afternoon I was strolling past the saloon and I saw a carriage draw up in front of the dance hall in back of the saloon. A bride and bridegroom got out, followed by families and guests. I saw my opportunity and strolled in; and nobody had the slightest objection to my presence. Everybody was willing to talk to me, even the policeman who was there as a precaution. It was a Lithuanian family and I was told all about them, and little by little I realized that I had all the characters for my novel. I didn't tell them what I was doing, because I was just a friendly observer from a world somewhat above their own. I listened to the music, I joined in the singing—in Lithuanian, but it didn't matter. Some of the friends told me all about them, even the policeman was friendly and told me what he thought about them. And at one or two o'clock in the morning I went back to the stockyards Hotel and put it all down in my notebooks right away. (Sinclair, 1965a, 2–3)

In the printed version of this preface (which became a foreword), the fact that Sinclair sang in Lithuanian was deleted, but it included the supplementary information that "friends of the couple told me about them, including their *names*" (Sinclair, 1965b, vi).

Probably the last account was given by Laurinčiukas, who said that Sinclair told him:

> Once I found my way into a Lithuanian wedding party. It made such a striking impression on me; its contrast was so immense that when I was returning home from the wedding, I created the first chapter of my novel in my thoughts. (Laurinčiukas, 1981, 163)

First of all, Sinclair confessed that in the wedding party "I watched the people . . . Everything which I had previously planned seemed in some miraculous way to fit in with them . . . the opening chapter of *The Jungle* began to take form. There were my characters—the bride, the groom, the old mother and father, the boisterous cousin, the children, the three musicians, everybody." Sinclair also emphasized that "No one who knows anything about literature will need to be told that I saw the wedding feast with my own eyes." The wedding made an extremely strong impact on Sinclair. He was involved emotionally in the event to the point that he sang Lithuanian songs and "it didn't matter" if they were vocalized in Lithuanian!

Also, the only place Sinclair used the device of flashback in *The Jungle* was this wedding scene (Mookerjee, 1988, 48), which chronologically fits in chapter seven. Otherwise the entire novel is written in chronological order. In this regard, the first wedding chapter is conspicuously different from the others; thus, it is compositionally unique. Unlike most of the following chapters, it is also very bright, friendly, optimistic, and even beautiful. This chapter is a nexus among all the Lithuanian characters of the story as well.

The importance of the Lithuanian wedding in the creation of a Lithuanian aura is also signified by the number of Lithuanian words and phrases Sinclair included in the first chapter. . . . [T]here are 46 new Lithuanian words in chapter one (used 68 times), which make up the preponderance of Lithuanian words of the novel. . . . Clearly, the more Lithuanian words used, the stronger the Lithuanian atmosphere. Several other chapters that contain some new Lithuanian words have fewer that ten such occurrences. . . . Also, the preponderant majority of Lithuanian names and surnames used in *The Jungle* are introduced in the first chapter. . . .

At this point, the issue remains of whether Sinclair made the final decision to select Lithuanians, leaving aside Poles or Slovaks, on the basis of the wedding feast he witnessed. There is no very direct answer to this question, but there is no evidence, either, that before he saw the wedding he had deliberately gathered any specific Lithuanian data. Conversely—since Sinclair *fitted* wedding participants into the story, he presumably had the story drafted in his mind *by* the time he saw the wedding feast. Then the assumption seems quite plausible that Sinclair could have selected Lithuanians as characters for the novel *because of* that fortuitously spotted wedding. Quite recently Tom Gregg published an article entitled "The Truth about 'The Jungle'" in the Chicago Lithuanian magazine *Lithuanian Heritage* (2002); he reflected on the wedding party that "maybe that alone persuaded him to cast Lithuanians rather than Poles or Slovaks" (Gregg, 2002, 15).

The uniqueness of Sinclair's experience and of his emotional involvement, which made the first chapter exceptional in the context of the entire novel, makes the connection between this experience and his decision to opt for Lithuanians undisputable.

3.2. Ernest Poole's (Kaztauskis's) Text

Journalist Ernest Poole had "taken up his residence in Packingtown so as thoroughly to investigate the strike at first hand." His article "The Meat Strike" on the Chicago Packingtown strike appeared in the 28 Jul. 1904 issue of *The Independent* (Poole, 1904b, 179). In the next issue of the journal he printed an ostensibly autobiographical story by a Lithuanian immigrant, Antanas Kaztauskis. Poole gathered data from Lithuanians in Packingtown and told the story as if by one of them.

There is a typographical error in the last name *Kaztauskis*; it should read *Kazłauskis* (according to the spelling of that period, the letter <l> with a stroke <ł> signified a nonpalatal [l]), corresponding to today's Lithuanian surname *Kazlauskas*; it is one of the most widespread Lithuanian last names, like the English *Smith* or Indian *Patel*; the selection might have been made deliberately by Poole to symbolize that this character did not represent a particular Lithuanian, but many thousands of them. For the sake of tradition I shall use Poole's original spelling with a typographical error.

Speaking as "Kaztauskis," Poole depicted Lithuanian political, cultural, and material life, both in Lithuania and in Chicago, quite thoroughly. It contained information about smuggling Lithuanian newspapers and prayer books across the frontier from Germany into Lithuania; the prohibition against reading and writing in Lithuanian or having Lithuanian schools; it describes paying eighty roubles for taxes, an old wife plowing behind oxen, Chicago Lithuanians reading the Lithuanian newspaper *Katalikas*, singing the song by P. Brandukas, and other scenes of Lithuanian life. It is obvious that Poole was familiar with Lithuanians not just in Chicago, but in Lithuania as well. He must have heard many stories by Lithuanians to be able to come up with this kind of detailed picture of Lithuanian life. In his autobiography Poole described the following encounter with a Lithuanian in the stockyards:

> Many could speak no English yet. When I tried it on one big Lithuanian, he kept dumbly shaking his head, till at last I ventured the one word:
>
> "Strike?" It worked like magic. Out shot his fist.
>
> "Yo' bet yo'!" this new American cried. (Poole, 1940, 93)

Poole mentioned that president Theodore Roosevelt had noticed his text about the Lithuanian Kaztauskis:

> It must have been read by the man in the White House, for only a few days later an agent from Washington came and said:
>
> "The President has sent me here to check up on that Lithuanian story of yours and get the facts. Where's your man?" I smiled back and answered:
>
> "He's not one man; he's forty thousand. You'll find him all around the yards." (Poole, 1940, 95)

Surely if Roosevelt knew the text, it had to be known quite widely, and this might have made an impression on Sinclair as well. Sinclair published his own articles in *The Independent* often, hence he probably read it regularly and would have known Kaztauskis's text even before he came to Chicago, as it was published in August of 1904.

In Chicago, Sinclair met Ernest Poole personally at least a few times. Poole recorded the meeting in his autobiography:

> Into our headquarters one day breezed a lad in a wide-brimmed hat, with loose-flowing tie and a wonderful warm expansive smile.
>
> "Hello! I'm Upton Sinclair!" he said. "And I've come here to write the Uncle Tom's Cabin of the Labor Movement!"
>
> He already had a man digging for "the inside dope" on conditions in the Yards, and I gave him some tips on where to get more, and the color that he wanted. Then he dived into the strike and I lost track of him for two weeks.
>
> "Well?" I asked when we met again. "Have you made a good start on your job?"
>
> "Start? I've finished!" he replied. "I've got all that I need to get on the spot and now I'm going home to write!" (Poole, 1940, 95–96)

In her article "Upton Sinclair and the Writing of *The Jungle*," Christine Scriabine listed some topics of Kaztauskis's story that may have affected the plot of *The Jungle*:

> Among other things, Kaztauskis described how real estate agents cheated immigrants who attempted to buy houses on the installment plan, and how these newcomers became the tools of politicians and saloonkeepers. Even more important, his writing revealed the feelings of Lithuanian immigrants as they reached Chicago and later reflected on their life in the old country. The contrasting images of the polluted Chicago landscape and the flowers and green woods of Lithuania which are integral to the structure of the first part of *The Jungle* may well have been inspired by Kaztauskis's article. (Scriabine, 1981, 28–30)

Scriabine asserted that "although the figure of Jurgis Rudkus cannot be regarded simply as a fictionalized portrayal of Antanas Kaztauskis, he is nevertheless a better developed character because of Kaztauskis's 'autobiography'" (30). She had no doubts about the impact of Kaztauskis's story upon Sinclair (cf. also her dissertation *Upton Sinclair: Witness to History*, 1973, 63). Barrett, too, agreed that this story "probably helped to shape the character of Jurgis Rudkus" (Barrett, 1988a, xxxi).

These assertions are very persuasive. Scriabine mentioned agents, politicians, and saloonkeepers that emphasized Lithuanian life in Chicago, not in the far-away country. An addition to Scriabine's observations can be made—certain traces of Kaztauskis's story of the events that occurred in Lithuania can likewise be uncovered in Sinclair's. For instance, both Kaztauskis and Rudkos had to travel quite a long distance to see their fiancées in Lithuania—only it was ten miles for Kaztauskis (Poole, 1904a, 244), and ten times more for Rudkos—one hundred miles (*FE* 18; Ch 2). Musteikis criticized Sinclair's choice of a hundred mile distance as very unrealistic in a country as small as Lithuania (Musteikis, 1971, 30); it seems reasonable to believe that the substitution of the distances occurred because of Sinclair's attempts to change the details of Kaztauskis's story. Also, both Kaztauskis and Rudkos left Lithuania for America because of the circumstances created by the death of family members; Kaztauskis's mother died and then his father finally let him go (243–244), and Rudkos's fiancée's father passed away and no one was hindering their trip to America any more as well (*FE* 18; Ch 2). In addition, the oldest brother of Kaztauskis was killed serving in the Russian army during the war with Turkey (242), and the older brother of Rudkos "had been drafted into the army; that had been over ten years ago, but since that day nothing had ever been heard of him" (*FE* 17; Ch 2).

Of significance here is that the *Lithuanian* influence of Kaztauskis's story was, incorporated into the beginning of *The Jungle*. After the opening wedding party scene, the second chapter chronicled all the events that had taken place in Lithuania. Indeed, the second chapter is the *chronological* beginning of *The Jungle*.

Kaztauskis's story obviously affected Sinclair's novel; it was an important source of his Lithuanian information. Poole's advice may also have influenced Sinclair. Poole "gave him [Sinclair] some tips on where to get . . . the color that he wanted." The *color* for Poole might mean *Lithuanians*, the nationality whose representatives he spent much time communicating with. Thus, not only the written text, but also Poole's suggestion to depict the lives of Lithuanian immigrants might have been partly decisive in Sinclair's selection of a nationality.

There were also Sinclair's other helpers in the stockyards. No palpable evidence is available to show, however, that their impact might be of equivalent importance. For instance, Scriabine wrote about the first person Sinclair interviewed in the stockyards—the socialist Algie Martin Simons. She claimed that "it was Simons who introduced Sinclair to the workers . . . He undoubtedly provided Sinclair with a copy of his pamphlet, *Packingtown*" (Scriabine, 1981, 28). Kent and Gretchen Kreuter were of the opinion that:

> Simons liked Sinclair at once. The two men, though very different in tastes and temperament, still had much in common. . . . In short order, the preparations were made for Sinclair to enter the yards and begin gathering material for his projected novel. (Kreuter and Kreuter, 1969, 78)

But no known biographical detail betrays any particular attention Simons may have paid to aspects of the Lithuanian immigrant life that would have influenced Sinclair's choice. In the pamphlet *Packingtown* (1899), Simons never even mentioned Lithuanians or any other nationalities. Hence there is no hint of a possibility that Simons influenced Sinclair's selection of Lithuanians. Conversely, in 1906 Simons defended *The Jungle* from its critics as a very truthful story in the following words:

> This story is hung upon a group of Lithuanians, who, in any other book, would be called the "principal characters." But in this book the real characters are social classes and industrial conditions. (Simons, 1906, 712)

Simons beheld only social classes and industrial conditions, as though nationalities might threaten to distract readers' minds from socialist ideology.

4. The Wedding, Kaztauskis's Story, and Lithuanian

The more general or more "objective" reason for Sinclair's decision to opt for Lithuanians was the demographic situation in the neighborhoods adjacent to the Chicago stockyards—if Sinclair wanted to soak his characters in any national color, he needed to select from the most prevalent ethnic groups—Poles, Bohemians, Lithuanians, and Slovaks. The chances of his picking any one of these may seem to be equal. It appears plausible that Sinclair did not set out to portray Lithuanians specifically before he arrived at the stockyards.

The choice of Lithuanians was the result of Sinclair making concrete use of chance. More concrete and tangible subjective reasons for this turn out to be the two salient sources of inspiration: (1) the Lithuanian wedding feast and (2) Kaztauskis's story and the advice written and given by Ernest Poole. The conjunction of these two influences might have been even more decisive for Sinclair than if any one of them were taken separately. Even so, if only emotionally, Sinclair put the emphasis on the first chapter, making the wedding the stronger candidate for the title of *decisive* source.

The structure of *The Jungle* obviously supports the idea of these two sources as the main factors for deciding on Lithuanians. Both were used in the first and the second chapters of the novel. In the following chapters, Sinclair seemingly ran out of Lithuanian material. Had more Lithuanian data sources been available, the disproportional concentration of Lithuanian redolence or color in the two opening chapters might not be as conspicuous as it is. It is certain that Sinclair did not try to acquire any ample collection of specific Lithuanian cultural or historical materials.

One more feature that accented the Lithuanian color in *The Jungle* was the Lithuanian language. Sinclair employed Lithuanian words, phrases, and names in his English text. The Lithuanian language may be considered a device that Sinclair used to instill the Lithuanian aura into his *chef-d'oeuvre*.

How did he collect the language data and what were his Lithuanian linguistic sources? These questions are addressed in the next chapter of this book.

MICHAEL MOGHTADER

Discursive Determinism in Upton Sinclair's The Jungle

> There is one kind of prison where man is behind bars, and everything that he desires is outside; and there is another kind where the things are behind bars like language, and the man is outside the bars of language. (*The Jungle* 278)

Literary scholars of Upton Sinclair have generally agreed on the triple significance his novel *The Jungle* has in American literature. First, the novel is recognized as a classic example of muckraking fiction whose description of Chicago's meatpacking industry influenced the United States Government to change the food spoilage laws in the early part of the twentieth century. Second, the novel is generally acknowledged as an important example of American proletarian fiction and as a definitive statement about Sinclair's socialist convictions. Finally, the novel is often singled out as a classic example of American literary naturalism. While it is relatively easy to find consensus about the first two claims, critics have been reluctant to agree on the last claim.

The first two-thirds of the novel, critics routinely point out, illustrate quite vividly Jurgis Rudkus's struggle to survive in the determinist world of Packingtown's urban jungle. But the overt political propaganda in the final chapters of the novel undermine its literary qualities. For example, critics like William Bloodworth, L. S. Dembo, Jon Yoder, Michael Brewster

From *The CEA Critic* 69, no. 3 (Spring and Summer 2007): 13–27.

Folsom, and Jacqueline Tavernier-Courbin all recognize *The Jungle* as a key work of American literary naturalism; but they do so with significant reservations. "Without the specifically socialist conclusion," Dembo writes in his book-length study of socialist fiction, "Jurgis's story would be that of a naturalist man in a naturalist world" (*Detotalized* 169). Or consider Jacqueline Tavernier-Courbin's assessment of the novel, which Donald Pizer includes in his 1995 collection of essays, *The Cambridge Companion to American Realism and Naturalism*:

> Unfortunately, in [*The Jungle*] as well as [in] many of his other works, Sinclair tends to assault the reader with the message he wants to carry, subordinating plot, character development, and verisimilitude to propaganda. In Sinclair's own words, *The Jungle* was misread: he had 'aimed at the public's heart, and by accident [had] hit it in the stomach.' Not really accidental, the misreading was caused by the vividness of his descriptions of the stomach-turning conditions of work in the Chicago meat-packing plants, the deceitful and unsanitary practices of the meat industry as a whole, and, at the same time, by the presence of characters who are not lifelike, and a plot that loses credibility in the last third of the novel. The sympathy and pity one initially experiences eventually give way to exasperation, as Sinclair manipulates his protagonist out of character for socialist purposes. (250)

These pathos-evoking details, such criticisms point out, combined with Sinclair's overt politicizing overwhelm the more literary qualities of this naturalist novel. Indeed, as Tavernier-Courbin reminds us, even Sinclair himself downplayed the novelistic qualities of his book despite the admiration he received for his descriptive and propagandistic talents.[1]

Such critical assessments exert tremendous influence over the way English teachers approach Sinclair's novel—in both their critical scholarship and their curricular approaches as teachers. This is particularly true for courses that introduce students to literary naturalism, courses designed to help students assess the literary qualities of naturalist works by using criteria like those mentioned in Tavernier-Courbin's remarks. And yet, as those of us who include *The Jungle* in such courses will attest, it's difficult to teach the book as literary naturalism because we cannot reconcile its more literary qualities with the naturalistic characteristics of the book. Readings of *The Jungle* as a unified novel with a coherent plot and narrative seem incompatible with its dimensions as a work of economic, biological, or sociological determinism: Because of the overt socialist propaganda in the final chapters of the book, teachers have been unable to teach it as successful literary naturalism. In fact, confronted by these sorts of challenges, teachers may be less inclined to give the novel the attention it deserves (and, at worse, to give it a place in their courses).

One mode of determinism that has not been applied to the novel, however, is that of "discourse"—language as it is actually used among members of specific communities in their written and verbal communication. Discourse also includes forms of reasoning and thinking unique to a given community that establish and regulate the conventions of communication. "Discursive determinism," then, would examine how discourse and discursive fluency operate as naturalistic forces to influence the individual's struggle for survival. Apart from its novelty, what makes this mode so useful in readings of *The Jungle* as a work of naturalism is its compatibility with more literary readings of the novel. In fact, the qualities of discursive determinism we find in the book are not just compatible with its literary qualities; they are inseparable. Just how prominent, though, *is* the theme of discourse in *The Jungle*? How does discourse thwart the Lithuanian family's struggle to survive in the jungle-like American "Packingtown"? And does this thematic approach help the novel cohere in ways that elude other approaches teachers and students traditionally apply to works of literary naturalism?

From the opening chapters of *The Jungle*, readers immediately sense the struggle that awaits Jurgis and his family as non-native English speakers. What we may not fully appreciate, however, is the *extent* to which language acquisition contributes to the novel's theme and plot. As R. N. Mookerjee has summarized, "Until chapter IX, when Jurgis becomes 'desirous of learning English' . . . , none of the characters seem to know the language in which the novel is written. Therefore, for over a full quarter of the novel's length, . . . the author himself becomes the voice of the chief" character among the others (51). What makes Mookerjee's observation so significant is how Sinclair's choice of third-person narrative in these initial chapters makes it easy for readers to overlook the Rudkus's inability to speak English. When members of the family speak to one another, their dialogue is in English; only when Sinclair forces them into conversation with Americans are we reminded of their complete dependence on those who can speak English.

Indeed, from these opening chapters, we quickly understand the severe helplessness of these immigrants and their over-reliance on others to help them develop the cultural literacy needed to succeed in the new world of Packingtown. And this helplessness is best illustrated in their interactions with those outside the family unit. Consider, for example, their relationship to Jokubas Svedvilas. Although a mere delicatessen vender, Svedvilas serves as a key agent in the family's survival in America. It is through Svedvilas's "many acquaintances" that Jurgis gets an interview with "one of the special policemen employed by Durham [the processing plant], whose duty was to pick out men for employment" (Sinclair 35). Judging from the brokenness of Jurgis's English in the dialogic exchange in the beginning of Chapter 3, we can safely assume that without Svedvilas's influence, the interview may never have occurred.

But even Svedvilas's fortuitous role as translator cannot compensate for the ominous, naturalistic force that discourse exerts over Jurgis and his family. The rental of the house in Chapter 4 provides a vivid example of how powerful this discursive force can be. Sinclair equates the "smooth and florid, elegantly dressed" rental agent with his ability to speak "their language freely, which gave him a great advantage in dealing with [the Rudkus family]" (51). Along with his dapper, professional, "gentlemanly" appearance, the agent's facility with the Lithuanian language, we may infer, cements his credibility, which bullies the family into silence and, eventually, into accepting the number of discrepancies in the lease agreement: "To press the matter would have seemed to be doubting [the agent's] word, and never had any one of them ever spoken to a person of the class called 'gentleman' except with deference and humility" (51). As the rental transaction unfolds, even Svedvilas's skill as translator cannot decipher the legal jargon of the contract that the family is asked to sign. Svedvilas can only "stammer" questions regarding the language of the contract even he cannot understand: "This was not a deed of sale at all, so far as he could see—it provided only for the renting of the property! It was hard to tell, with all this strange legal jargon, words he had never heard before" (54). The family's translator baffled, the agent offers them the service of a lawyer—with whom the agent is suspiciously familiar—to help decipher the language for them. And as the lawyer and Svedvilas discuss the language of the contract (and the subsequent fate of the family's dream to own a house), "the women folks were fixed upon [them] in mute agony. They could not understand what he [the lawyer] was saying, but they knew that upon it their fate depended. . . . How . . . [to] know if this lawyer were telling the truth—that he was not in the conspiracy?" (55). Here, both the literal language of English and the figurative language of legal contractual discourse further alienate the immigrants and intensify their dependence on various interpreters. Ironically, instead of translating and deciphering these languages for the family, the interpreters themselves further complicate the terms of the transaction until the family is left "mute," compliant, and utterly dependent. We begin to see that the family's fate rests with those who possess some discursive facility with these languages.[2]

The rental scene reveals how the Rudkus family's material needs depend on their discursive facility. But discourse also thwarts their desire for spiritual and emotional solidarity with those outside of their Lithuanian culture. For example, in Chapter 8, Jurgis discovers the appeal of unionization: "A wonderful idea [unions] seemed to Jurgis, this of the men—that by combining they might be able to make a stand and conquer the packers" (91). Soon, "all the working members of his family had union cards, and wore their union buttons conspicuously and with pride. For fully a week they were quite blissfully happy, thinking that belonging to a union meant an end of all their troubles" (91–92). That happiness is short-lived, however, because the Lithuanians' inability to articulate their needs at these meetings jeopardizes their membership and weakens their faith in the power of community. Inflamed by her anger over the closing of the canning factory that had once employed her, "Marija got up and made a speech about it. It was a business meeting and was transacted in English, but that made no difference to Marija; she said what was in her, and all the pounding of the chairman's gavel and all the uproar and confusion in the room could not prevail" (92). Unable to articulate her rage in ways others can understand, her anger amounts to very little. All she can manage to do is to vent her frustrations in her Lithuanian language, which, to all those outside her culture, sounds like the ramblings of a madwoman.

Jurgis, too, attempts to establish ties with others, like those who attend the union meeting. Yet, his inability to understand Tommy Finnegan's speech alienates, rather than liberates, Jurgis. Assuming that Jurgis can understand his broken English, Finnegan singles out the Lithuanian as the beneficiary of his speech. To Jurgis, though, who cannot understand a word Finnegan says, the incident only embarrasses him in front of the entire crowd:

> Tommy Finnegan went on, expounding a system of philosophy, while the perspiration came out on Jurgis's forehead, so great was his agitation and embarrassment. In the end one of the men, seeing his plight, came over and rescued him, but it was some time before he was able to find any one to explain things to him [Jurgis], and meanwhile his fear lest the strange little Irishman should get him cornered again was enough to keep him dodging about the room and the whole evening. (93)

Jurgis's alienation is symbolized quite vividly in this passage, as the "fearful," "cornered" Jurgis "dodges" detection—dodges full membership into the union. His inability to speak English, then, reinforces the very alienation he sought to alleviate by joining the union in the first place. Not surprisingly, his "I will work harder" spirit helps Jurgis salvage something positive from the incident: He manages to turn the experience into a positive, productive encounter and begins, informally, to learn the English language. In fact, of all the benefits that Jurgis sees in his membership, "one of the first consequences . . . was that Jurgis became desirous of learning English. He wanted to know what was going on at the meetings, and to be able to take part in them" (93–94). The unions are important, in other words, for what they teach Jurgis of the English language. What's more, this opportunity leads to his enrollment in school where he may develop an awareness of democracy: "It was a little state, the union, a miniature republic; its affairs were every man's affairs, and every man had a real say about them. In other words, in the union Jurgis learned to talk politics" (94). Once again, we see just how significant language acquisition is. In this case, Jurgis has the opportunity to "talk politics," a privilege afforded to those who belong to a democracy-based culture. In this way, Jurgis's ability to speak English is a key factor in his successful transformation into an American citizen.[3]

Discourse, then, clearly serves as a central plot element and theme that help the novel cohere. Scenes like the union meeting remind us of the important role language acquisition plays in determining the Rudkus family's fate. The scene at the union meeting, though, suggests another, more complex theme. A knowledge of English is one way language determines the fate of the Lithuanians. What is more significant, though, is their acquisition of *cultural* knowledge—an understanding of the "thinking" (in Jurgis's case, socialist thinking) accessible only to English speakers. Perhaps more than language acquisition, cultural literacy is a powerful factor in the individual's struggle for survival in *The Jungle*. Knowledge of a culture's worldview—its rhetorical, philosophical, and epistemological foundations—regulates communication and action within that culture. What Jurgis and his family lack, then, is not just the ability to speak English; they also lack the ability to think and act within that culture through a familiarity with its bodies of knowledge and the metaphorical and tropical systems used to organize that knowledge.

Among the many scenes in the novel that illustrate the importance of cultural literacy, there are three that dramatize its effects particularly well. In each case, we can appreciate just how detrimental cultural illiteracy can be. We might think of the first culture as that of *profit*, and those who regulate the literate practices within that culture as the creators of Packingtown. What intensifies this instance of cultural literacy is its contrast with Lithuanian sensibilities and values. Consider, for example, the *veselija* or "wedding feast" scene early in the novel. According to William Bloodworth, the scene "illustrates the desperate desire for order and community on the part of the Lithuanian immigrants who are struggling to make a living in Packingtown" (50). From scenes like this one, we can infer the values and laws that generate familial harmony in Lithuanian culture. "It was one of the laws of the *veselija*," says the narrator,

> that no one goes hungry, and while a rule made in the forests of Lithuania is hard to apply in the stockyard district of Chicago, with its quarter of a million inhabitants, still they did their best, and the children who ran from the street, and even the dogs, went out again happier. A charming informality was one of the characteristics of this celebration. (9)

The celebration spills out into the street, and the family's charitable sensibilities and their sense of communal bonding are so strong that they willingly invite the thousands of Packingtown inhabitants to revel in the festivities. "It is the music which makes [the occasion] what it is"—the melody both from the band's instruments and from the celebrators' waves of "laughter and shouts and endless badinage and merriment" (10). And while the family increasingly equates money to happiness later in the novel, they clearly do not do so here; instead, they are willing "to spend such a sum, all in a single day . . . at a wedding feast! . . . It is very imprudent, it is tragic, . . . it is [also] so beautiful! Bit by bit these poor people have given up everything else; but to this they cling with all the power of their souls—they cannot give up the *veselija*!" (18).[4]

The *veselija* scene clearly depicts the Rudkus family's knowledge of and desire to preserve their cultural heritage. They soon learn, however, that this cultural knowledge does very little to help them survive in the material culture of Packingtown. The immigrants soon are faced with the difficult task of retaining desirable aspects of an old way of life—their music, their religion, their concept of family—within a new culture that determines success by the individual's ability to compose a materialistic "self" through his economic strength (Yoder 32). As the family soon learns, a cultural knowledge based on familial solidarity and communal responsibility means very little in the profit-driven culture of Packingtown. Consequently, the Rudkus family's inability to compose themselves materialistically—through thought and language—leaves them powerless. According to Michael Brewster Folsom, "As we are introduced to the methods of the stockyards in company with Jurgis and the other immigrants, we might almost be in the hands of [the stockyard's] public relations department. The new arrivals are in constant wonder at the order and efficiency of it all, how nothing is wasted" (242). Figuratively struck dumb, the immigrants, once again, need a translator to decipher for them the strange cultural literacy one must learn to, speak in Packingtown. And what is that translator? The discursive voice of Packingtown. With each proclamation of Jurgis's "I will work harder," the exploitative voice of Packingtown answers, "Then I will work you to death." Their inability to negotiate a Lithuanian cultural literacy within a profit-oriented culture leaves them at the mercy of a translator whose sole agenda is to keep Packingtown running smoothly and productively. One culture's literacy, in other words, is deliberately "lost in the translation." Ingrid Kerkhoff is right when she says that the family is "little prepared for the dramatic struggle for survival with which they are confronted in the New World" (178). What makes that struggle particularly hopeless for Jurgis and his family is that they cannot read and manipulate the discursive signs and symbols of Packingtown culture and, thus, must rely on others who, in the best interests of Packingtown, exploit the culturally illiterate Lithuanian.[5]

Jurgis's escape to the country in Chapter 22 sets the stage for yet another example of the determinism of cultural literacy and its consequences. In this case the literate practices within the culture of *criminality* control his fate. In the moment between the death of his son and Jurgis's train ride out into the country, Jurgis undergoes a radical change in his sense of "self":

> He had been a fool, a fool! He had wasted his life, he had wrecked himself, with his accursed weakness; and now he was done with it—he would tear it out of him, root and branch! . . . Now he was going to be free, to tear off his shackles, to rise up and fight. He was glad that the end had come—it had to come sometime, and it was just as well now. This was no world for women and children, and the sooner they got out of it the better for them. . . . [H]e was going to fight for himself, against the world that had baffled him and tortured him! (210)

Jurgis is eager to give up the "weakness" of an old-world discourse, informed by domesticity and family, that had been such an organic part ("root and branch") of him but which had "shackled," "baffled," and "tortured him" since his birth in the new world. "Tearing up all the flowers from the garden of his soul, and setting his heel upon them" (210), Jurgis kills his Lithuanian cultural self—he lets the decorative "flowers" of the symbolic *veselija* whither—so that he can better adapt to and adopt a new literacy.

With this new perspective, Jurgis is reborn into a world of deceit and crime and, almost immediately, demonstrates the acquisition of his newfound literacy—he lies. When asked by a prospective employer if he has "ever worked in Chicago before," Jurgis responds in a way new to him and to us readers: "Whether it was a good angel that put it into Jurgis's mind, or an intuition of his sharpened wits, he was moved to answer, 'No, sir'" (220). Whereas a culturally illiterate Jurgis would probably have told the truth in this underworld, this new Jurgis demonstrates his competence to think and act within the culture of what the narrator calls "the high-class criminal world of Chicago"

(249). Leaving behind his literate proficiency in the old-world culture, Jurgis tries to develop an underworld cultural literacy in a number of ways. He helps to "tunnel all Chicago with a system of railway freight subways" to throttle "the teamsters' union by the throat" (221). By doing so, Bloodworth argues, Jurgis "becomes a burglar; burglary leads to political connections and to a position as a ward heeler for the Democratic machine in Packingtown. When a strike erupts in the plants, . . . Jurgis sees his opportunity for a good job after the packers break the strike, and he goes to work as a strikebreaker . . ." (54). Jurgis also knows enough to change the one-hundred dollar bill that Master Freddie gives him: "What would they think, seeing a bum like him with a hundred dollars? He would probably be arrested . . ." (241); and he even goes so far as to offer a crooked bartender a "kickback" to change the bill for him. Ironically, though, Jurgis does end up in jail, for while he does exhibit increased fluency in speaking the new discourse of crime, the bartender turns out to be much more fluent—that is, he keeps the bill and Jurgis is arrested for trying to get it back. Jailed again, Jurgis meets up with Jack Duane who, in the course of the conversation, sees (as we have) that Jurgis has "learned some things" since they last met (246).

Developing literacy in the culture of *socialism* represents a final example of discursive determinism, its consequences, and the extent to which it influences the individual's fitness to survive. Sinclair would have made a rather brutal indictment against immigrants—if not the entire working class—had Jurgis continued to learn and speak the criminal discourse of the Chicago underworld. But in Chapters 26 and 27, Jurgis's desire to assimilate into the culture of crime wanes; in its place, he desires the ability to manipulate the signs and symbols that make up the literate practices within a socialist culture. During one of the strikes, Jurgis, in the capacity of a strike-breaking manager, sees a familiar face of the Packingtown culture he had left behind: Phil Connor. Connor's sudden voice from the past unsettles Jurgis, in part because he associates Connor's voice with those of Ona and Lithuanian culture. Forgetting all that he had learned as a member of socialist culture, Jurgis attacks Connor. In doing so Jurgis jeopardizes his developing socialist literacy and, consequently, loses his position as manager. "An outcast and tramp once more" (276), Jurgis runs across Marija who has since become a whore, and with this physical reminder of all that he once was and is, Jurgis's head throbs with a cacophony of discursive voices that drive him nearly to the brink of insanity:

> He heard the old *voices* of his soul, he saw its old ghost beckoning to him, stretching out their arms to him! But they were far off and shadowy, and the gulf between them was black and bottomless;

> they would fade away into the mists of the past once more. Their *voices* would die, and never again would he *hear* them—and so the last faint spark of manhood in his soul would flicker out. (290 emphasis added)

All at once, Jurgis hears the multiple discourses that have, in turn, controlled his fate. What he needs is a single, meta-discourse that helps him think and act in ways that give him some reason and the means to live. But, much like the indifferent universe that answers the man in Crane's famous poem, there is no meta-discourse. For Jurgis, there are only the multiple voices that clamor in his head.

Clearly, a dominant thematic presence of discourse runs throughout *The Jungle*. Too illiterate to speak and think within the various discursive cultures of America, the protagonist and his Lithuanian family's struggle to survive is destined to fail. Just as much as economic and biological forces, discourse regulates their individual and collective attempts to join and succeed in the cultures they encounter.

Given the thematic prominence of discourse in *The Jungle* and the coherence it lends to the novel's narrative and plot, it seems cdd that the novel's final chapters have frustrated readers who attempt to appreciate the novel as successful literature. Instead, critics as well as Sinclair himself have suggested a whole host of possible explanations for what they claim to be a "tacked-on" ending.[6] What's noteworthy about such criticisms is that they obsess over the novel's preoccupation with socialist politics. To be sure, no one would dispute the socialist propaganda in the novel's final chapters, and analyzing those chapters within the frame of socialism, does, indeed, support arguments about the novel's thematic and narrative discontinuity.

But if we approach *The Jungle* from the perspective of discourse, these final chapters fit nicely with the thematic concerns Sinclair has pursued throughout the novel. To begin, consider what happens to Jurgis as he stumbles into the socialist meeting hall in Chapter 28. "Suddenly," the narrator tells us, "Jurgis looked up. A tremendous roar had burst from the throats of the crowd, which by this time had packed the hall to the very doors. Men and women were standing up, waving handkerchiefs, shouting, yelling. Evidently the speaker had arrived . . ." (294). Having practiced reading and interpreting a number of cultural discourses, Jurgis seems poised in this scene to demonstrate his intellectual strength to read, interpret, and manipulate the discursive conventions that authorize members to speak within socialist meeting hall.

Distracted by the din of voices in his head, Jurgis sits in the back of the noisy meeting hall: "Speaking had been going on all the time, and the audience was clapping its hands and shouting, thrilling with excitement; and little by little the sounds were beginning to blur in Jurgis's ears, and his thoughts were beginning to run together, and his head to wobble and nod" (295). Standing at the threshold of this new culture, Jurgis suddenly "sat up with . . . a terrified start! . . . And now what?" (295). Jurgis is eager for the opportunity to display his socialist literacy. And, at that moment, a cultural insider gives him that opportunity: "And then suddenly came a voice in his ear, a woman's voice, gentle and sweet. 'If you would try to listen, comrade, perhaps you would be interested'" (295). Aside from the sexual suggestiveness, the exchange tells Jurgis that he is not only invited into this culture but also *expected*, as if a new cultural identity, "comrade," had been waiting for him. Sensing this opportunity, Jurgis turns away from the voice and, looks at the orator:

> Jurgis had an unpleasant sensation, a sense of confusion, of disorder, of wild and meaningless uproar. The man was tall and gaunt, as haggard as his auditor himself; . . . he was *speaking* rapidly, in great excitement; he used many gestures—as he *spoke* he moved here and there upon the stage, reaching with his long arms as if to seize each person in his audience. His *voice* was deep like an organ; it was some time, however, before Jurgis thought of the *voice*—he was too much occupied with his eyes to think of what the man was *saying*. But suddenly it seemed as if the *speaker* had begun pointing straight at him, as if he had singled him out particularly for his *remarks*; and so Jurgis became suddenly aware of the *voice*, trembling, vibrant with emotion, with pain and longing, with a burden of things *unutterable*, not to be compassed with *words*. To *hear* it was to be suddenly arrested, to be gripped, transfixed. (296 emphasis added)

The numerous references to "speech" and the "voice" in this passage help us see just how well Jurgis has learned to understand both English and socialist discourse.

His newly acquired cultural literacy is all the more impressive when compared to his reaction at the first union meeting, when Finnegan's fluency in English "corners" Jurgis. But unlike Jurgis's reaction in the earlier union meeting, he is strangely attracted to what the socialist orator has to say. In fact, one could attribute Jurgis's "transfixion" to his ability not only to understand what the orator says but also to appreciate fully the *thinking* behind the orator's remarks and the desire to converse about the speech with those around him. Moreover, the fact that this speaker is given seven pages of narrative while Finnegan is given but a brief paragraph suggests just how proficient Jurgis's literacy appears to be. As the narrator says in the aftermath of the speech,

> suddenly, in one awful convulsion, the black and hideous fact was made plain to [Jurgis]! There was a falling in of all the pillars of his soul, the sky seemed to split above him—he stood there, with his clenched hands upraised, his eyes bloodshot, and the veins standing out purple in his face, roaring in the voice of a wild beast, frantic, incoherent, maniacal. And when he could shout no more he still stood there, gasping, and whispering hoarsely to himself: 'By God! By God! By God!' (303–304)

It is quite possible that Jurgis's animalistic response conveys how eager he is to participate in the socialist discourse community. As Alfred Hornung has said of this scene, Sinclair "presents in the spokesperson of socialism a new kind of hero whose message works a miracle in Jurgis and makes him feel free like a new-born man" (30). Time and again Jurgis has struggled to develop the cultural literacies needed to help him succeed in the new world. And, in this scene, that acquisition appears certain.

Not surprisingly, that does not happen. "An important point is easily overlooked in the flow of the [orator's] rhetoric," Dembo argues: "Revelation is only the first step in a socialist education; it must be followed by hard study and experience. The conclusion of *The Jungle* is [supposedly] optimistic not simply because it envisions a socialist victory at the polls, but because it marks the socialization of a man who without the doctrine would be wholly lost" (166). The last scene, in other words, illustrates not political socialism but *socialization* and the process of acculturation. Dembo, of course, is optimistic about Jurgis's fate. After all, Jurgis is invited to exercise his newfound cultural literacy; but he never gets that opportunity because the orator's pretentious verbosity and the narrator's omniscient voice deny him that chance. Instead, following his frenzied and animalistic response to the orator's speech, he suddenly disappears, confirming what we already know: his struggle to survive, once again, ends in failure. Despite his understanding of and enthusiasm to practice speaking a new discourse, he still lacks what he always has: a cultural literacy that allows him to manipulate discourse and compose a new sense of self with this culture. Consequently, it is not Jurgis's voice that resonates in our heads in the closing chapters of the novel. Intellectually bullied, he sits "spellbound" (326) as Dr. Schliemann and Mr. Lukas appropriate Jurgis's opportunity to speak for himself.

Despite the clear allusions to speaking, language, and discourse, this is the scene that critics recall to support their claim that *The Jungle* fails as a unified novel. Scenes like this one "prevent the reader from taking Jurgis seriously as a man and as a Socialist" (Folsom 257). "In the last chapter," Folsom adds, "in final ignominy and social insignificance, Jurgis virtually disappears from the novel, swallowed up in the parlor debate of the Socialist intelligentsia"; and "although he has been invited [to debate] as an expert on the crimes of the meat packers, 'he was terrified lest they should ask him to talk.' He is not asked to talk. . . . Jurgis merely evaporates" (258). According to Bloodworth, Sinclair in these final chapters "has . . . shifted the focus of the novel from Jurgis to the Socialist movement itself. Up to his accidental stumbling into the Socialist lecture, Jurgis's story is almost entirely his own" (56). The overt political propaganda in the final chapters explains why critics like Folsom and Bloodworth insist that the novel be read as a socialist text. As such, why, they ask, is Jurgis established as the beneficiary of this socialist program when he is left stammering at the conclusion of the orator's speech? Why isn't Jurgis invited to participate within this socialist culture? "What was Sinclair's intention?" Folsom asks: "Certainly he must have believed that this whole embarrassing episode was doing what everything else in the book was meant to do: convince the reader of the necessity for and validity of socialism" (257).

These are valid criticisms. But note how they all take socialism to be the novel's main theme. As a novel about discourse and the struggle to acquire cultural literacy, however, such criticism is unwarranted. In fact, within the context of the discursive determinism readers have witnessed throughout the novel, the last scene is a fitting, even artful, ending.

A re-evaluation of Sinclair's novel in light of its discursive features reveals two ironies. First, contrary to critical consensus, the disjointed quality of the novel is not a "flaw" per se but a rare opportunity to see a writer working within the tradition of the novel to pioneer a new type of literary naturalism. Admittedly, *The Jungle* may not succeed as a model of the more recognizable modes of determinism that we expect of naturalist texts—modes oriented around the work of Darwin, Marx, Comte, or Freud. But as a vivid illustration of discursive determinism, the novel unquestionably succeeds.

Overlooking the discursive theme in *The Jungle* creates a second and, perhaps, more significant irony. If teachers were more inclined to approach the novel from this thematic perspective, they might understand better why their own students often struggle in the English classroom. Particularly in writing-intensive literature classes, college English teachers know how difficult it is for students to acquire a facility with the sort of academic discourse that determines their success as college readers and writers. After all, understanding literary texts entails much more than plot summation and character memorization. It entails developing interpretive strategies that give readers the authority to critique or "speak back" to those literary texts. As Robert Scholes reminds us in *Textual Power*, his classic book on literary theory and English studies, many students come to our English classes with a sense of alienation. For much of their education, they have been bullied by difficult literary texts and, as a result, feel isolated as readers of literature because they lack a knowledge of the discursive conventions needed to succeed in our classes. After reading *The Jungle*, we have a much better appreciation for how hard that knowledge is to come by. Much like Jurgis and his family, our students succeed only if they learn to "move from 'reading' to 'interpretation'" and then "from 'interpretation' to 'criticism'" (40)—"from a submission to textual authority in reading, through a sharing of textual power in interpretation, toward an assertion of power through opposition in criticism" (39).

As a pioneering novelist exploring new forms of naturalism, Sinclair responds to the call Donald Pizer makes in the introduction to his 1995 collection of naturalism criticism. "Indeed," he appeals to scholars of American literary naturalism,

> one of the more striking characteristics of [American naturalism] has been its adaptability to fresh currents of idea and expression in each generation while maintaining a core of naturalistic preoccupations. The nature of this core is not easy to describe, given the dynamic flexibility and amorphousness of naturalism as a whole in America, but it appears to rest on the relationship between restrictive social and intellectual environment and the consequent impoverishment both of social opportunity and of the inner life. (13)

As teachers of English, we have an obligation to respond to Pizer's call, as well, and explore with that next generation of scholars—our students—what these "fresh currents of idea and expression" might sound like. Examining with our students the discursive current that runs throughout *The Jungle* is a good way to begin that important work.

Notes

1. According to R. N. Mookerjee, Sinclair himself never even attempted to defend the flaws of the novel. Instead, he offered a number of excuses for it, including increasing financial difficulties, his inability to travel to Chicago to complete the novel "properly," and the inevitable disjointedness that accompanies a novel's serialization (56).

2. The extent of this realization becomes more clear later in Chapter 6 when Jurgis, Ona, and Teta Elzbieta learn through translation by English-speaking Grandmother Majauszkiene yet another surprising detail of their lease—interest. As the family bemoans this new information, "There sat Grandmother Majauszkiene, unrelenting, typifying fate. No, of course it was not fair," the narrator reminds us, "but then fairness had nothing to do with it. And of course they had not known it" (73). The ambiguity of the unspecified pronoun "it" in this passage certainly leaves

open the possibility that discourse—as much as any other naturalistic force—determines the fate of these newly arrived immigrants.

3. In Chapter 20 Jurgis finds yet another opportunity to continue his learning of English while working at the harvester plant: "All day," the narrator reports, Jurgis "sat at a machine turning bolts; and then in the evening he went to the public school to study English and learn to read" (199). Ironically, though, the plant suddenly closes and, once again, Jurgis's education is disrupted. By this point in the novel, Sinclair demonstrates the crucial role that discourse plays in controlling Jurgis's fate. Only when he is successfully speaking English with others does he find a sense of camaraderie and community as an American. And those incidents in the novel when Jurgis cannot "find the right words" are precisely those when his feelings of isolation and alienation are most acute. His Lithuanian accent, his "stammering" of English, his need for a "translator" of some kind to mediate his expression of the present and his recollection of the past—all reinforce his helplessness and mark him as different, as "other."

4. A family profile begins to emerge from scenes like this one. We begin to appreciate the contrast between the Lithuanian culture and the materialistic culture of America. From the world they leave, this community-oriented family believes that an individual's survival depends on the harmony between that individual and her community. Consider, for example, Jurgis's familiar response within the context of the *veselija*. When his family's traditional ceremonies are threatened by their residence in Packingtown, he responds, "[D]o not worry—it will not matter to us. . . . I will work harder" (22). According to Jon Yoder, this "response to increasing trouble" (31) is both admirable and complements the "neighborliness, obedience, [and] respect" of Lithuanian culture (32).

5. Armed only with his Lithuanian work ethic, Jurgis's proclamation "I will work harder" translates into the language of the new world as "a cog in the machine." The factories work the "cog-like" Jurgis with relentless drive, and, consequently, his "teeth" begin to wear. Yet, despite the number of unfortunate incidents that befall Jurgis as a result of this gradual wear, he instinctively responds in the language he knows best: "I will work harder." Lacking the appropriate discursive knowledge to respond in this culture, Jurgis is forced to work under constant strain until he sprains his ankle. The restlessness he feels while recovering suggests just how unfit he is to survive in the Packingtown culture: "In truth, it was almost maddening for a strong man like him, a fighter, to have to lie there helpless on his back. It was for all the world the old story of Prometheus bound" (118).

6. Bloodworth, Yoder, and Folsom are among those critics who question the literary worth of *The Jungle* on this point alone, faulting the novel as an unintentionally fractured work. See also Mookerjee (56) on this point.

Works Cited

Bloodworth, William A. Jr. *Upton Sinclair*. Boston: Twayne, 1977.

Dembo, L. S. *Detotalized Totalities: Synthesis and Disintegration in Naturalist, Existential, and Socialist Fiction*. Madison: U of Wisconsin P, 1989.

———. "The Socialist and Socialite Heroes of Upton Sinclair." *Toward a New American Literary History: Essays in Honor of Arlin Turner*. Ed. Louis J. Budd et al. Durham: Duke UP, 1980. 164–80.

Folsom, Michael Brewster. "Upton Sinclair's Escape from *The Jungle*: The Narrative Strategy and Suppressed Conclusion of America's First Proletarian Novel." *Prospects: An Annual of American Cultural Studies* 4 (1979): 237–66.

Hornung, Alfred. "Literary Conventions and the Political Unconscious in Upton Sinclair's Work." *Upton Sinclair: Literature and Social Reform*. Ed. Dieter Herms. Frankfurt: Peter Lang, 1990. 24–38.

Kerkhoff, Ingrid. "A Closer Look at Upton Sinclair's Females." *Upton Sinclair: Literature and Social Reform*. Ed. Dieter Herms. Frankfurt: Peter Lang, 1990. 176–94.

Mookerjee, R. N. *Art for Social Justice: The Major Novels of Upton Sinclair*. Metuchen: Scarecrow, 1988.

Pizer, Donald. *The Cambridge Companion to American Realism and Naturalism: Howells to London*. Cambridge: Cambridge UP, 1995.

Scholes, Robert. *Textual Power: Literary Theory and the Teaching of English*. New Haven: Yale UP, 1985.

Sinclair, Upton. *The Jungle*. 1906. New York: New American Library, 1980.

Tavernier-Courbin, Jacqueline. "*The Jungle* and *The Call of the Wild*: London's and Sinclair's Animal and Human Jungles." Pizer 236–62.

Yoder, Jon A. *Upton Sinclair*. New York: Frederick Ungar, 1975.

ELIZABETH KRAFT

Writers that Changed the World: Samuel Richardson, Upton Sinclair, and the Strategies of Social Reform

The dust jacket blurb on the inside flap of the first and only edition of Upton Sinclair's 1950 novel, *Another Pamela*, cites with pride the novel's point of origin and stakes its claim to readership in the spectacular success of the novel on which it is modeled:

> Upton Sinclair has taken a busman's holiday to write this new novel, his first since he completed his ten-volume Lanny Budd series. He has gone back to that first great English bestseller, Richardson's Pamela of 1740, and used it as a model for a novel of our own times. His modern Pamela is a naive country girl, a devout Seventh Day Adventist, who goes to work as parlormaid for a wealthy and eccentric California family. In a series of letters to her mother and sister, she tells the story of her awakening to a bewildering world. Her battles against the seductions of the young master, a playboy of the twenties, provide a series of episodes that are comic, pathetic, and as true to life today as they were two hundred years ago; and they lead to the rewards of virtue just as they did in the eighteenth century.

Published by Viking Penguin, the novel did well enough for Sinclair to begin negotiations for *Pamela, the Musical*, a project that never materialized,

From *On Second Thought: Updating the Eighteenth-Century Text*, edited by Debra Taylor Bourdeau and Elizabeth Kraft, pp. 141–57.

sadly enough.[1] The cast of characters alone would have produced memorable lyrics, for in addition to Pamela and her rich employers is a host of incidental types—"Hindu sages, criminal syndicalists, birth control fanciers, peripatetic poets, Wobblies, movie stars, and cultists of all varieties"—brought to the "great house" by Pamela's mistress, who is, according again to the dust jacket, "a parlor pink." Richardson's *Pamela was* indeed the source of paintings, artifacts, and—yes—an opera libretto; but Sinclair's version remained a curiosity of print culture alone.[2]

Even as a curiosity of print culture, *Another Pamela* can hardly be said to command our attention today. The book seems to have little antiquarian value as a rarity, for copies can be found fairly easily for around $10.00, not too much more than the original price of $3.00. Aesthetically, the claim to our attention is even more tenuous; one would be hard-pressed to make an argument that Upton Sinclair has produced in his response to an eighteenth-century work a masterpiece of parodic or philosophic response (as J. M. Coetzee does in *Foe*, for example, or Jean Rhys does in *The Wide Sargasso Sea*, or as Henry Fielding, for that matter and more to the point, does in *Shamela*). Yet its very failure to tap into the cultural energies of its time is an interesting fact, given Sinclair's success as doing just that—both in his early novel *The Jungle* and in the later Lanny Budd series, as well as in other novels written in between.[3] Still, I hesitate to deem *Another Pamela* an unqualified failure. Although certainly reform was on Sinclair's mind, as it always was, he also seems to have written *Another Pamela* as a tribute, an act of homage, to the first example of a novelist whose pen managed to cut through the divide between the fictional and the real to effect a change,in the society he depicted.[4] As such, *Another Pamela* repays our attention. The club to which Sinclair belongs—novelists who changed the world for the better—is a small one. His novel *The Jungle* was credited with the passing of the Pure Food and Drug and the Meat Inspection Acts of 1906, which had been stalled in Congress before the novel appeared.[5] If Richardson's *Pamela* did not precipitate social legislation, it did stimulate positive social change. Eighteenth-century scholars, of course, have examined and recorded and analyzed that change from the point of view of social and cultural historians.[6] In updating Richardson's tale, however, Sinclair divorces *Pamela* from her moment in history. As the blurb says, Pamela is as "true to life" today as she ever was. The implication is that there are essential, universal values to which the novelist/reformer subscribes—and perhaps essential, universal techniques the novelist/reformer employs as well. This essay wishes to consider the validity of Sinclair's implied assumption through, first, an examination of *Another Pamela* and, second, a brief consideration of *The Jungle*.

Early on, *Another Pamela* seems only loosely related to Richardson's novel in that the point is more often the mildly satiric effect of the naive narrator commenting on an unfamiliar world than on the evolving relationship between master and servant in which social and spiritual systems of value come into conflict. The first 120 pages of *Another Pamela* often read like episodes of *The Beverly Hillbillies* or a rendition of Andy Griffith's "What It Was Was Football" in that Pamela interprets literally the unfamiliar language she encounters or she tries to accommodate the language she has to the unfamiliar sights she sees.[7] For example, she writes to her sister: "As you know, I was hired for a parlormaid, but it seems there is no parlor; it is called the drawing room, but I have never seen anybody drawing in it," and she describes a woman's bathing suit as "a little tight thing with no arms and very little legs."[8] But on page 123, this twentieth-century Pamela is given a book to read, Richardson's *Pamela*, and from that point on the novel can be said to shift from a kind of Menippean satire to a rather complex psychological study of the process of self-construction through the mediation of a literary text.

Sinclair's Lanny Budd series had featured a protagonist who interacts with real people—George Bernard Shaw, Hitler, Franklin Roosevelt, Einstein. The series was so popular that Sinclair's contemporaries actually requested appearances. Isadora Duncan proposed that Lanny Budd and she become lovers in one of the novels—a suggestion that Sinclair rejected.[9] The series provoked criticism, many objecting to the combination of history and fiction, but some readers—some important readers—found the novels not only entertaining but educational as well. Sinclair's biographer Leon Harris quotes Lady Bird Johnson as saying she "gained a more vivid recollection of foreign affairs (the rise of fascism and the American involvement in the Second World War) through the adventures of Lanny Budd, than she did through reading the newspapers at that time!"[10] *Another Pamela* retains the patina of the Lanny Budd series in that central to its vision and plot is a blurring of what some take to be the harsh lines of demarcation between fiction and reality.

Up until the moment when Sinclair's Pamela is given Richardson's novel by a visiting literary magazine editor, the parallels between the texts are relatively few. But Sinclair's Pamela, similar to her namesake, is subjected to the amorous advances of her employer's nephew prior to the presentation of the text. Indeed, it is that fact which leads the editor to think the young parlor maid would find Richardson's book interesting and instructive in the first place. But the parallel is thin up until this point, and Sinclair seems torn between the satiric use of his protagonist's naive innocence and his commitment to the notion that seems to have been the genesis of his novel—that a modern

Pamela could exist and that her virtue could prevail in the twentieth-century fictional landscape as it had in the eighteenth-century novel. Occasionally, Sinclair seems to strain for connections, as when he has Pamela write to her sister early on that she is "not letting anyone see the letters [she] write[s]." She continues: "I have made myself a little flat bag and I put the letter in it and pin it inside my bodice and so it is safe. When I find myself in town I drop it in the mailbox and no one is the wiser" (*Another Pamela*, 22). There seems no need for this secrecy, however, in terms of Pamela's own personal safety. True, some of the things she tells about her mistress's Sunday afternoon gatherings of communist sympathizers of various sorts could perhaps bring sanctions against the Harries family, but Pamela understands so little of what is going on that her letters would serve scant use as evidence in any kind of legal action. And no one seems particularly interested in her letters, anyway. The obsessive curiosity exhibited by Richardson's characters when someone retires to compose a letter is absent from the world Sinclair's Pamela inhabits. She is an odd little country girl with a strange religion that disallows most of the behavior around which the fashionable world centers its life. The notion that anyone would want to read what she reports home is so ludicrous that her care here would seem eccentric to the point of paranoia, if we did not know the literary precedent that had provoked Sinclair to invent it.

On page 123, however, Sinclair discovers a use for his literary model. He brings Richardson into the text overtly, and from that point on the "first Pamela" serves to frame and legitimize the second Pamela's personal struggle to resist and reclaim her young master. As Sinclair's Pamela reads the 1740 novel, she copies out significant scenes for her sister's perusal, commenting on the differences and the similarities between herself and "Pamela One," as she calls her. The first scene she reproduces is the one in which Mr. B surprises Pamela writing: "I broke off abruptly my last letter; for I feared he was coming; and so it happened. I put the letter in my bosom, and took up my work" (146). The image recalls the earlier unmotivated echo of Richardson's text, and it focuses our attention on Pamela Two's personal crisis—not a crisis requiring secrecy, but one demanding some moral and ethical decisions. As she herself articulates the problem: "[W]ould I be satisfied to end like her and marry the cruel man who had pursued me? I admit to myself that I have sometimes dreamed that Charles might ask me to marry him, though he has never spoken that word. I know that I would never marry a man who did not take the pledge against liquor, and I cannot see how I could marry a man who did not believe in God and keep the Sabbath. It is hard for me to imagine Charles doing these things; the second would be harder than the first, for he would have to humble his pride and I think he would rather go to hell" (151–52).

Hard as it is to imagine, however, turning Charles into a sober believer with honorable intentions becomes Pamela's goal, the end to which she directs her behavior for the rest of Sinclair's narrative. Inspired by a story two hundred years old, she learns the power—both spiritual and venal—of her sexuality, a power she uses, like her literary "great-great-great grandmother" for social reform and personal aggrandizement.

Sinclair's appropriation of Richardson's novel seems a straightforward-enough strategy, suggesting that for all the intervening two hundred years the choices of women—particularly women from poor families—are defined by their ability to make the most of youthful attractiveness and allure. Pamela Two, like Pamela One, chooses to play for the highest stakes—marriage—though she, like her literary forebear, is offered lesser material rewards in exchange for sex. Holding out for marriage is fashioned as the moral choice by Sinclair, just as it is by Richardson. The rigid sexual code endorsed by conservative Christianity enables Pamela Two to withstand the pressure brought to bear by both her would-be seducer and his aunt, who encourages Pamela to go to any lengths to keep Charles away from the bottle. The combination of social authority and moral imperative might have been too much for another parlor maid to withstand, but Pamela is never really tempted to allow more than the kisses and caresses of what she is taught to refer to as "petting parties." She finds herself very attracted to Charles, but his powers of coercion are more limited than those of Mr. B, and the obstacles to an honest marriage are fewer as well. Family concerns, in particular, carry less weight for Sinclair's Pamela than they do for Richardson's. After all, a "parlor pink" can hardly affect the umbrage of a Lady Davers without exposing herself to be the most blatant of hypocrites, and Sinclair's Mrs. Harries is not that. She overindulges her nephew out of excessive fondness, and she holds societal reform a higher priority than the feelings and fears of her excitable, socially conservative husband. But her treatment of Pamela is uniformly generous and kind. If anything, she becomes even more embracing after Charles and Pamela decide to marry, prompting Pamela to predict that her soon-to-be aunt-in-law will "do her best to spoil me as she has spoiled Charles" (305).

Mrs. Harries and Pamela in fact share a common trait. As Pamela says of her mistress: "She is good and kind but determined to have her own way and to impress her ideas upon everyone she meets" (305). She could well say the same of herself, for a few sentences later, she articulates her own plan: "What I mean to do, very tactfully, is to try to weaken the prejudice which she cherishes against the idea of God. I have the advantage over her, that she could not keep Charles from drinking, while with God's help I can" (305). In other words, what seems to be of interest to Sinclair is the power conferred by ideological positions from which to insist upon and effect social change.

Pamela's more rigid system of behavioral guidelines (shored up, as she presents it to Charles, by the power of an all-knowing God) stands a better chance of succeeding than Mrs. Harries's pleadings and threats. Communism provides no imperative for combating the abuse of alcohol or sex, but Christianity—of the Seventh-Day Adventist variety—certainly does.

There are ironies at work in *Another Pamela* similar to the ironies at the heart of Richardson's novel. When Mr. B, in frustration, says of the first Pamela that she could "corrupt a Nation," he as much as acknowledges the power of her adamant insistence on her own personal dignity and her right to sexual self-determination.[11] Richardson, of course, aimed at such a widespread effect, and he—and many of his readers—like Mr. B saw the servant girl as an agent of reform, corrupting, so to speak, the corrupt values and behavior of the upper class. Some, of course, argued for the more literal interpretation of Mr. B's remarks, insisting that the prurience of the novel was indeed corrupt and corrupting. Those ironies made for a widely appealing narrative that managed to satisfy opposite tastes and appetites.[12]

Sinclair does not exactly match the ironic complexity of Richardson's achievement in this regard. *Another Pamela* is not at all titillating. Scenes of kissing and "petting" are reported without reference to heaving breasts and panting breathlessness. These scenes are seldom lingered over, and they are often contrasted to the more sensational passages in Richardson's book. For example, Pamela Two quotes at length the scene in which Mr. B masquerades as the drunken Nan and "put[s] his hand in [Pamela's] bosom" causing her to faint (*Another Pamela*, 231). She follows that excerpt with the report of "another battle with Satan for the soul my young master" (241): "He started trying to kiss me again, and I told him that they were not sisterly kisses. He was provoked, and went off to Hollywood, and came back with liquor on his breath" (241). Even the "petting party" is described primarily in terms of talk, and it ends when Charles verbally reneges on his promise to build houses for poor people. Pamela says: "When he starts kissing me again my heart is dead and when he starts pressing me more closely I say, 'No, Charles, that is enough now; you promised you wouldn't do that; you must stop now.' When he tries not to heed me, I start to weep, and he says, 'Oh, God, that crybaby stuff again!' I say, 'You promised not to go any farther,' and he takes the name of Jesus in vain and says it is a way to drive a man crazy" (179–80). Granted, this was written in 1950 for a readership that had no doubt participated in such "conversations" themselves; but the formulaic presentation of passion recalling memories of adolescent sexual exploration seems unlikely to have aroused the prurient *imaginations* of readers in the same way that Richardson's *Pamela* did. Sinclair's Pamela is so cool in her responses, so staunchly resolved to adhere to a conventional set of sexual mores, there is never a question as to whether or not she will succumb. We do wonder about Richardson's Pamela. Indeed, in the scene just invoked, she wonders about herself. "Your poor Pamela cannot answer for the Liberties taken with her in her deplorable State," she writes, inviting the reader to imagine for himself or herself.[13]

Sinclair's ironies are of another sort, though in an important sense they speak to the same end. The seduction that *his* Pamela has difficulty withstanding, the "attack" that leaves her defenseless and on the verge of emotional collapse and spiritual compromise, is not a sexual seduction but a literary one. Seventh-Day Adventists, according to this novel anyway, disapprove of novel reading.[14] Like movies and liquor and premarital sex, novels are banned. Yet Pamela is drawn to *Pamela*, and she finds a way around her church's injunction. She justifies reading the novel by a rather specious argument: "I am permitted to read letters," she explains to Mr. MacKenzie, taking refuge in the fuzzy generic boundaries that Richardson himself exploited. Rachel, Pamela's sister, seems to know a rationalization when she hears (or reads) one, as Pamela's defensiveness suggests: "I have not written you much about it, in view of your fear that it is really a novel in spite of being in the form of letters" (*Another Pamela*, 187–88). Later, she argues even more strongly for the efficacy of reading this work, as she is also learning from Mr. Mackenzie the historical background necessary to place the book in context. (He explains why Pamela cannot just call the police when Mr. B mistreats her early on, and he lectures about the "rigid class system" in answer to the question "How can it be possible that a girl would be willing to marry a man who has shown himself so wicked and so treacherous?") Pamela tells her sister, "I am sure this book cannot harm me. It takes me out of one time into another, and is like history; at the same time it does not fail to strengthen my virtue, being full of moral sentiments most uplifting." When she concludes "Someday I may persuade you to read some of it and see," we realize that she is not just content to break the rules of her faith; she wants others to do so as well, implying a need to rethink and perhaps revise the regulatory precepts that govern the behavior of the sect (226). When in the end, Pamela marries Charles, she reports a "concession" she has decided to make: "I have been going to shows with him." She has decided that "the main point" of the Adventist prohibition on shows is "the corrupting of the young. . . . [and she deems herself] no longer young in that sense." Besides, she explains, "I have to balance the evil of breaking our church's rule against the evil of managing my husband too strictly and so losing my hold on him" (311–12). One suspects that had there been an *Another Pamela II*, we might see her taking an occasional drink in the interest of retaining and restraining her husband.

Sinclair's Pamela is given psychological depth through her interaction with a literary text; she learns to see herself and her choices as more significant than she would have thought them to be without the mediation of Richardson's novel. She also demonstrates, however, the seductiveness of being right, of "maintaining hold," as she puts it, of converting others to one's own point of view. The power conferred her by her religion is significant, but one suspects the power of novels and film are just as important to her sense of control. Centered on individuals like herself, they teach her to find herself interesting and to make herself so beyond the interest conferred by youth and desirability.

Like Mrs. Harries, Pamela seems determined to make the world a better place as she defines that phrase. Through his novels, Sinclair hoped to do the same thing. In *The Jungle*, of course, he did just that. If *Another Pamela* did not contribute substantially to the betterment of society, it is perhaps because the issues it treats are ones pertaining to a world that had been created by an earlier social revolution—a revolution given vision and voice by Richardson himself. In *Pamela*, Richardson presented a heroine whose resistance to the heretofore uncontested power of class difference gave the novel's readership new ideas, prompting a rethinking of the basic assumptions of their world. "It is no ordinary moment in political history" Nancy Armstrong observes, "when a male novelist imagines a woman whose writing has power to reform the male of the dominant class."[15] Such reformation comes through the redirecting of male desire from the body of the woman to her mind, thus according her a power over male desire she had never experienced before. In Richardson's text, the social revolution resulting from such power is indicated by a shift in the regulation of domestic space. As Armstrong points out, imprisoned in Lincolnshire, Pamela exists in a panopticon as an object of continual surveillance by Mr. B's servants. Though he himself is not present, Pamela is completely subject to Mr. B's control. The Lincolnshire home resembles, again in Armstrong's words, "nothing so much as a paranoid conspiracy"; the servants "are bound only by the principle of satisfying their master's desire." Such a bond, however, is so powerful and coercive that the staff, Mrs. Jewkes in particular, will stop at nothing to satisfy Mr. B's needs. When the master's desire is transformed by Pamela's words, when Mr. B himself internalizes, through the reading of her letters, Pamela's moral authority, that authority extends to the household. Armstrong concludes: "Because a well-regulated household depends entirely on the moral qualities of the female in charge, it cannot succumb to the double tyranny of male desire and aristocratic whim."[16] The revolution effected by Richardson, as Armstrong so convincingly argues, is the transfiguration of male desire, which in turn transfigures the eighteenth-century estate, and, thus, the eighteenth-century world.

Attitudes that were revolutionary in Richardson's texts are accepted facts in the world of Sinclair's *Another Pamela*. What troubles this world is not the autocratic, venal power of male authority over the women in his family. In fact, women seem firmly in charge of all domestic space, and domestic space is the location of most of the novel's action, suggesting that the world is morally and ethically centered on the home. What seems to be the real source of trouble is the abdication of the male from the matriarchal home, not to the world of business or politics (those activities are domestically centered in Sinclair's novel), but to the world of mindless pleasure—alcohol, fast cars, and impersonal, casual sex. This male must be won back to the household through love, and he must be held to strict codes of sexual and spiritual conduct by the woman who loves him. While Mr. B becomes the proper head of household through the influence of his Pamela, Charles simply becomes a member of the home again, a novitiate, still, in the life of rectitude and sobriety—the foundation from which he can build a public identity and contribute positively to the society in which he lives. His presence is welcomed—indeed, desired—but the women remain in control of the domestic sphere, as they had for a century at least.

In short, Armstrong's analysis of the revolutionary power of Richardson's text simply does not apply to Sinclair's modernization of the tale. Sinclair's "master's" failings are self-destructive, aimed toward his own dissolution, not toward extreme tyranny over others in his world. In fact, there seems no center at all to this world to displace and replace, as there was in the first Pamela's world. Yet, like Richardson, Sinclair believed that fiction could change the world, and he always wrote with that end in mind. In his most remarkable success, *The Jungle*, in fact, his techniques for advocating change were very like Richardson's. He elaborated scenes that would encourage the sentimental involvement of readers in the lives of characters who suffer at the hands of those in power; he wrote in plain language that earned him little aesthetic acclaim but that seemed designed to attract the kind of readership and the response from that readership that he desired; and he forged an emotional link between Christianity and social reform.

Still, *The Jungle* failed to effect the change Sinclair hoped to bring about. He wanted to illustrate and thereby put a stop to "the breaking of human hearts by a system which exploits the labor of men and women for profits."[17] What he actually accomplished, as we have noted above, was the precipitation of an outcry against adulterated food that led to the passage of the Pure Food and Drug Act and the Meat Inspection Act. Sinclair memorably voiced his disappointment about the novel's effect on its readership: "I aimed at the public's heart, and by accident I hit it in the stomach."[18] Richardson, on the other hand, seems to have been pleased with the result of the fiction he wrote in pursuit of social reform. We cannot point to any act of legislation resulting from *Pamela*, but certainly our sense is that the book made exactly the difference Richardson intended it to make: it got its readership thinking and talking about morality, propriety of behavior, and religion. Both authors wished to bring into accord the stated values of a Christian society and the social practices in which that society typically engaged. But the difference in outcome is significant enough to warrant examination of the techniques shared by the authors in approaching their didactic ends.

Sentimental identification is forwarded in both *The Jungle* and *Pamela* by situating the protagonist in relation to life-cycle events common to almost every reader's experience. Jurgis Rudkus, like Pamela, begins his narrative life in a scene of transition—a marriage, his own, to Ona Lukoszaite. We meet Pamela first after the death of her mistress, as the household comes under control of Mr. B. Jurgis too begins to establish a home for his wife and their extended families, all immigrants who have traveled together to America from Lithuania to live a life of freedom. Already in the early chapters, there are signs that the social fabric of immigrant life is being frayed beyond repair. The community does not honor the custom of contributing to the wedding expenses, which means Jurgis and his wife begin their married lives in debt. They are under pressure to meet their work obligations in the various units of the meat packing industry in which they have all taken jobs at ridiculously low pay for unbelievably hard work. The need to make it to work on time the day after the wedding does not mean the celebration is cut short, but the sense of pressure—the omnipresent concern over the repercussions of tardiness, illness, and unforeseen events that will characterize the entire novel—is immediately apparent. Pamela, too, tries to maintain a sense of decorum, of order, of an expected sequence of events in the aftermath of her mistress's death, but her master's behavior exerts pressure on her. In other words, both novels begin with well-intentioned, innocent characters living lives according to ordinary expectations that are quickly shown to be false fronts for alternate, sinister realities.

Our concern for their fates is complicated, however, by other details in the novels—details that in fact contribute more to the power of the stories than the creation of sentimental care for misled and oppressed innocence. In Richardson's case, estate ownership and its various accoutrements, attitudes, and sources of power are compellingly attractive. No one really wants Pamela to lose access to this world, for if she does, the reader must follow her back to a life of poverty and hard work. The scene in which she dresses as a country girl and captures the attention of Mr. B as an unknown rustic beauty titillates not only because of the voyeurism and display involved, but also because it references a mode of life that itself speaks to the power of the estate owner. Every life is attached to the life of Mr. B and his ilk. It is important to reform this class, but it is just as important to appease and appeal to them.

In Sinclair's case, the description of the wedding ceremony is interrupted by the first graphic description of the meat-packing industry, the feature for which *The Jungle* would be most famous, though, as Jon A. Yoder has pointed out, "only about half of the book is concerned" with "working conditions in Packingtown."[19] Here, in a passing reference to a wedding guest, Mikolas, we are treated to a digression having to do with the hazards of his trade. He is a beef-boner: "and that is a dangerous trade, especially when you are on piece-work and trying to earn a bride. Your hands are slippery, and your knife is slippery, and you are toiling like mad, when somebody happens to speak to you, or you strike a bone. Then your hand slips up on the blade, and there is a fearful gash. And that would not be so bad, only for the deadly contagion. The cut may heal, but you never can tell."[20] This passage is mild compared to later ones, but interjected into the middle of the happy scene of dancers and celebrants, it is shocking-enough preparation for what is to come.

Up until that passage in *The Jungle*, our readerly sensibilities have been at one with those of the immigrants. We are "in the moment," processing the sights, sounds, concerns, and emotions of the wedding celebration. With the graphic interruptive reference to the hazards of the beef-boning trade, we are suddenly in possession of information that takes us out of the scene and that makes us view the wedding guests in the light of tragic irony. The discordance felt by readers at this moment is interestingly similar to that felt in reading Pamela's report of Mr. B's summerhouse behavior. When Mr. B kisses Pamela, she is shocked and outraged, unprepared for such a violation. Readers, however, have suspected for some time that Mr. B's designs are not innocent. We and Richardson share a worldly perspective that is foreign to Pamela, and in this particular scene the distance between ourselves and the innocent heroine becomes clear. We read from this point on with a concern for her fate that prompts scrutiny of all she says. We are more alert than she is to the possibility of chicanery, machination, manipulation, and betrayal. In both *Pamela* and *The Jungle*, we, the readers, are aware of an authorial presence that admires innocence despite an awareness of the dangers to which such vulnerability opens itself. It will take some growing up for both Jurgis and Pamela to better their own lots, given the harsh realities they have to deal with and the distance of those realities from their own views of the world. These early scenes allow us to see the need for maturation and to regret the need as well.

The harsh reality that Pamela has to learn is that male estate-owners regard their serving girls as property to be used and then discarded. Her resistance is born of an innate sense of her own self-worth, which she derives from an earnest, almost puritanical approach to Christianity; that sense of self-worth, first startles and then reforms her master. The harsh reality of

Jurgis's life is that capitalism depends on an ignorant, oppressed workforce to perform the jobs no one else will do. The America of *The Jungle* is a network of graft and corruption; for the immigrant, surviving is unlikely, prospering next to impossible. Jurgis's resistance is born of despair, penury, and personal injury, but Sinclair, unlike Richardson, does not conceive the tale as an individual struggle that Jurgis can win. Sinclair's point, and the driving force behind his message, is that the machine of society is too powerful for one man to stand against. It takes money and organization to combat it; so Jurgis wins in the end only by joining the Socialist Party, to which he dedicates himself with the evangelical zeal of the newly converted, the same evangelical zeal with which Sinclair himself had embraced the party a few years before he published *The Jungle*.[21]

Sinclair and Richardson are both novelists who rely on the power of empirical observation to construct fictions that address and attempt to redress serious social ills. As James R. Barrett has put it, "Sinclair believed that citizens would demand reform, if only they understood the facts."[22] Such a belief encouraged an unrelenting realism, an unstinting commitment to graphic description, plain language, blunt observation. Richardson's meticulous attention to quotidian life invested his fiction with a power of persuasion all its own, as one of its first reader's comments on the effectiveness of *Pamela's* "Simplicity of . . . Style" and its rendering of "the immediate Impression of every Circumstance" would suggest.[23] While, of course, style was the central point on which negative critics of each novel would dwell in order to call into question each narrative's claim to the more refined and cultured readers of their respective days, style was also largely responsible for each work's impact on the society it addressed. *Pamela* and *The Jungle* are perhaps best described as "propaganda," but as Kenneth Burke pointed out long ago, all writers are propagandists. Some are simply more effective than others in deploying the "rhetorical textures, strategies, and structures of discourse" necessary to attain their ends.[24] In the narratives in which they made their most stunning social impact, Sinclair and Richardson are two of the best propagandists literary history has yet witnessed.

And of the two, the higher honor goes to Richardson. In *Another Pamela*, Sinclair himself suggests why. His Pamela knows that to change Charles, she has to bend a little herself. Rigid opposition is not the process by which social revolutions happen. In his meditation on Kenneth Burke's thought and writing, Frank Lentricchia articulates the principal by which literature that changes the world operates: "[T]here is no morally pure, no epistemologically secure, no linguistically uncontaminated route to radical change. . . . To attempt to proceed in purity—to reject the rhetorical strategies of capitalism and Christianity, *as if such strategies were in themselves responsible for human oppression*—to proceed with the illusion of purity is to situate oneself on the margin of history, as the possessor of a unique truth disengaged from history's flow. It is to exclude oneself from having any chance of making a difference for better or for worse."[25]

The early pages of Richardson's *Pamela* were provocative and exciting for readers—in a prurient sense. Readers did not know in the beginning whether or not the servant would succumb to her master's desires. Voyeuristic interest and erotic fantasies kept most readers reading, and Pamela's repeated references to religion, God, and heaven gave them permission to do so without guilty consciences. The radical change begins to occur with the transformation of the reader's own desire, an early prurient wish to read the story of seduction evolving into a desire to read a story of salvation—both in the secular (materialistic) and sacred sense. Pamela's rewriting of Psalm 137, her identification of herself as both oppressed by society and beloved of God, is just one example of Richardson's ability to employ textual and rhetorical strategies familiar to the readers of his time in the service of a radical re-visioning of the society in which they live. He takes readers from points of common interest and agreement and leads them through the character of his heroine to belief in attitudes that become the basis for social revolution.

Sinclair's failure in *The Jungle* occurs, as he himself knew, in the final third of the novel.[26] Pressed to complete the work by his own straitened economic circumstances, Sinclair yields tonal and emotional control to a "platform," an alien discourse. Although he attempts to invest our emotions by depicting Jurgis's turn to socialism as a religious conversion, we—and the audience he first addressed—do not respond in the way he had hoped. While Richardson hits the mark with Pamela's literary/emotional engagement with biblical texts and themes, Sinclair invokes a passion that can be experienced only firsthand: the psychosexual appeal of evangelical public performance, something that is not reproducible in the written word or on the printed page. Rhetorically, Sinclair's ending fails because, to echo Lentricchia again, it "appears foreign, disruptive," whereas "the revolutionary argument must be made implicitly, must be made to emerge as a necessary expression of our historical drift as a nation."[27] That Richardson accomplished as much in *Pamela* speaks to his genius as a writer of reform; that Sinclair did not accomplish as much in *The Jungle* is probably less important to us than what he did accomplish in that text. As for *Another Pamela*, with which this essay began, it is not a text that made a difference. It did not spawn a reform in the patterns of upper-class drinking nor did it prompt a rash of conversions to Seventh-Day Adventism. Yet, it is of interest to us as evidence of Sinclair's high regard for Richardson not only as a kindred spirit, but also as a master of the literary strategies of social reform through which he changed the world for the better.

Notes

1. In his 1962 autobiography, Sinclair refers to the fact that *Another Pamela* "is being prepared as a musical comedy." *The Autobiography of Upton Sinclair* (New York: Harcourt, Brace and World, 1962), 298.

2. For a brief summary of works based on *Pamela* by Richardson's contemporaries, see T. C. Duncan Eaves and Ben D. Kimpel, introduction to *Pamela; or Virtue Rewarded*, by Samuel Richardson (Boston: Houghton Mifflin, 1971), vi–vii. Fuller access to the eighteenth-century response is now available in the six-volume work edited by Thomas Keymer, Peter Sabor, and John Mullan entitled *The Pamela Controversy: Criticisms and Adaptations of Samuel Richardson's "Pamela," 1740–1750* (London: Pickering and Chatto, 2001). Joseph Dorman's 1742 opera libretto is included in volume 6.

3. Sinclair's 1918 novel *Jimmie Higgins* and his 1927 *Oil!* come to mind as two other instances of Sinclair's success as a novelist of reform. Nearly everything Sinclair wrote was in some way or another dedicated to the pursuit of "social justice," so much so that he himself felt that after his death, the curious might find those words written in his heart, "[f]or that is what I have believed in and fought for during sixty-three of my eighty-four years." *Autobiography*, 329. See also Leon Harris, *Upton Sinclair: American Rebel* (New York: Thomas Y. Crowell, 1975), 5, and 356.

4. Sinclair called the projected *Pamela Play* one of his "[i]ndirect demands for reform." *Autobiography*, 306.

5. See James R. Barrett's introduction to *The Jungle*, by Upton Sinclair, ed. Barrett (Urbana: University of Illinois Press, 1988), xi–xiii, and Harris, *Upton Sinclair*, 82–90. Harris is particularly insightful about the somewhat testy relationship between Sinclair and President Roosevelt, noting that each man "exaggerate[d] his own role in the passage of the first enforceable national Pure Food and Drug Act and Meat Inspection Act while downgrading the other's" (90). The nation seems to have sided with Sinclair, however. As Jon A. Yoder puts it, after publication of *The Jungle* "[t]he meat-packing scandal was front-page newspaper material for weeks, with Sinclair's name constantly attached," and even opponents of the bill recognized the ruckus the novel had stirred up. See his *Upton Sinclair* (New York: Frederick Unger, 1975), 41, 43. Indeed, Harris himself notes that *The Jungle* ranks with *Uncle Tom's Cabin* and *The Grapes of Wrath* as one of the "three most effective muckraking novels in America's history" (*Upton Sinclair*, 354).

6. Most notable among these studies is Nancy Armstrong's *Desire and Domestic Fiction: A Political History of the Novel* (New York: Oxford University Press, 1987), 108–34, to which I will refer again later in this discussion.

7. *The Beverly Hillbillies* was a CBS sitcom, produced from 1961 to 1972, featuring rural characters who struck oil and moved to a mansion in Beverly Hills. The game room with a pool table became, to them, the "fancy eating room" used for large dinner parties where pool cues served as "pot passers." Similarly, Andy Griffith's stand-up comic routine "What It Was Was Football," recorded in 1953, features a country bumpkin who does his best to describe a college football game: "I don't know friend, to this day, what it was that they was a doin' down there, but I have studied about it. I think it's some kindly of a contest where they see which bunchful of them men can take that pumpkin and run from one end of that cow pasture to the other without gettin' knocked down or steppin' in somethin.'" Quoted from a transcript of the recording on http://www.ziggazoomba.com/whatitwaswasfootball.php; accessed

August 31, 2003 (site now discontinued). Other, more literary, uses of the naive narrator as a comically satiric technique, of course, feature the characters Huck Finn and Lemuel Gulliver.

8. Upton Sinclair, *Another Pamela* (New York: Viking Penguin, 1950), 13, 57. Further references will be cited parenthetically in the text.

9. Harris, *Upton Sinclair*, 333.

10. Ibid., 335.

11. Samuel Richardson, *Pamela, or, Virtue Rewarded*, ed. T. C. Duncan Eaves and Ben D. Kimpel, Riverside ed. (Boston: Houghton Mifflin, 1971), 144.

12. The materials included in the six-volume *Pamela Controversy* cited above make abundantly clear the widespread—and varying—appeal of Richardson's novel.

13. Richardson, *Pamela* (ed. Eaves and Kimpel), 177.

14. Actually, the disapproval of fiction would seem to be in line with the Seventh-Day Adventist ban on theatrical performances and films during the early twentieth century. According to a Seventh-Day Adventist of my acquaintance, Eric Rochester, these strictures have been relaxed, a point one can confirm by consulting any recent history of the faith. In fact, Sinclair's novel and his heroine address this topic at a crucial juncture in Seventh-Day Adventist history, as during the 1940s and 1950s, the popularity of films and television would prompt serious debate within the faith about the proper and improper uses of media and the proper and improper indulgence in these entertaining pleasures.

15. Armstrong, *Desire and Domestic Fiction*, 120.

16. Ibid., 125.

17. From Sinclair's announcement of his forthcoming novel, published in the Populist-Socialist journal, *Appeal to Reason*, February 11, 1905; quoted by William A. Bloodworth Jr., *Upton Sinclair* (New York: Twayne, 1977), 48.

18. Sinclair wrote this famous statement in an article for *Cosmopolitan Magazine* published in October 1906, quoted by Yoder, *Upton Sinclair*, 40, and by Sinclair himself in his *Autobiography*, 126.

19. Yoder, *Upton Sinclair*, 38.

20. Sinclair, *Jungle* (ed. Barrett), 12.

21. See Barrett, introduction, xxv.

22. Ibid., xv.

23. Letter to Samuel Richardson from Jean Baptiste de Freval, published in Richardson, *Pamela* (ed. Eaves and Kimpel), 4.

24. Burke says as much in an essay entitled "Revolutionary Symbolism in America," in *American Writers' Congress*, ed. Henry Hart (New York: International Publishers, 1935), 87; quoted in Frank Lentricchia, *Criticism and Social Change* (Chicago: University of Chicago Press, 1985), 26.

25. Lentricchia, *Criticism and Social Change*, 35–36.

26. See Yoder, *Upton Sinclair*, 45.

27. Lentricchia, *Criticism and Social Change*, 35.

Chronology

1878	Born on September 20 in Baltimore to Upton Beall and Priscilla.
1888	Family moves to New York City.
1892	Enrolls in College of the City of New York.
1897	Writes novels to finance education at Columbia University.
1900	Marries Meta H. Fuller.
1901	*Springtime and Harvest* is published. In December, son David is born.
1903	*The Journal of Arthur Stirling* is published.
1904	*Manassas* is published. Travels to Chicago to conduct research for *The Jungle*.
1906	*The Jungle* is published. Founds Helicon Hall in Englewood, New Jersey, an experiment in communal living.
1907	Helicon Hall destroyed by fire.
1908	*The Metropolis* and *The Money-Changers* are published.
1911	*Love's Pilgrimage* is published.
1912	Divorces in Amsterdam.
1913	Marries Mary Craig Kimbrough in Virginia.

1915	Moves to California.
1917	*King Coal* is published. Resigns from Socialist Party but later rejoins.
1918	*The Profits of Religion* is published.
1919	*Jimmy Higgins* is published.
1920	*The Brass Check* and *100%* are published.
1923	*The Goose-Step* is published.
1924	*The Goslings* is published.
1925	*Mammonart* is published.
1927	*Oil!* is published.
1928	*Boston* is published.
1930	*Mental Radio* is published.
1932	*American Outpost* is published.
1933	*Upton Sinclair Presents William Fox* and *I, Governor of California* are published.
1934	Wins Democratic nomination for governor of California; narrowly loses election.
1935	*I, Candidate for Governor* is published.
1936	*Co-Op* is published.
1937	*The Flivver King* is published.
1940	Begins Lanny Budd series with *World's End.*
1941	*Between Two Worlds* is published.
1942	*Dragon's Teeth* is published.
1943	*Dragon's Teeth* wins Pulitzer Prize. *Wide Is the Gate* is published.
1944	*Presidential Agent* is published.
1945	*Dragon Harvest* is published.
1946	*A World to Win* is published.
1947	*Presidential Mission* is published.
1948	*One Clear Call* is published.

1949	*O Shepherd, Speak!* is published.
1953	*The Return of Lanny Budd* is published.
1956	*The Cup of Fury* is published.
1960	*My Lifetime in Letters* is published.
1961	Mary Craig Sinclair dies at age 78.
1962	Marries May Hard. *The Autobiography of Upton Sinclair* is published.
1967	May Hard Sinclair dies on December 18.
1968	Dies on November 25 in New Jersey.

Contributors

HAROLD BLOOM is Sterling Professor of the Humanities at Yale University. Educated at Cornell and Yale universities, he is the author of more than 30 books, including *Shelley's Mythmaking* (1959), *The Visionary Company* (1961), *Blake's Apocalypse* (1963), *Yeats* (1970), *The Anxiety of Influence* (1973), *A Map of Misreading* (1975), *Kabbalah and Criticism* (1975), *Agon: Toward a Theory of Revisionism* (1982), *The American Religion* (1992), *The Western Canon* (1994), *Omens of Millennium: The Gnosis of Angels, Dreams, and Resurrection* (1996), *Shakespeare: The Invention of the Human* (1998), *How to Read and Why* (2000), *Genius: A Mosaic of One Hundred Exemplary Creative Minds* (2002), *Hamlet: Poem Unlimited* (2003), *Where Shall Wisdom Be Found?* (2004), and *Jesus and Yahweh: The Names Divine* (2005). In addition, he is the author of hundreds of articles, reviews, and editorial introductions. In 1999, Professor Bloom received the American Academy of Arts and Letters' Gold Medal for Criticism. He has also received the International Prize of Catalonia, the Alfonso Reyes Prize of Mexico, and the Hans Christian Andersen Bicentennial Prize of Denmark.

G. S. BALARAMA GUPTA has been a professor of English at Gulbarga University in India. He has been director of the National Institute for Research in Indian English Literature. He is coauthor of *New Perspectives in Indian Literature in English* and author of *Critical Gleanings* and other works.

WILLIAM A. BLOODWORTH has been part of the faculty at East Carolina University, where he also has been head of the English department and a vice chancellor. He is the author of Twayne's *Upton Sinclair* and, part of the same series, *Max Brand.*

MATTHEW J. MORRIS has been a visiting assistant professor at the College of Charleston.

STEVEN ROSENDALE is an associate professor at Northern Arizona University. He is editor of the Dictionary of Literary Biography's *American Radical and Reform Writers* and coauthor of *Radical Relevance: Toward a Scholarship of the Whole Left.*

J. MICHAEL DUVALL is an assistant professor at the College of Charleston. Prior to his work there, he was associate director of the Writing Across the Curriculum program at Georgia State University, where he also taught English. His work includes presentations at the American Literature Association Convention, of which he also was a panel organizer and chair.

ORM ØVERLAND is a professor in the Department of Foreign Languages at the University of Bergen in Norway. He is an author, editor, and translator. His published work includes *Immigrant Minds, American Identities: Making the United States Home, 1870–1930.*

GIEDRIUS SUBAČIUS is a professor in the Department of Slavic and Baltic Languages and Literature at the University of Illinois at Chicago. He has published *The Lithuanian Language* and other books and is editing the annual scholarly journal *Archivum Lithuanicum.*

MICHAEL MOGHTADER is an associate professor in The School of Writing, Rhetoric and Technical Communication at James Madison University. He has published work on rhetorical theory, first-year writing, and English graduate student culture.

ELIZABETH KRAFT is a professor at the University of Georgia. She is the author of *Character and Consciousness in Eighteenth-Century Comic Fiction* and *Women Novelists and the Ethics of Desire 1684–1814* and other works. Also, she is on the editorial team producing the Cambridge edition of Samuel Richardson's *Sir Charles Grandison*, and she has edited and coedited other titles as well.

Bibliography

Abrahamson, David. "An Inconvenient Legacy: *The Jungle* at 100: A Century of the Journalism of Reform." *Journalism History* 34, no. 3 (2008): 163–165.

Arthur, Anthony. *Radical Innocent: Upton Sinclair.* New York: Random House, 2006.

Barrett, James R. "Life in 'The Jungle': An Immigrant Working-Class Community on Chicago's South Side in Fiction and in Fact, 1900–1910." In *Transactions of the Illinois State Historical Society*, edited by Mary Ellen McElligott and Patrick H. O'Neal, pp. 97–106. Springfield: Illinois State Historical Society, 1988.

Benson, Peter. "Possession and Dispossession in Crèvecoeur's, Sinclair's, and Dos Passos's America." *Bridges: An African Journal of English Studies/Revue Africaine d'Etudes Anglaises* 4 (December 1992): 91–112.

Blinderman, Abraham, ed. *Critics on Upton Sinclair.* Coral Gables, Fla.: University of Miami Press, 1975.

———. "The Social Passions of Upton Sinclair." *Chicago Jewish Forum* 25 (1967): 203–208.

Bloodworth, William A., Jr. *Upton Sinclair.* Boston: Twayne Publishers, 1977.

Boylan, James. "The Long and the Short of *The Jungle*." *Journalism History* 34, no. 3 (2008): 165–167.

Chalmers, David Mark. *The Social and Political Ideas of the Muckrakers.* Freeport, N.Y.: Books for Libraries Press, 1970, 1964.

Colburn, David R., and George E. Pozzetta. *Reform and Reformers in the Progressive Era.* Westport, Conn.: Greenwood, 1983.

Connery, Thomas. "Fiction/Nonfiction and Sinclair's *The Jungle*." *Journalism History* 34, no. 3 (2008): 167–170.

Cook, Timothy. "Upton Sinclair's *The Jungle* and Orwell's *Animal Farm*: A Relationship Explored." *MFS: Modern Fiction Studies* 30, no. 4 (Winter 1984): 696–703.

Dawson, Hugh J. "Winston Churchill and Upton Sinclair: An Early Review of *The Jungle*." *American Literary Realism* 24, no. 1 (Fall 1991): 72–78.

DeGruson, Gene, ed. *The Lost First Edition of Upton Sinclair's* The Jungle. Atlanta: Peachtree, 1988.

Dell, Floyd. *Upton Sinclair; a Study in Social Protest.* New York: AMS Press, 1970, 1927.

Dembo, L. S. "The Socialist and Socialite Heroes of Upton Sinclair." In *Toward a New American Literary History: Essays in Honor of Arlin Turner*, edited by Louis J. Budd, Edwin H. Cady, and Carl L. Anderson, pp. 164–180. Durham, N.C.: Duke University Press, 1980.

Den Tandt, Christophe. "Abjection and Oratory in Upton Sinclair's *The Jungle*: The Contradictions of Political Discourse in American Naturalism." *BELL: Belgian Essays on Language and Literature* (1993): 15–34.

Derrick, Scott. "What a Beating Feels Like: Authorship, Dissolution, and Masculinity in Sinclair's *The Jungle*." *Studies in American Fiction* 23, no. 1 (Spring 1995): 85–100.

Dickstein, Morris. *A Mirror in the Roadway: Literature and the Real World.* Princeton, N.J.: Princeton University Press, 2005.

Duram, James C. *Upton Sinclair's Realistic Romanticism.* Wichita, Kan.: Wichita State University, 1970.

Durant, Will, and Ariel Durant. *Interpretations of Life: A Survey of Contemporary Literature, the Lives and Opinions of Some Major Authors of Our Time.* New York: Simon and Schuster, 1970.

Folsom, Michael Brewster. "Upton Sinclair's Escape from *The Jungle*: The Narrative Strategy and Suppressed Conclusion of America's First Proletarian Novel." *Prospects: An Annual Journal of American Cultural Studies* 4 (1979): 237–266.

González Diáz, Isabel. "Whose Chicago, Anyway?: 'Aesthetics' vs. 'Propaganda' in Upton Sinclair's Ending for *The Jungle*." *Revista Canaria de Estudios Ingleses* 32–33 (April–November 1996): 93–106.

Gottesman, Ronald. *Upton Sinclair: An Annotated Checklist.* Kent, Ohio: Kent State University Press, 1973.

Gottesman, Ronald, and Charles L. P. Silet. *The Literary Manuscripts of Upton Sinclair.* Columbus: Ohio State University Press, 1972.

Grover, Dorys Crow. "Upton Sinclair: Never Forgotten." *MidAmerica* 22 (1995): 41–49.

Harris, Leon. *Upton Sinclair, American Rebel.* New York: Crowell, 1975.

Hicks, Granville. "The Survival of Upton Sinclair." *College English* 4 (January 1943): 213–220.

Hornung, Alfred. "The Political Uses of Popular Fiction in the Muckraking Movement." *Revue Française d'Etudes Américaines* 8, no. 17 (May 1983): 333–348.

Howard, June. *Form and History in American Literary Naturalism.* Chapel Hill: University of North Carolina Press, 1985.

Karolides, Nicholas J. *Literature Suppressed on Political Grounds.* New York: Facts On File, 2006.

Koerner, J. D. "The Last of the Muckrake Men." *South Atlantic Quarterly* 55 (April 1956): 221–232.

Little, William G. *The Waste Fix: Seizures of the Sacred from Upton Sinclair to the Sopranos.* New York: Routledge, 2002.

Mattson, Kevin. *Upton Sinclair and the Other American Century.* Hoboken, N.J.: John Wiley & Sons, 2006.

Michaels, Walter Benn. *The Gold Standard and the Logic of Naturalism: American Literature at the Turn of the Century.* Berkeley: University of California Press, 1987.

Mookerjee, R. N. *Art for Social Justice: The Major Novels of Upton Sinclair.* Metuchen, N.J.: Scarecrow Press, 1988.

Parry, Sally E. "Upton-Sinclair-Lewis: The Crossed Paths of Two American Reformer Novelists." *Connecticut Review* 16, no. 1 (Spring 1994): 81–92.

Pickavance, Jason. "Gastronomic Realism: Upton Sinclair's *The Jungle*, the Fight for Pure Food and the Magic of Mastication." *Food and Foodways* 11, nos. 2–3 (April–September 2003): 87–112.

Quint, Howard H. "Upton Sinclair's Quest for Artistic Independence." *American Literature* 29 (June 1957): 194–202.

Scott, Ivan. *Upton Sinclair, the Forgotten Socialist.* Lewiston, N.Y.: Edwin Mellen Press, 1997.

Sesplaukis, Alfonsas. "Lithuanians in Upton Sinclair's *The Jungle*." *Lituanus: Lithuanian Quarterly* 23, no. 2 (1977): 24–31.

Simon, Linda. "Socialism at Home: The Case of Upton Sinclair." *New Jersey History* 107, no. 1/2 (1989): 48–57.

Sinclair, Upton. The Jungle: *An Authoritative Text, Contexts and Backgrounds, Criticism.* New York: Norton, 2003.

Suh, Suk Bong. "Lithuanian Wedding Traditions in Upton Sinclair's *The Jungle*." *Lituanus: Baltic States Quarterly of Arts & Sciences* 33, no. 1 (Winter 1987): 5–17.

Tavernier-Courbin, Jacqueline. "*The Call of the Wild* and *The Jungle*: Jack London's and Upton Sinclair's Animal and Human Jungles." In *The Cambridge Companion to American Realism and Naturalism: Howells to London*, edited by Donald Pizer, pp. 236–262. Cambridge, Mass.: Cambridge University Press, 1995.

Vadon, Lehel. "Hungarian Attitudes toward Upton Sinclair." *Gulliver* 9 (1981): 199–208.

Walcutt, Charles Child. *American Literary Naturalism, A Divided Stream*. Minneapolis: University of Minnesota Press, 1956.

Welland, Dennis. "Upton Sinclair: The Centenary of an American Writer." *Bulletin of the John Rylands University Library of Manchester* 61 (1979): 474–494.

Wilson, Edmund. "Lincoln Steffens and Upton Sinclair." *New Republic* 72 (September 28, 1932): 173–175.

Yoder, Jon A. *Upton Sinclair*. New York: Ungar, 1975.

Acknowledgments

G. S. Balarama Gupta, "A Note on Upton Sinclair's *The Jungle*." From *Indian Studies in American Fiction*, edited by M. K. Naik, S. K. Desai, and S. Mokashi-Punekar. Published by Macmillan of India. Copyright © 1974 by Karnatak University, Dharwar.

William Bloodworth, "From *The Jungle* to *The Fasting Cure*: Upton Sinclair on American Food." From *Journal of American Culture* 2, no. 3 (Fall 1979): 444–53. Copyright © 1979 by Ray B. Browne.

Matthew J. Morris, "The Two Lives of Jurgis Rudkus." From *American Literary Realism 1870–1910* 29, no. 2 (Winter 1997): 50–67. Copyright © 1997 by McFarland and Company.

Steven Rosendale, "In Search of Left Ecology's Usable Past: *The Jungle*, Social Change, and the Class Character of Environmental Impairment." From *The Greening of Literary Scholarship: Literature, Theory, and the Environment*, edited by Steven Rosendale. Copyright © 2002 by the University of Iowa Press.

J. Michael Duvall, "Processes of Elimination: Progressive-Era Hygienic Ideology, Waste, and Upton Sinclair's *The Jungle*." From *American Studies* 43, no. 3 (Fall 2002): 29–56. Copyright © 2002 by the Mid-America American Studies Association.

Orm Øverland, "*The Jungle*: From Lithuanian Peasant to American Socialist." From *American Literary Realism, 1870–1910* 37, no. 1 (Fall 2004): 1–23.

Copyright © 2004 by Board of Trustees of the University of Illinois. Used with permission of the University of Illinois Press.

Giedrius Subačius, "Sinclair's Sources and His Choice of Lithuanian Characters." From *Upton Sinclair:* The *Lithuanian* Jungle. Copyright © 2006 by Editions Rodopi B.V.

Michael Moghtader, "Discursive Determinism in Upton Sinclair's *The Jungle*." From *The CEA Critic* 69, no. 3 (Spring and Summer 2007): 13–27. Copyright © 2007 by the College English Association.

Elizabeth Kraft, "Writers that Changed the World: Samuel Richardson, Upton Sinclair, and the Strategies of Social Reform." From *On Second Thought: Updating the Eighteenth-Century Text*, edited by Debra Taylor Bourdeau and Elizabeth Kraft. Published by University of Delaware Press. Copyright © 2007 by Rosemont Publishing and Printing.

Every effort has been made to contact the owners of copyrighted material and secure copyright permission. Articles appearing in this volume generally appear much as they did in their original publication with few or no editorial changes. In some cases, foreign language text has been removed from the original essay. Those interested in locating the original source will find the information cited above.

Index

Characters in literary works are indexed by first name (if any), followed by the name of the work in parentheses